KT-372-047

BAINTE DEN STOC

WITHDRAWN FROM
DUN LAOGHAIRE-RATHDOWN COUNTY
LIBRARY STOCK

BY CLAMP

2

TOKYOPOP
PRESS ™

Chix Comix
Pocket Edition ®

TOKYOPOP Press Presents
Cardcaptor Sakura by CLAMP
Chix Comix Pocket Edition is an imprint of Mixx Entertainment, Inc.
ISBN: 1-892213-50-8
First Printing December 2000

10 9 8 7 6 5 4 3 2 1

This volume contains the Cardcaptor Sakura installments from
Cardcaptor Sakura Chix Comix No.6 through No.10 in their entirety.

English text ©2000 Mixx Entertainment, Inc. Original Japanese version ©1997 CLAMP.
All rights reserved. First published in Japan by Kodansha, Ltd., Tokyo. English publication rights arranged through Kodansha, Ltd. Original artwork reversed for this edition. No part of this book may be reproduced by any means, without permission in writing from the copyright holders. The stories, characters, and incidents in this publication are entirely fictional. Printed in the USA.

Translator-Mika Onishi. Retouch Artist-Bernard San Juan, Ryan Caraan.
Graphic Assistant-Steve Kindernay. Graphic Designer-Akemi Imafuku.
Editor-Jake Forbes. Editor-Mary Coco. Production Manager-Fred Lui.
Vice President, Publishing-Henry Kornman.

Email: editor@press.Tokyopop.com
Come visit us at www.TOKYOPOP.com.

TOKYOPOP
Los Angeles - Tokyo

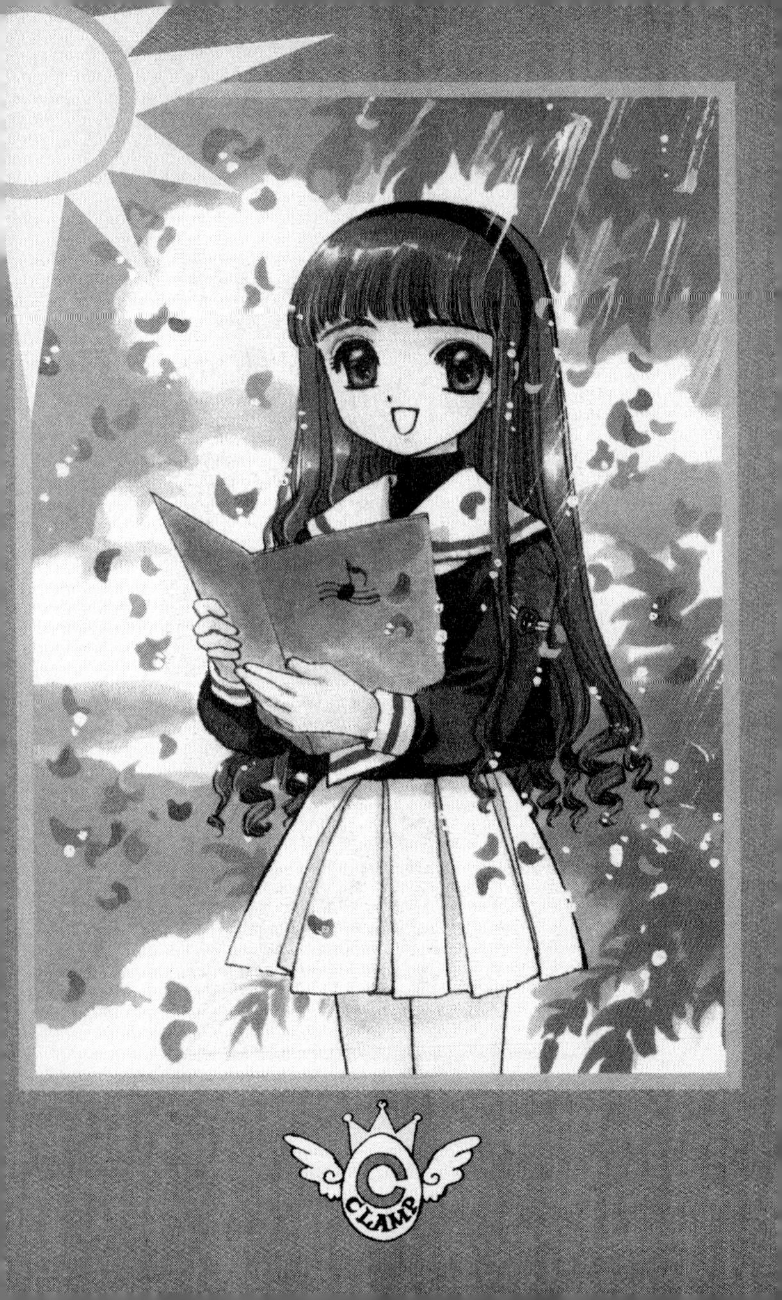

CLAMP

CLOW CARD

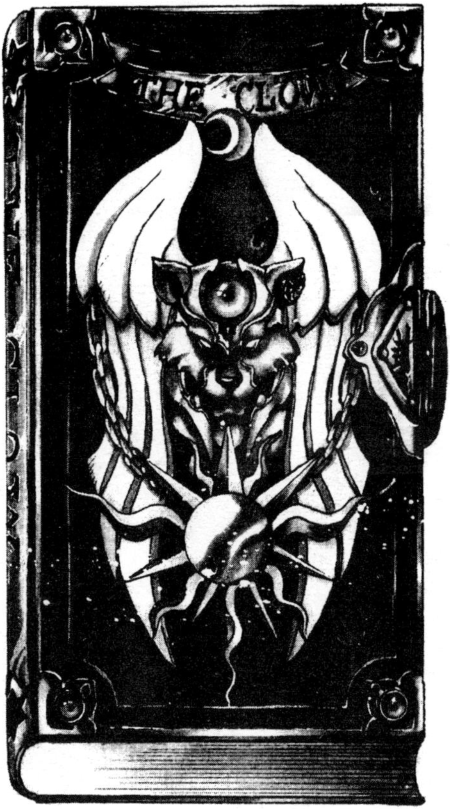
THE CLOW

When the seal is broken...

Evil will befall this world...

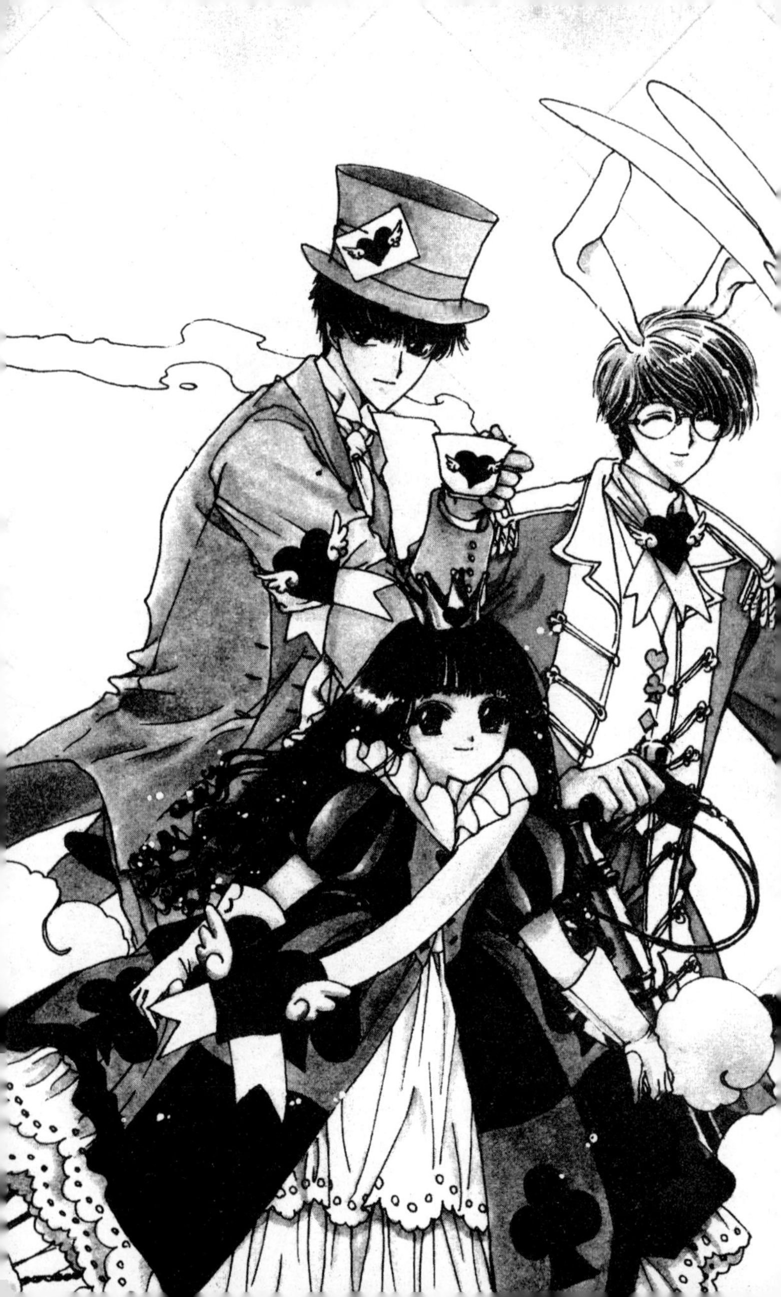

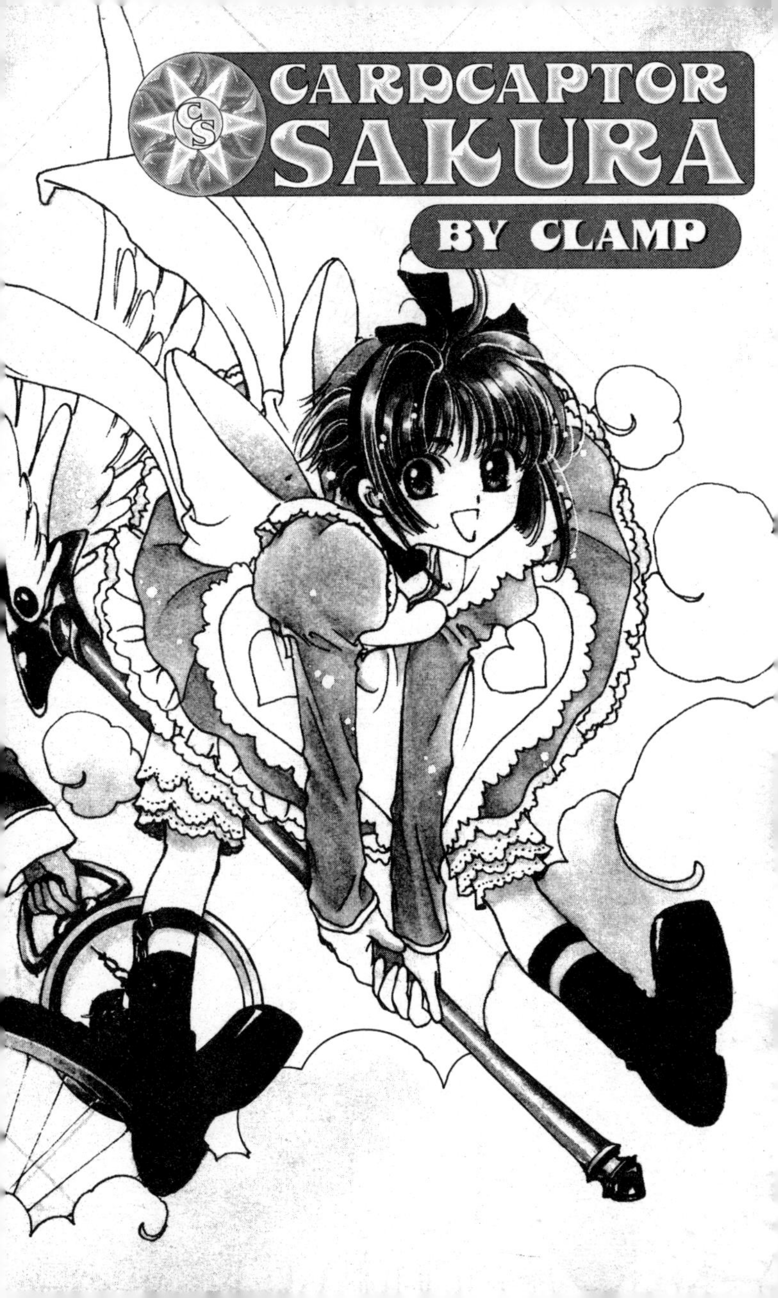
CARDCAPTOR SAKURA
BY CLAMP

BAINTE DEN STOC

WITHDRAWN FROM
DÚN LAOGHAIRE-RATHDOWN COUNTY
LIBRARY STOCK

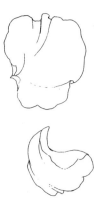

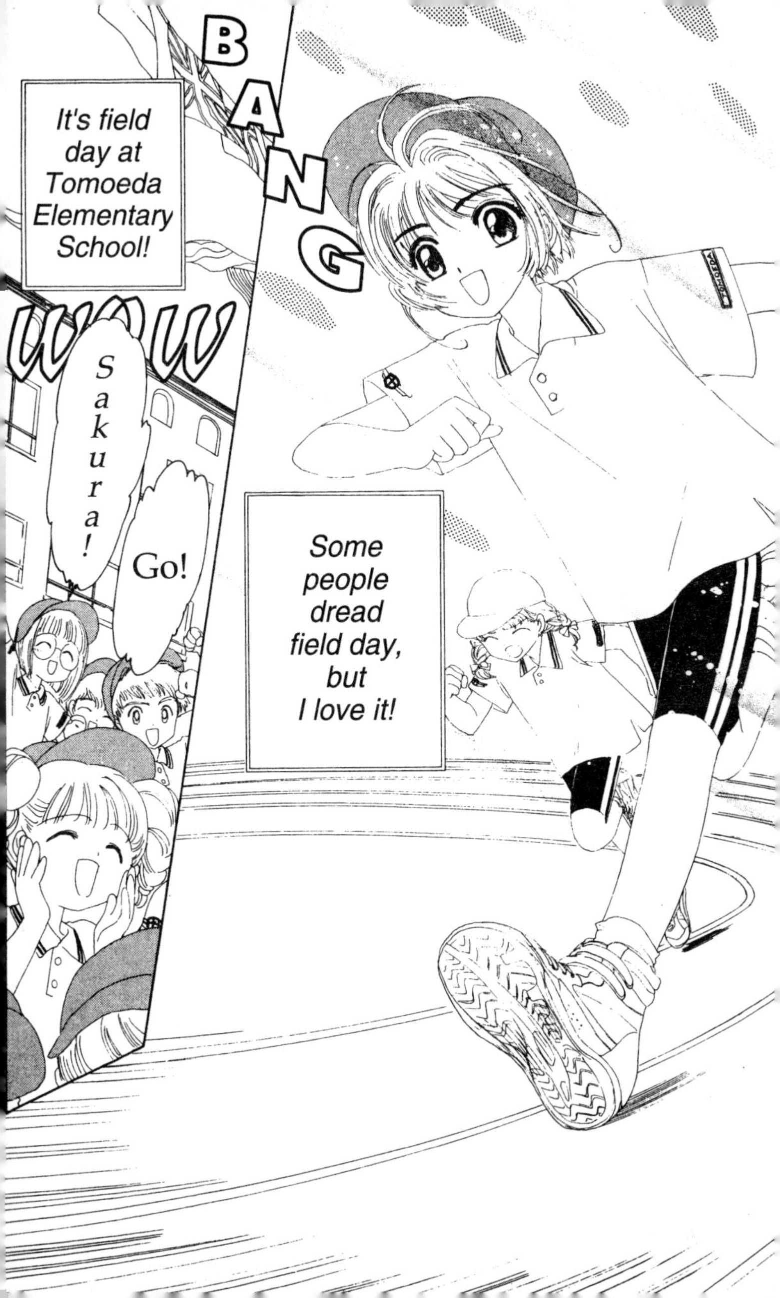
It's field day at Tomoeda Elementary School!
WOW
Sakura!
Go!
BANG
Some people dread field day, but I love it!

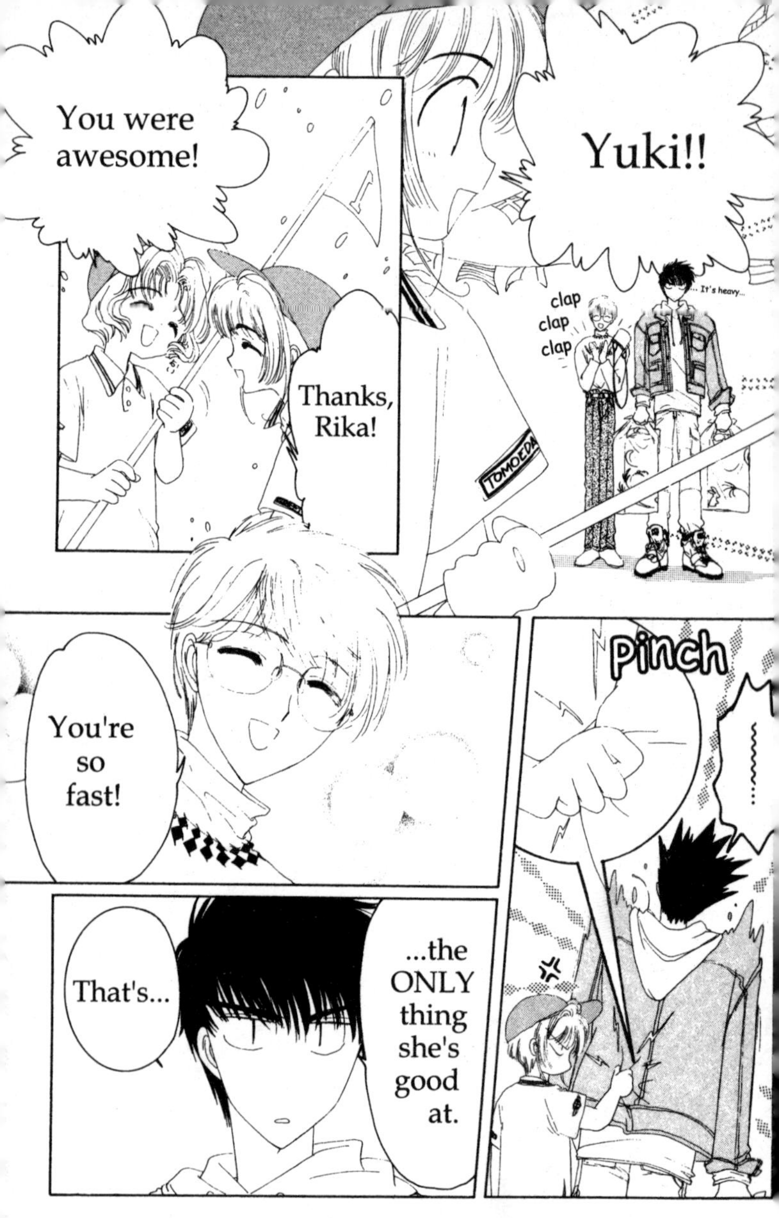
You were awesome!
Thanks, Rika!
Yuki!!
clap clap clap
... It's heavy...
You're so fast!
Pinch
......
That's...
...the ONLY thing she's good at.

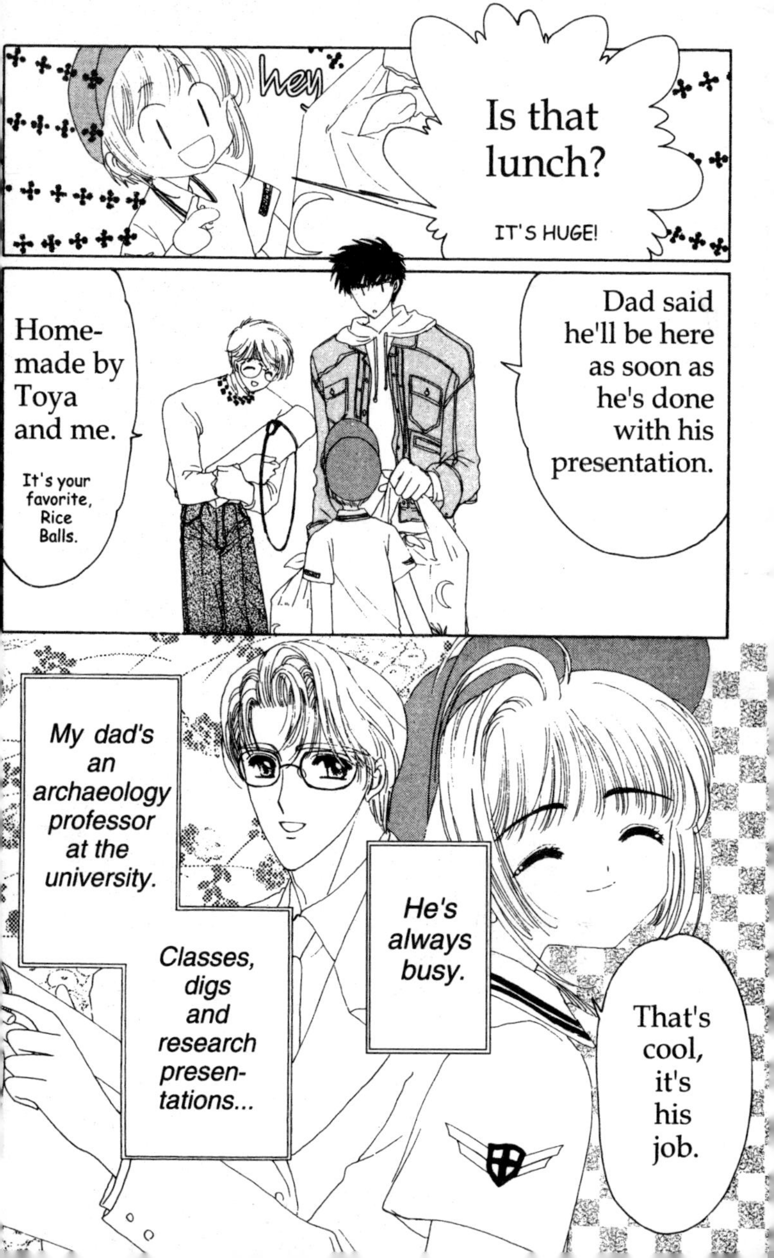
hey
Is that lunch?
IT'S HUGE!
Home-made by Toya and me.
It's your favorite, Rice Balls.
Dad said he'll be here as soon as he's done with his presentation.
My dad's an archaeology professor at the university.
Classes, digs and research presen-tations...
He's always busy.
That's cool, it's his job.

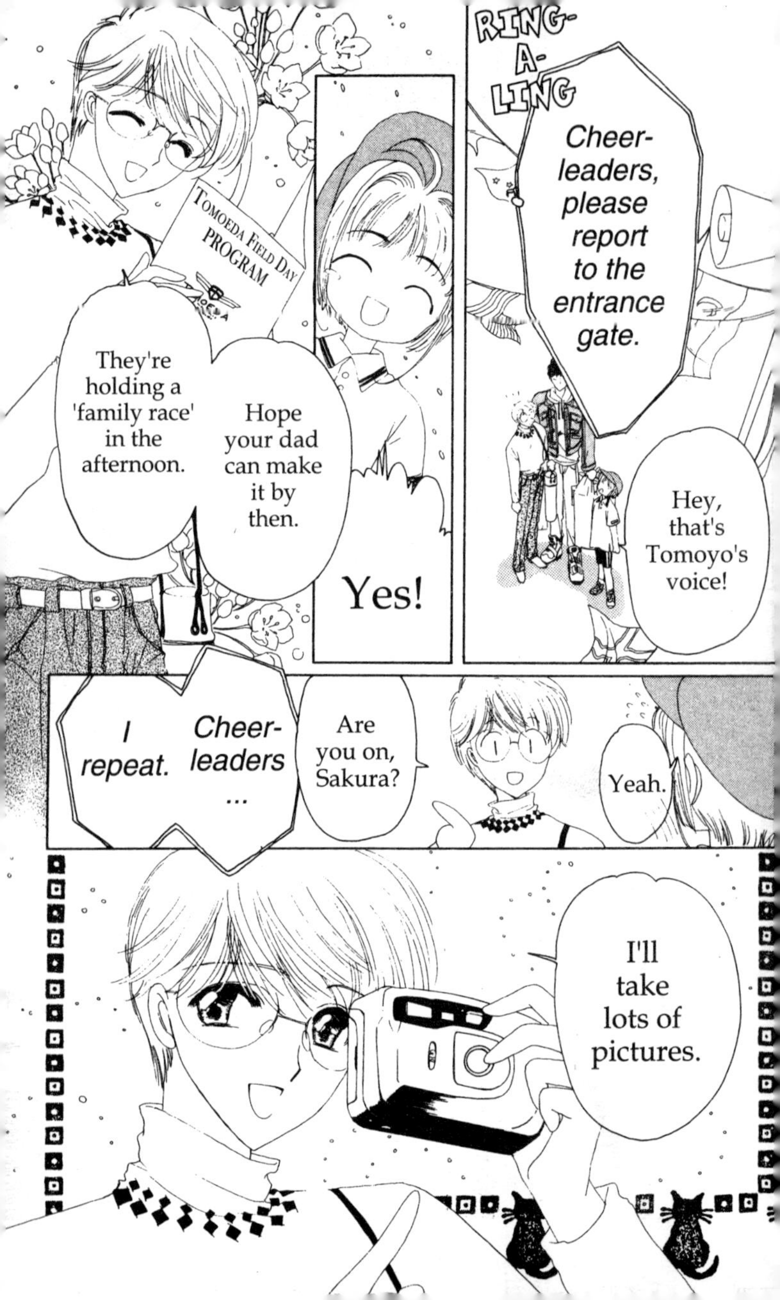
TOMOEDA FIELD DAY PROGRAM
They're holding a 'family race' in the afternoon.
Hope your dad can make it by then.
Yes!
RING-A-LING
Cheer-leaders, please report to the entrance gate.
Hey, that's Tomoyo's voice!
I repeat. Cheer-leaders ...
Are you on, Sakura?
Yeah.
I'll take lots of pictures.

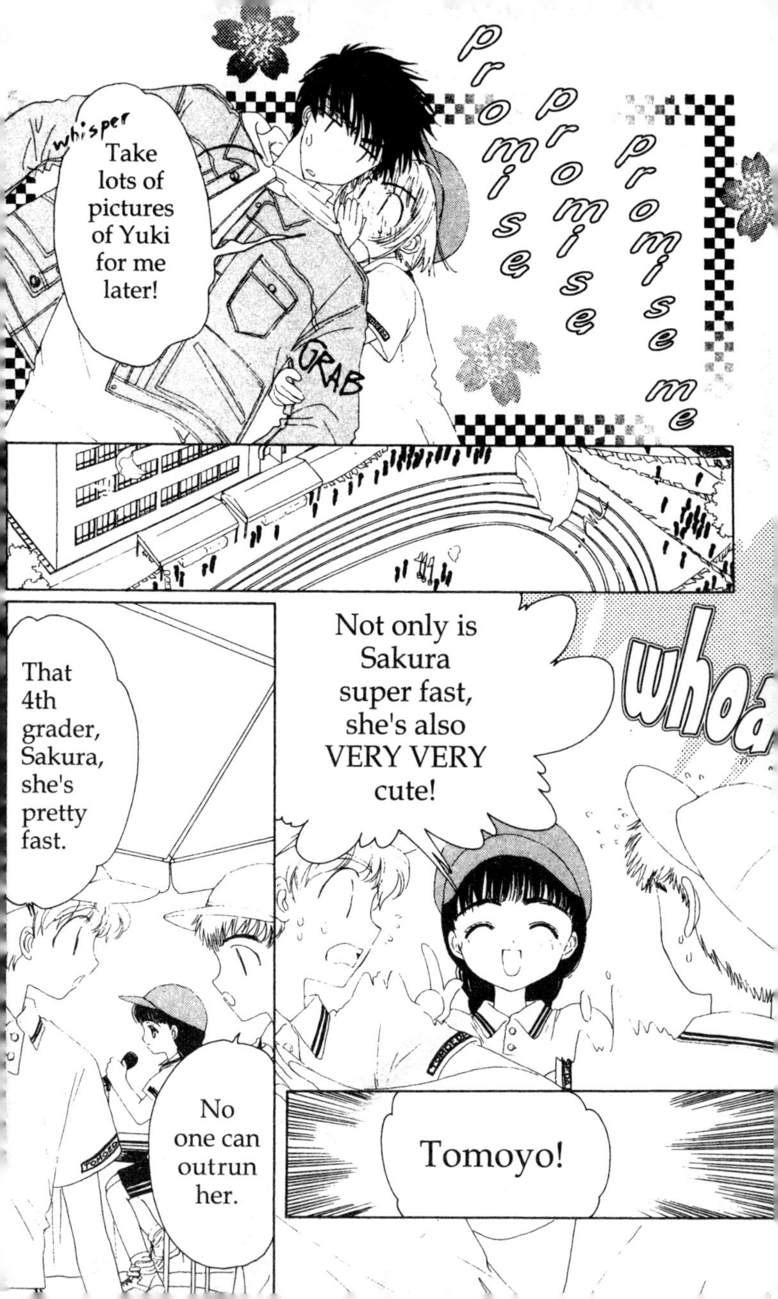
whisper
Take lots of pictures of Yuki for me later!
GRAB
promise promise promise me
That 4th grader, Sakura, she's pretty fast.
No one can outrun her.
Not only is Sakura super fast, she's also VERY VERY cute!
whoa
Tomoyo!

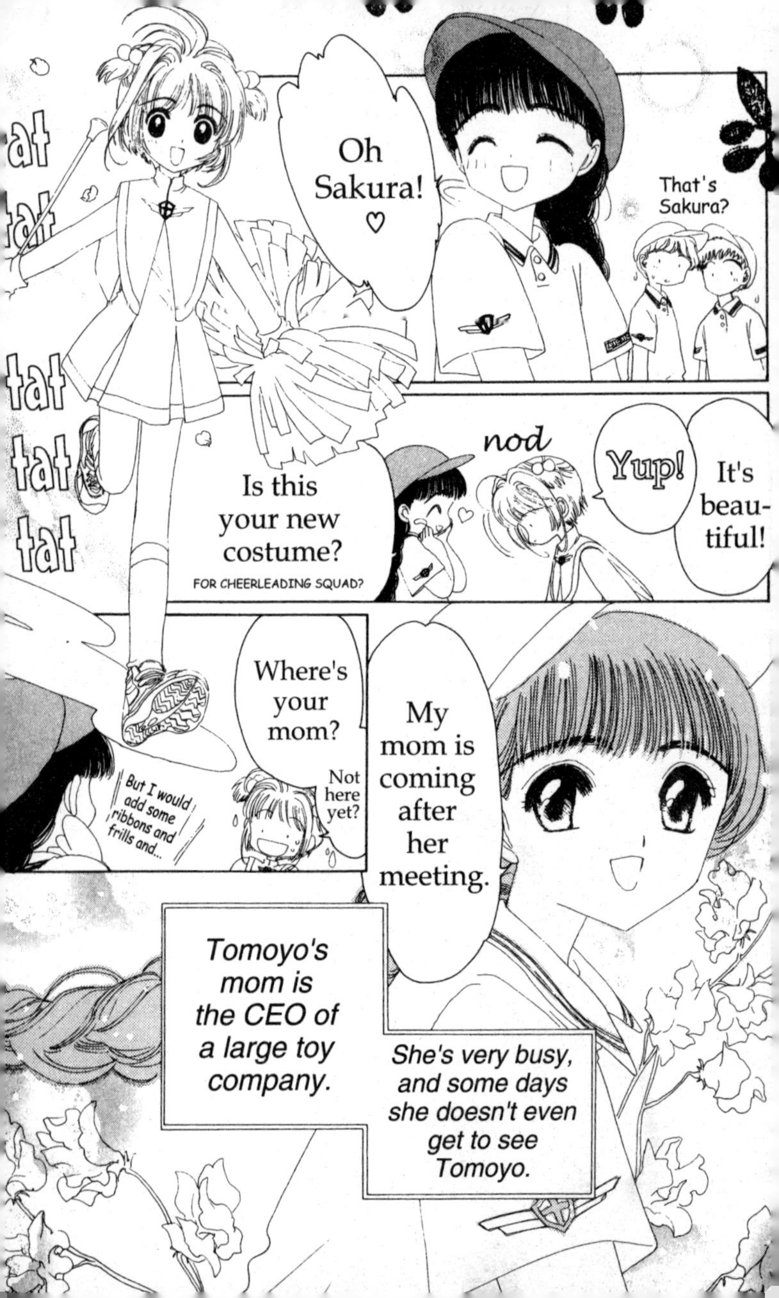
tat tat tat tat tat
Oh Sakura! ♡
That's Sakura?
Is this your new costume?
FOR CHEERLEADING SQUAD?
nod
Yup!
It's beau-tiful!
But I would add some ribbons and frills and...
Where's your mom?
Not here yet?
My mom is coming after her meeting.
Tomoyo's mom is the CEO of a large toy company.
She's very busy, and some days she doesn't even get to see Tomoyo.

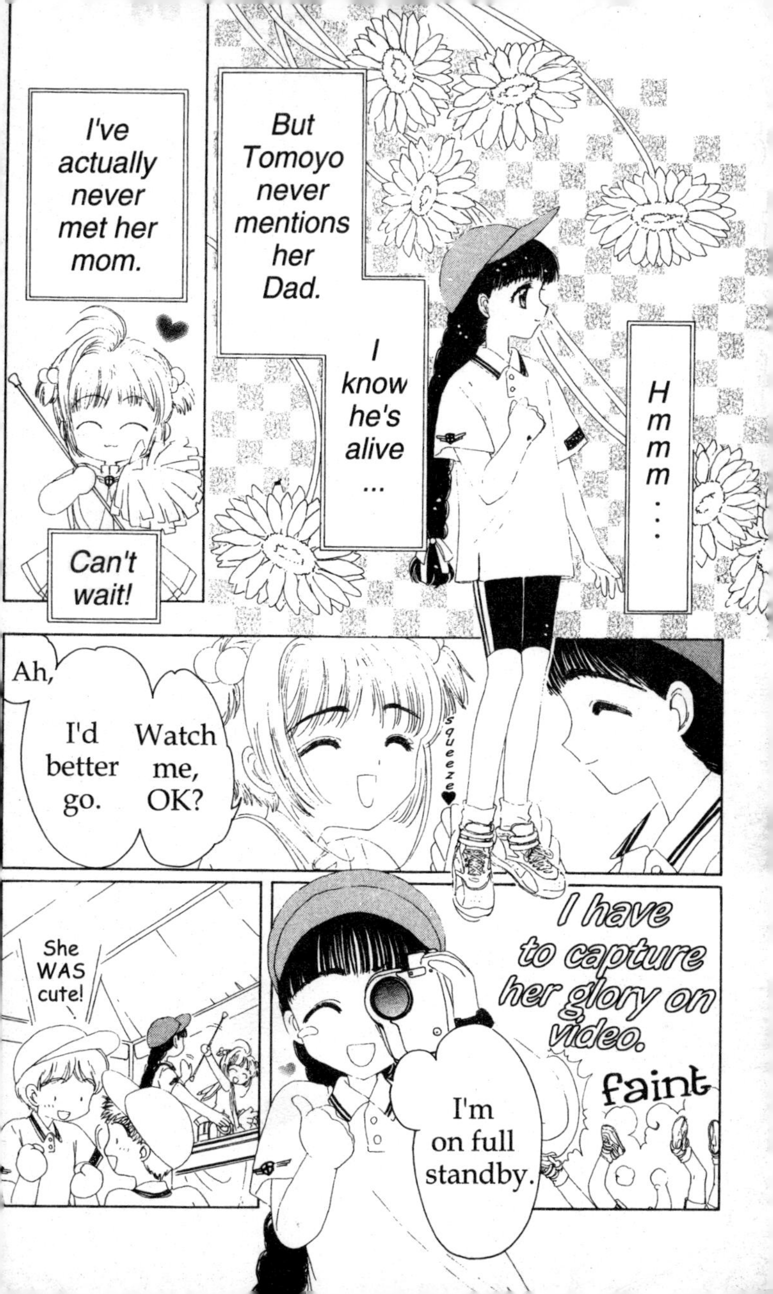
I've actually never met her mom.
But Tomoyo never mentions her Dad.
I know he's alive...
Hmmm...
Can't wait!
Ah,
I'd better go.
Watch me, OK?
squeeze
She WAS cute!
I have to capture her glory on video.
faint
I'm on full standby.

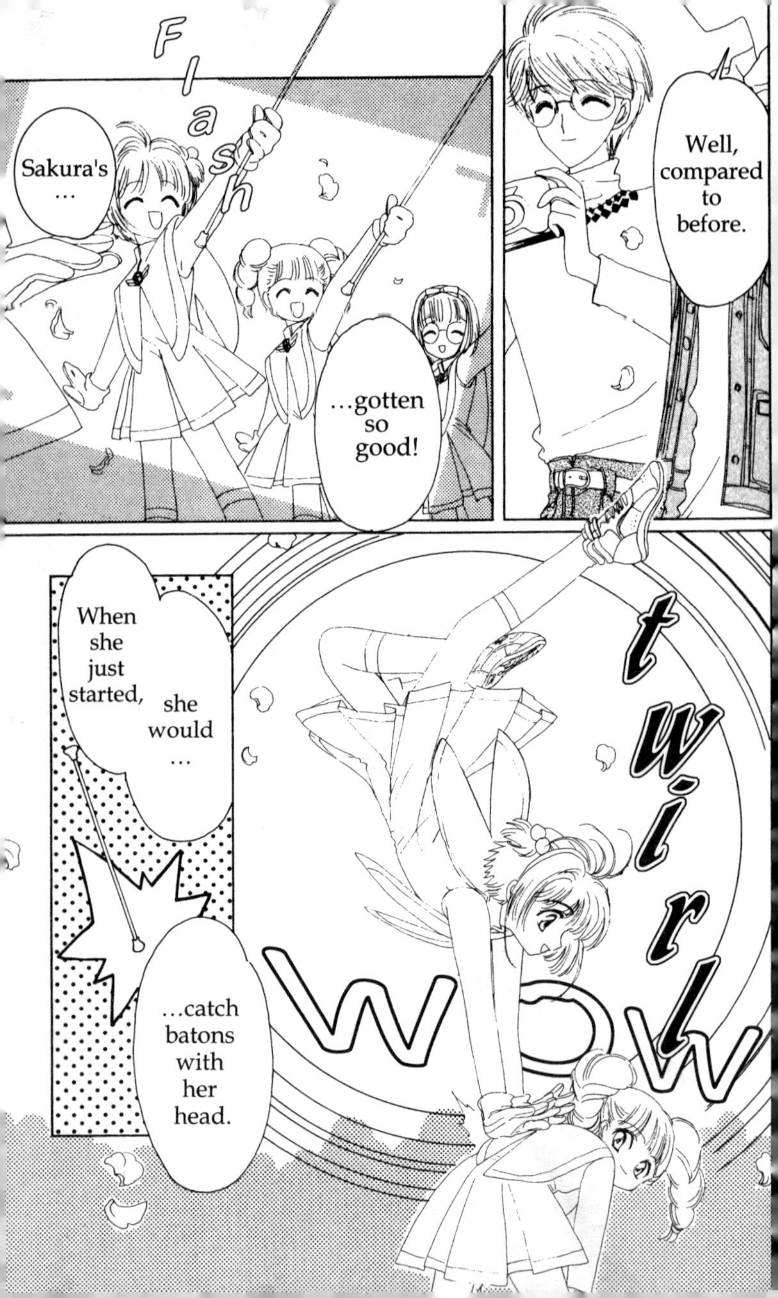
Flash
Sakura's ...
...gotten so good!
Well, compared to before.
When she just started,
she would ...
...catch batons with her head.
twirl
WOW

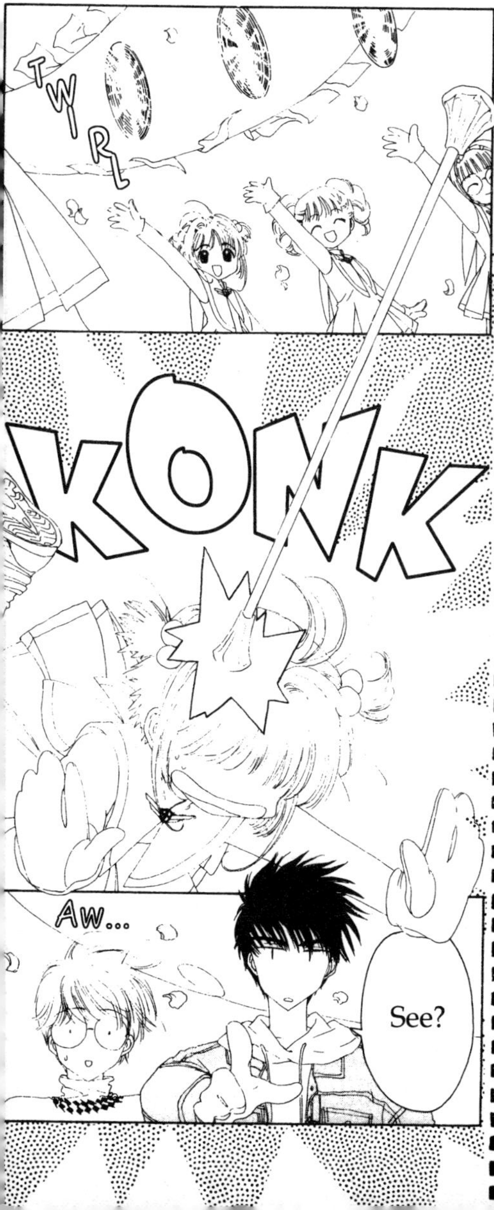
TWIRL
KONK
Aw...
See?

5

Kerberos

Nickname:
Kero
Birthday:
Secret
Favorite Foods:
Sweets
Least Favorite Foods:
Hot and spicy foods
Favorite Pastime:
Video games
Favorite Colors:
Red and Orange
Favorite TV Shows:
Quiz shows
Favorite Flower:
Sunflowers
Wish List:
A new video game
Where I live:
Sakura's room
My true form:
Unknown

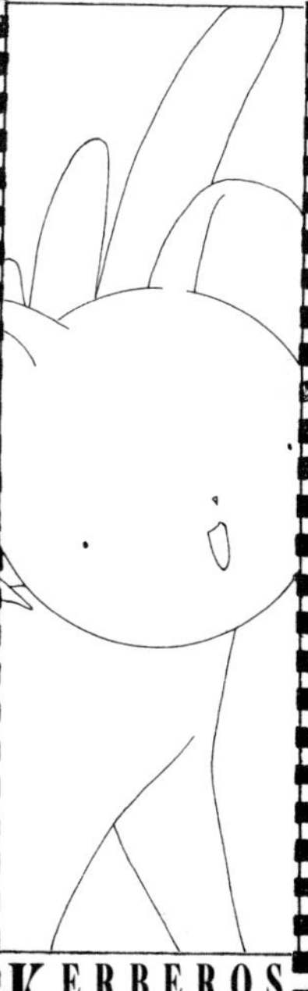

KERBEROS

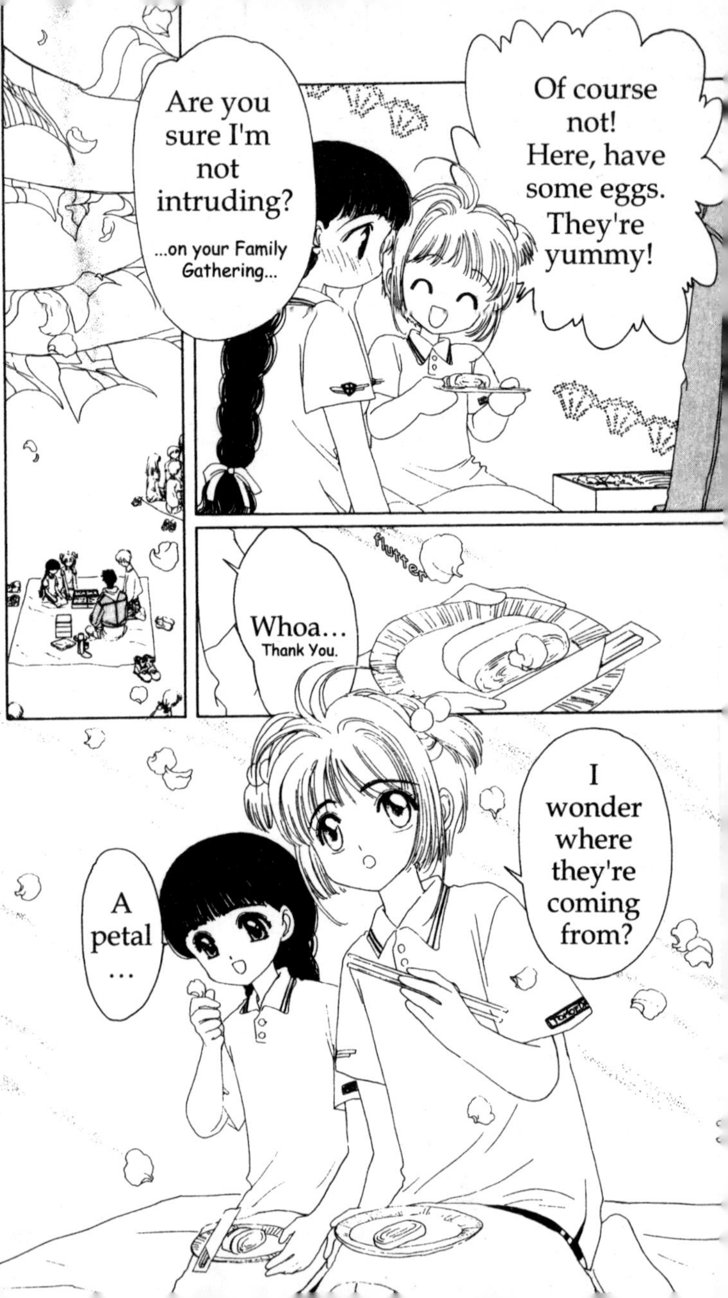
Are you sure I'm not intruding?
...on your Family Gathering...
Of course not! Here, have some eggs. They're yummy!
Whoa... Thank You.
flutter
A petal ...
I wonder where they're coming from?

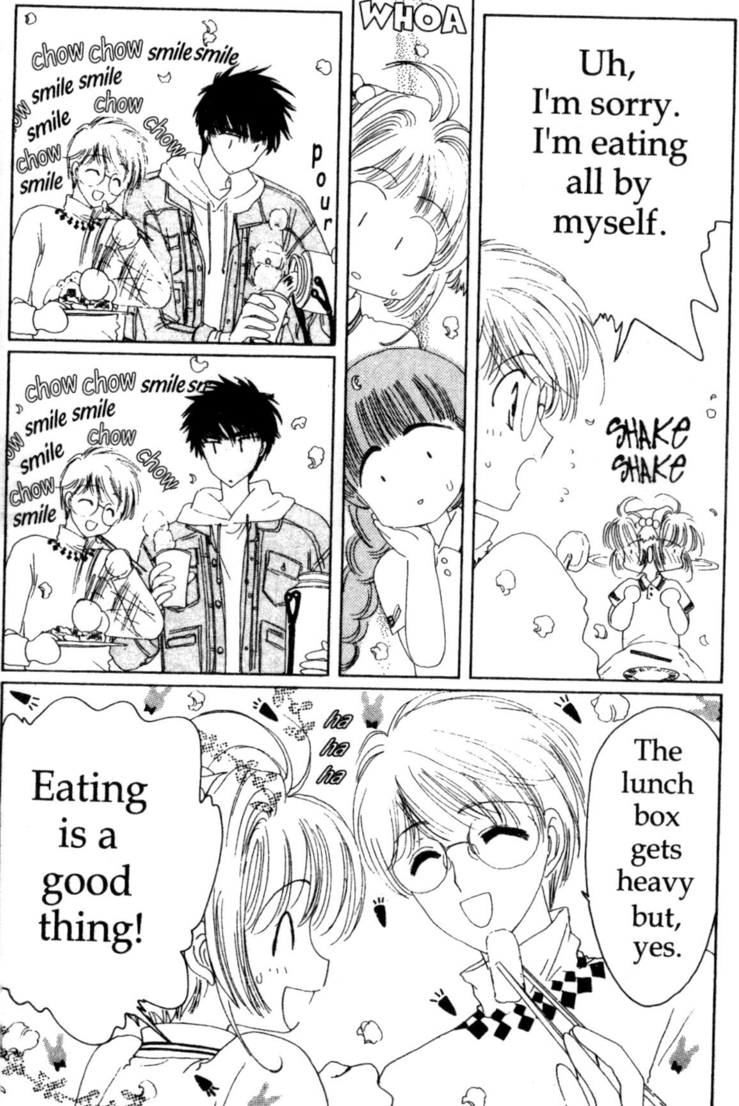

chow chow smile smile
smile smile
chow
smile
chow
chow
smile
pour
chow chow
smile smile
chow
smile
chow
chow
smile
WHOA
Uh, I'm sorry. I'm eating all by myself.
SHAKE SHAKE
Eating is a good thing!
ha ha ha
The lunch box gets heavy but, yes.

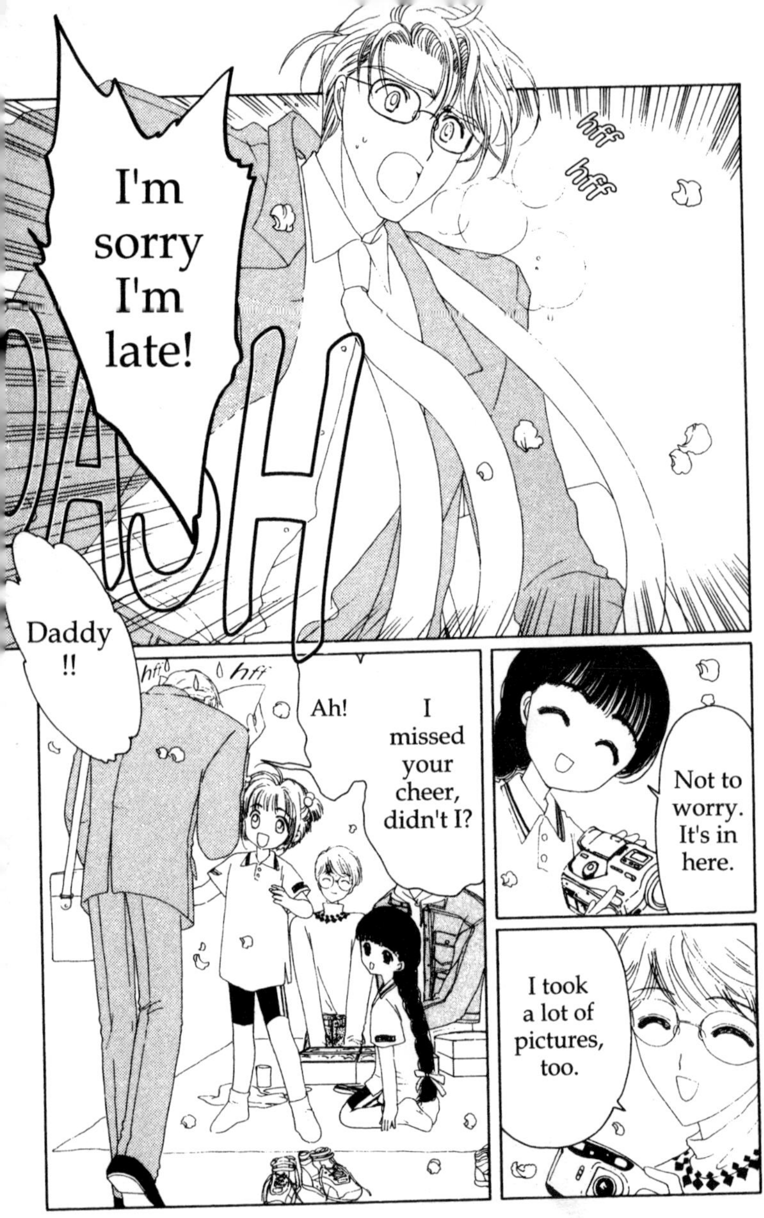
I'm sorry I'm late!
hff
hff
Daddy !!
hff
hff
Ah!
I missed your cheer, didn't I?
Not to worry. It's in here.
I took a lot of pictures, too.

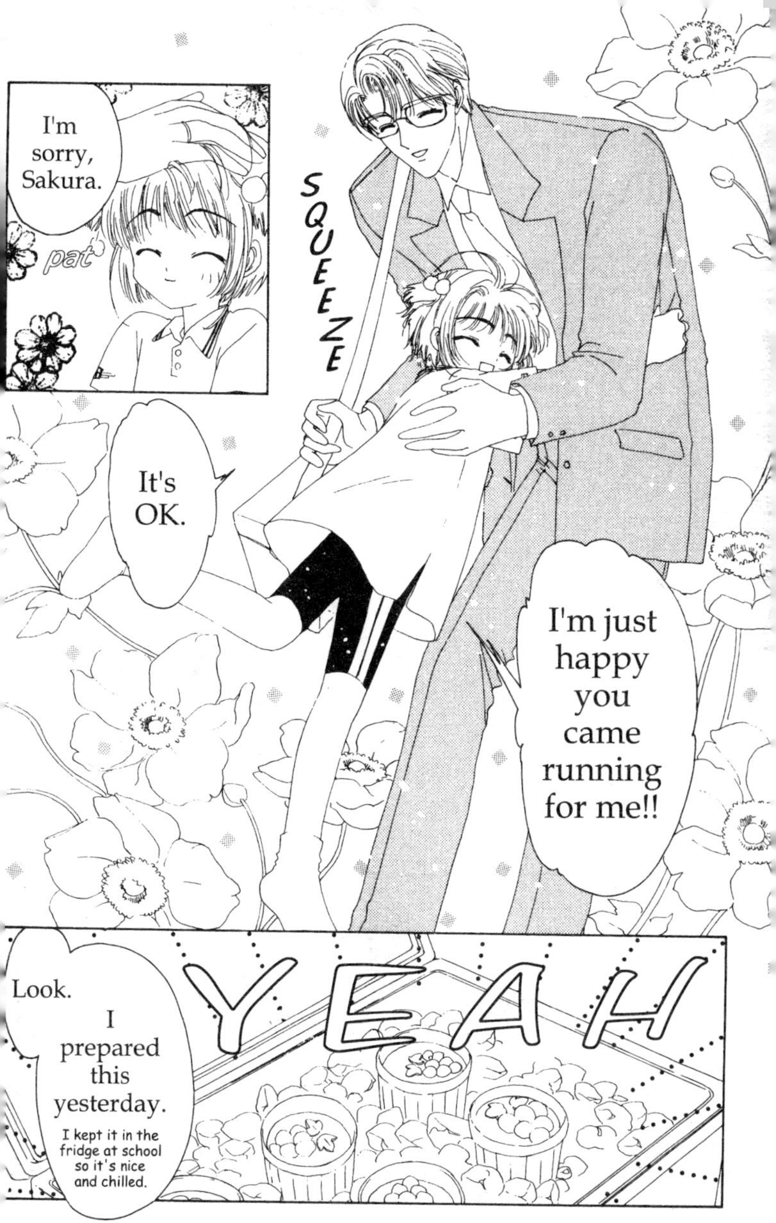

I'm sorry, Sakura.
pat
SQUEEZE
It's OK.
I'm just happy you came running for me!!
Look.
I prepared this yesterday.
I kept it in the fridge at school so it's nice and chilled.
YEAH

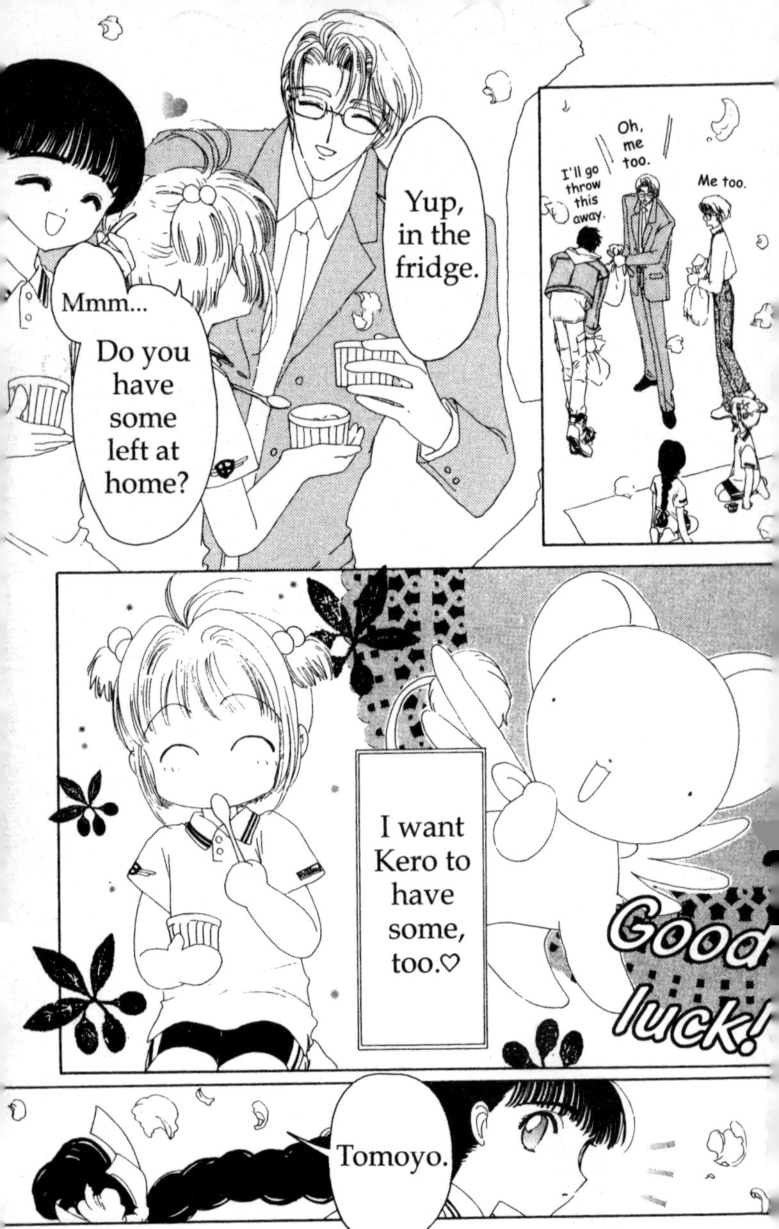
Mmm...
Do you have some left at home?
Yup, in the fridge.
I'll go throw this away.
Oh, me too.
Me too.
I want Kero to have some, too.♡
Good luck!
Tomoyo.

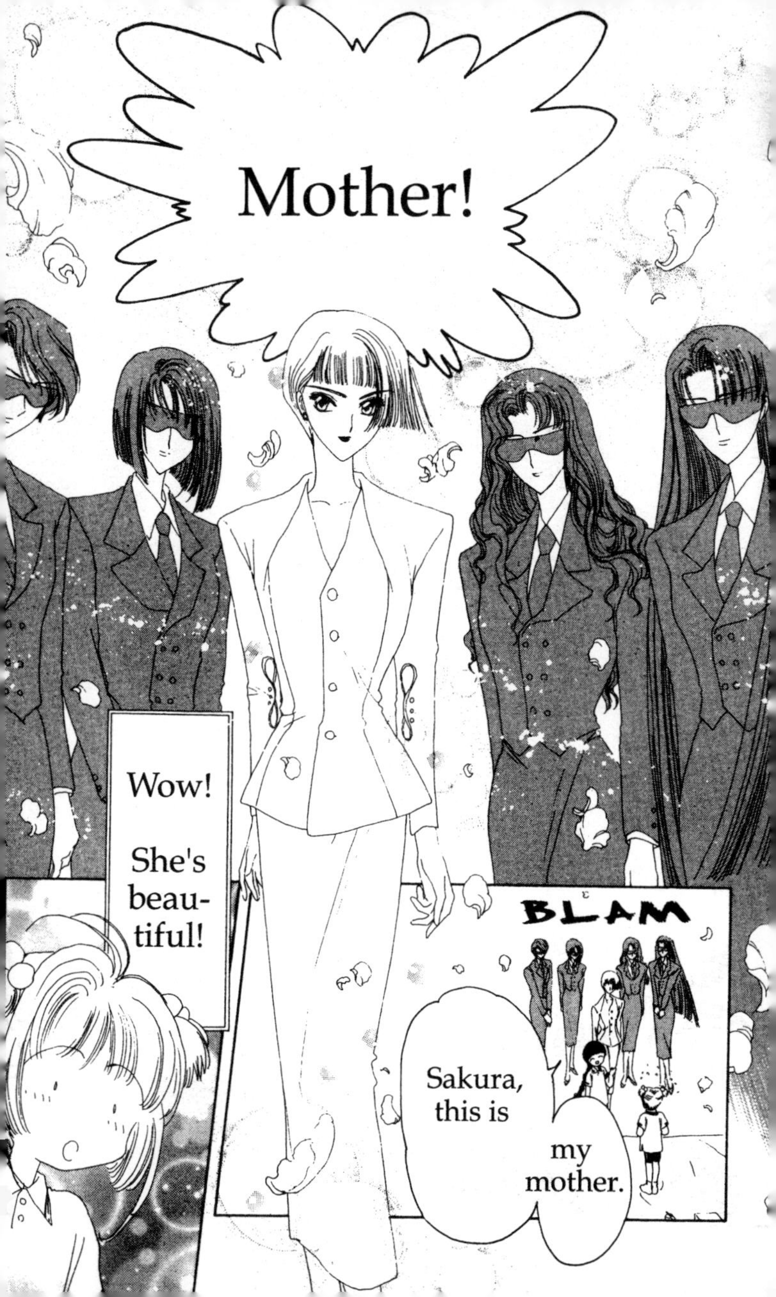
Mother!
Wow! She's beau-tiful!
BLAM
Sakura, this is my mother.

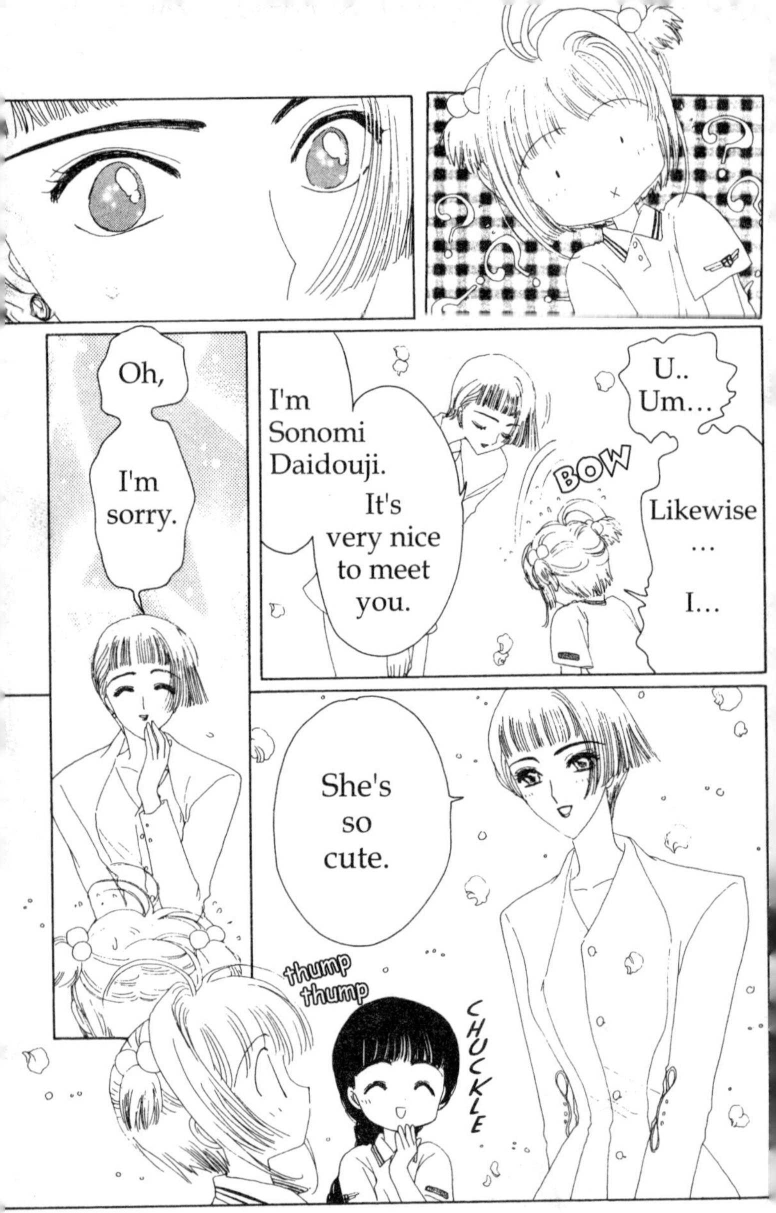
Oh,
I'm sorry.
I'm Sonomi Daidouji.
It's very nice to meet you.
BOW
U.. Um...
Likewise ...
I...
She's so cute.
thump thump
CHUCKLE

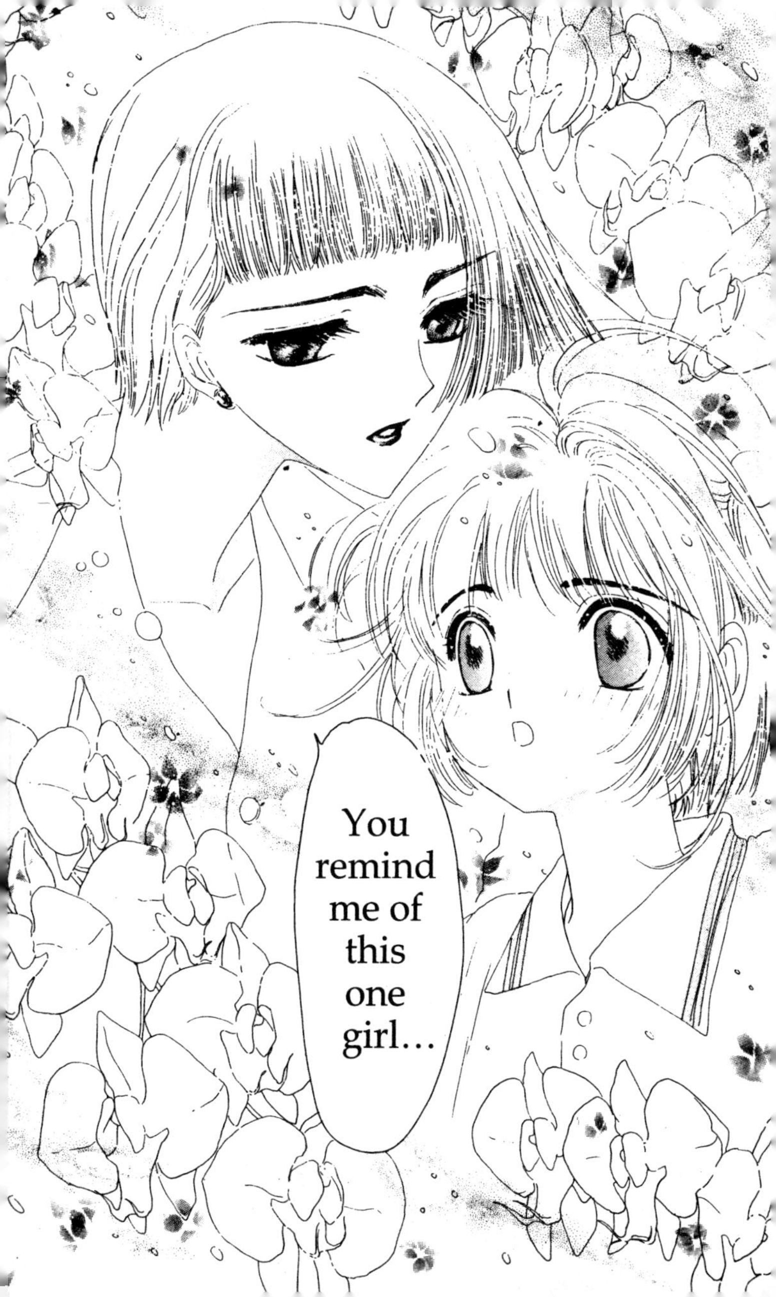
You remind me of this one girl…

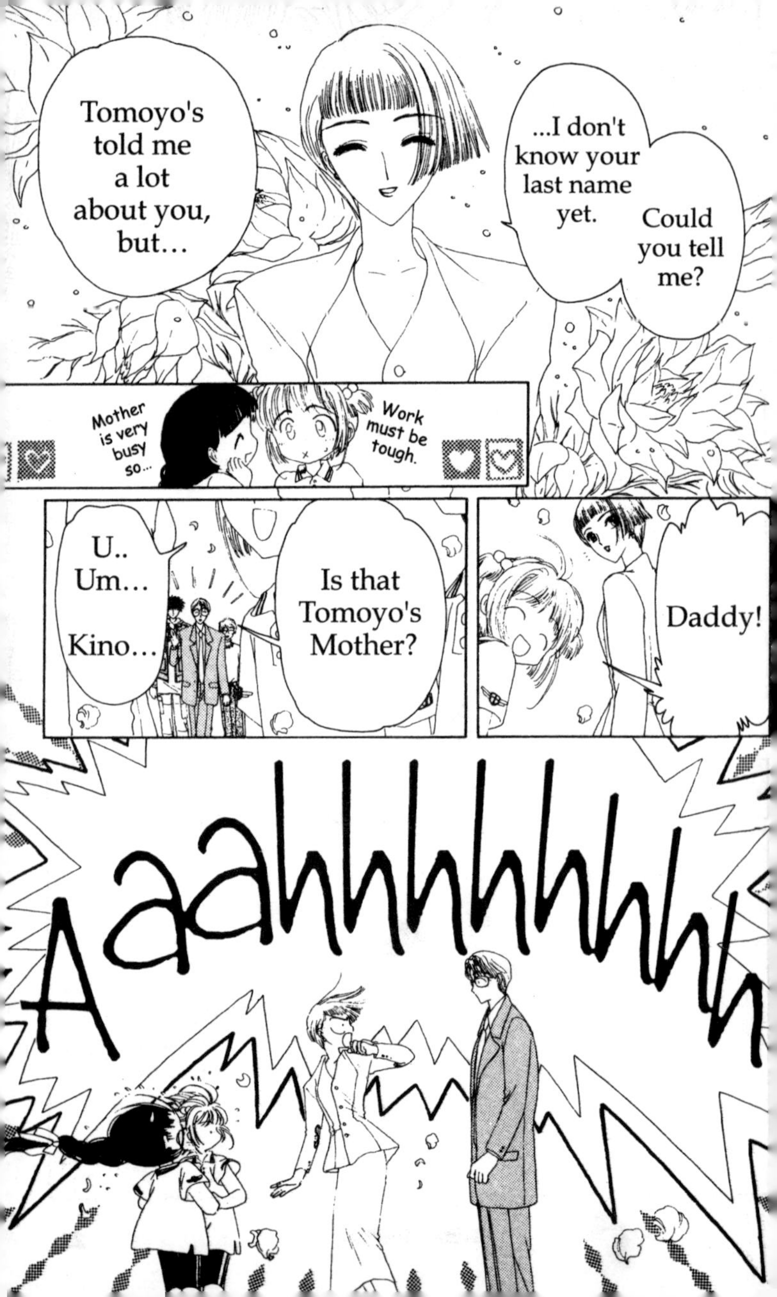
Tomoyo's told me a lot about you, but...
...I don't know your last name yet.
Could you tell me?
Mother is very busy so...
Work must be tough.
U.. Um... Kino...
Is that Tomoyo's Mother?
Daddy!
Aaahhhhhhh

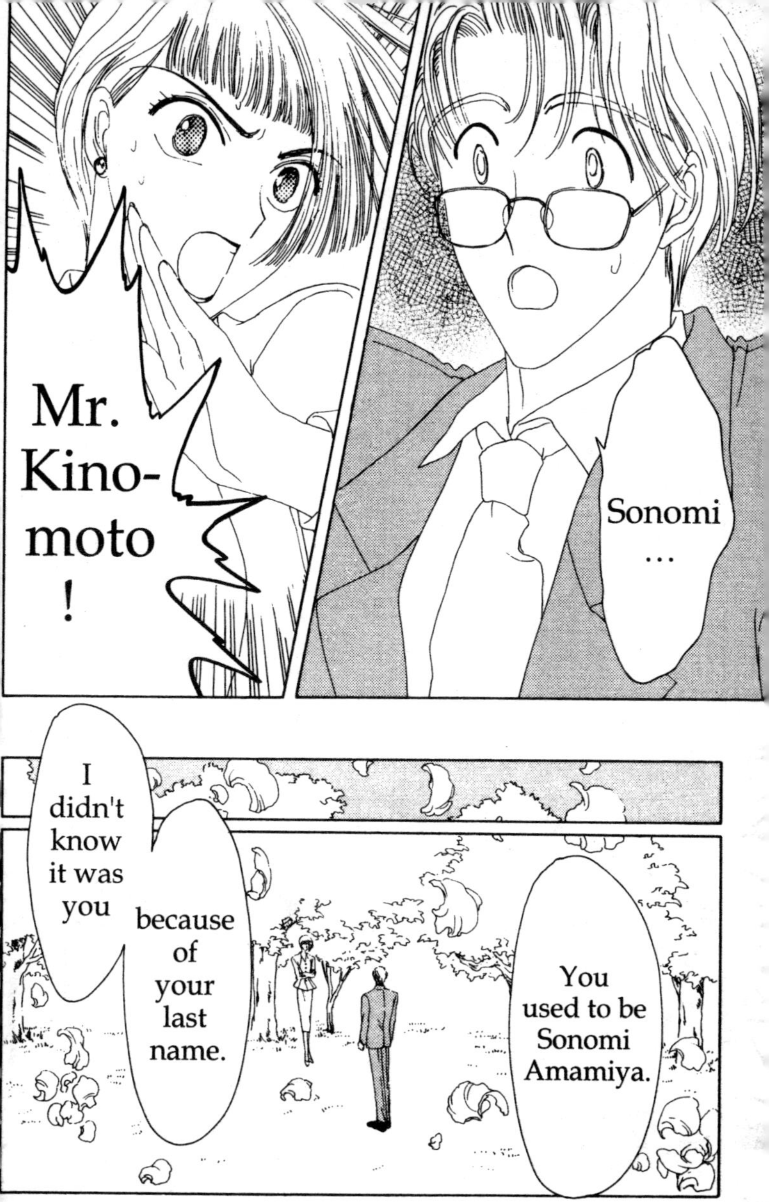
Mr. Kino-moto!
Sonomi...
I didn't know it was you
because of your last name.
You used to be Sonomi Amamiya.

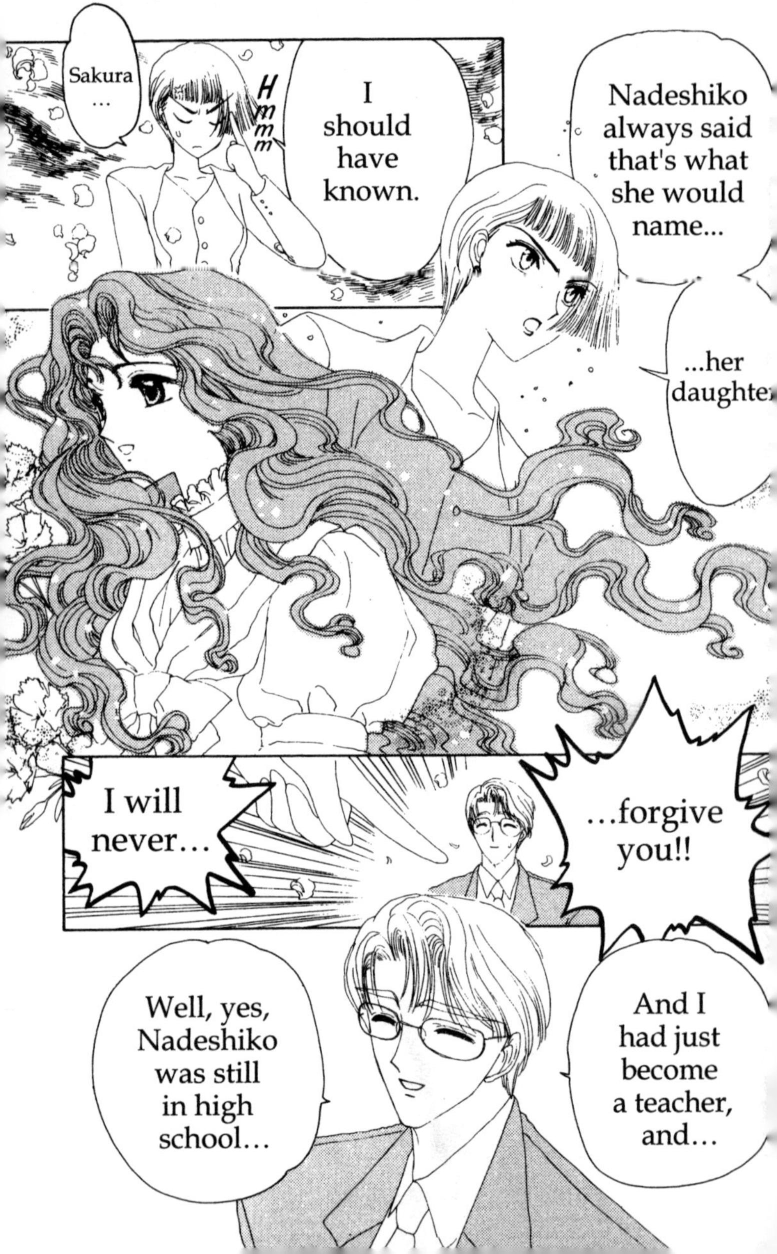
Sakura ...
Hmmm
I should have known.
Nadeshiko always said that's what she would name...
...her daughte
I will never...
...forgive you!!
Well, yes, Nadeshiko was still in high school...
And I had just become a teacher, and...

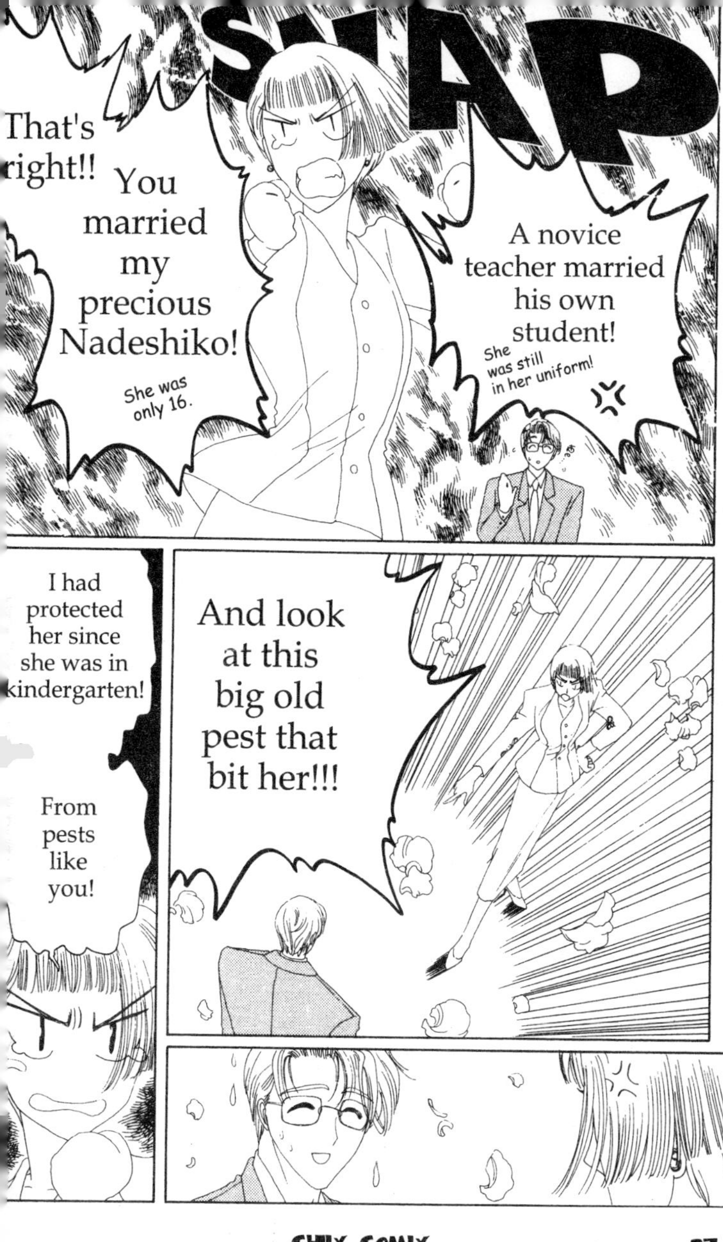
SNAP
That's right!!
You married my precious Nadeshiko!
She was only 16.
A novice teacher married his own student!
She was still in her uniform!
I had protected her since she was in kindergarten!
From pests like you!
And look at this big old pest that bit her!!!

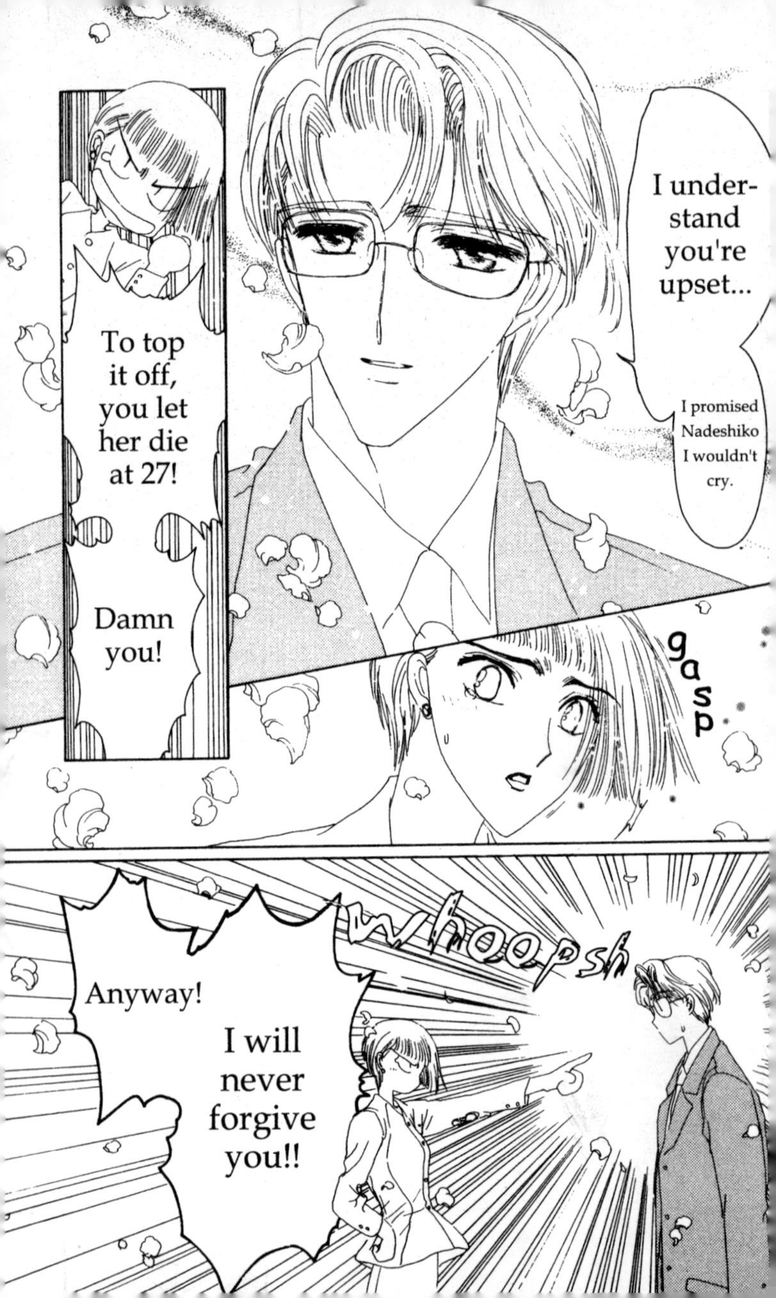
To top it off, you let her die at 27!
Damn you!
I under-stand you're upset...
I promised Nadeshiko I wouldn't cry.
gasp
Anyway!
I will never forgive you!!
whoopsh

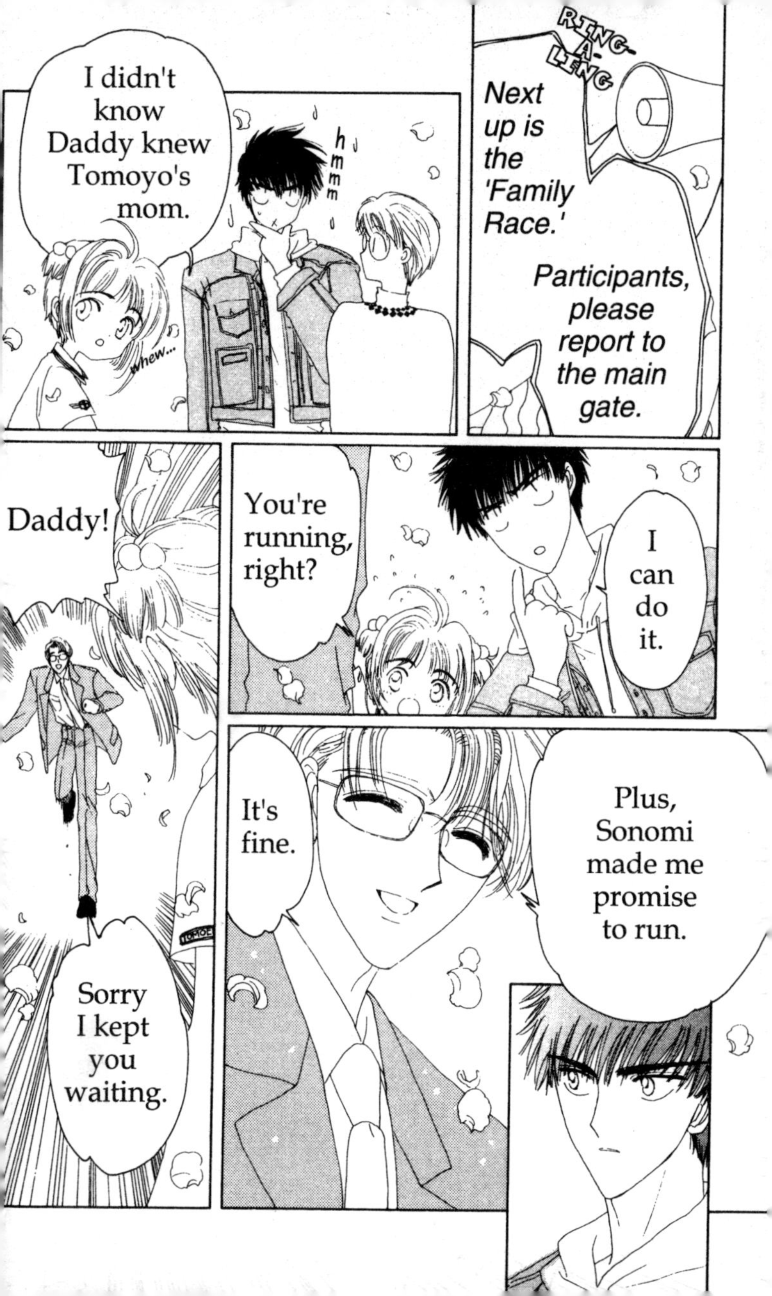
I didn't know Daddy knew Tomoyo's mom.
hmmm
whew...
RING-A-LING
Next up is the 'Family Race.'
Participants, please report to the main gate.
Daddy!
Sorry I kept you waiting.
You're running, right?
I can do it.
It's fine.
Plus, Sonomi made me promise to run.

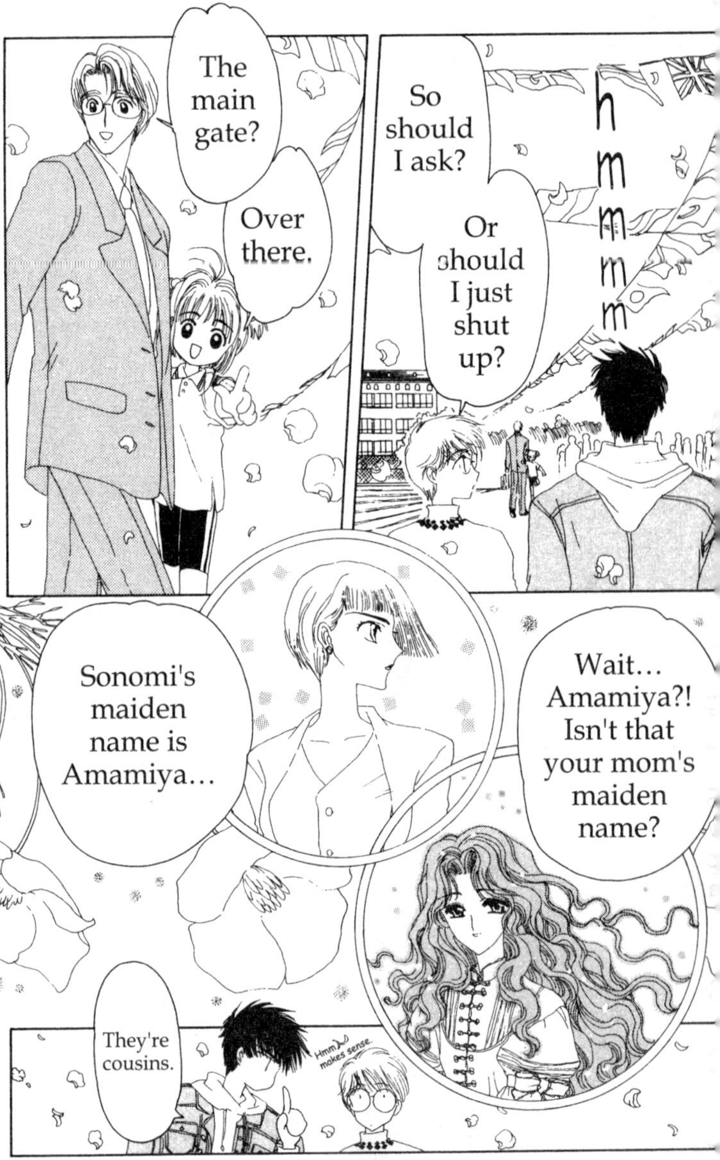

The main gate?
Over there.
So should I ask?
Or should I just shut up?
hmmmm
Sonomi's maiden name is Amamiya...
Wait... Amamiya?! Isn't that your mom's maiden name?
They're cousins.
Hmm makes sense.

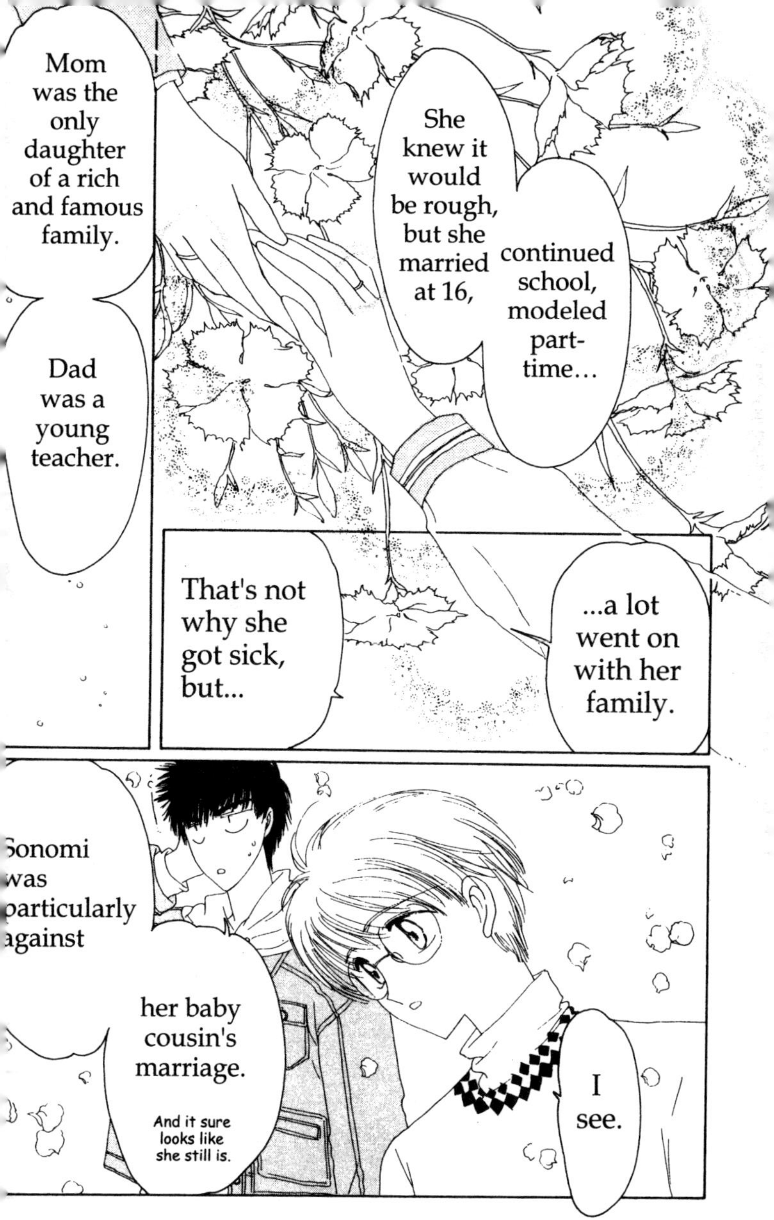
Mom was the only daughter of a rich and famous family.
Dad was a young teacher.
She knew it would be rough, but she married at 16,
continued school, modeled part-time...
That's not why she got sick, but...
...a lot went on with her family.
Sonomi was particularly against
her baby cousin's marriage.
And it sure looks like she still is.
I see.

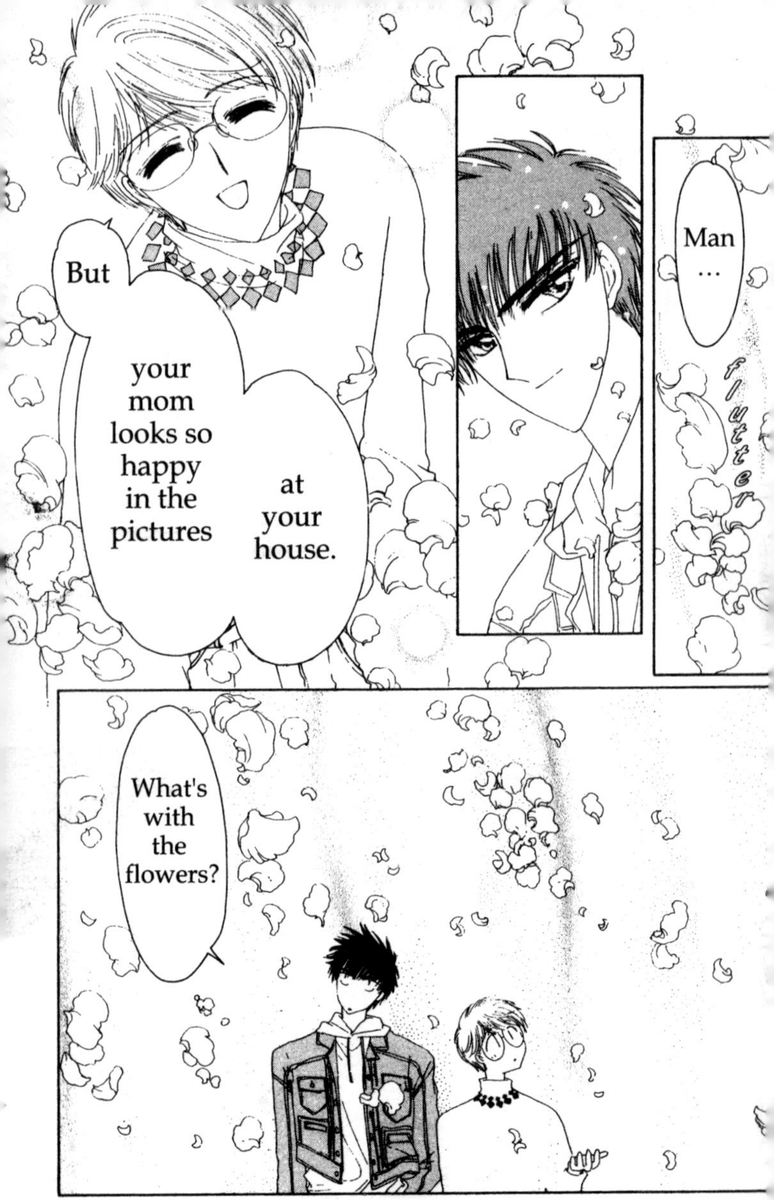
But
your mom looks so happy in the pictures
at your house.
Man ...
flutter
What's with the flowers?

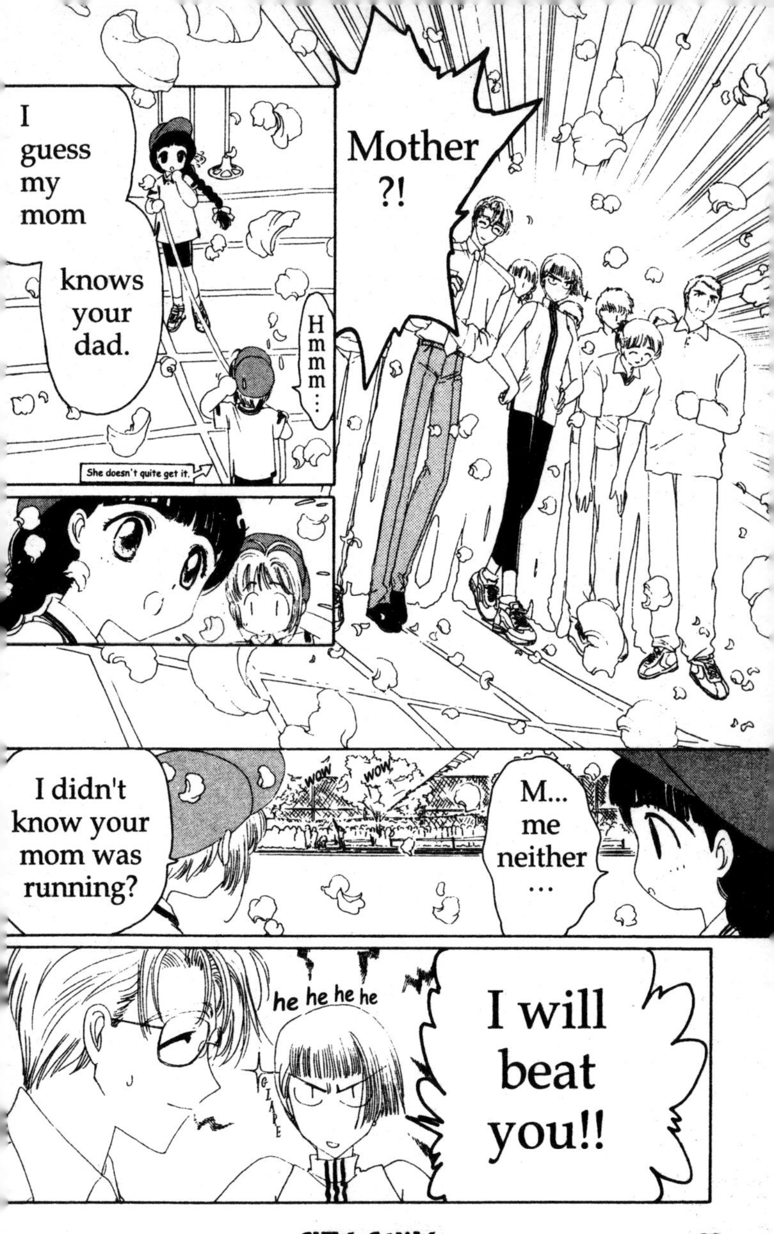
I guess my mom
knows your dad.
Hmmm...
She doesn't quite get it.
Mother?!
WOW
WOW
I didn't know your mom was running?
M... me neither...
he he he he
GLARE
I will beat you!!

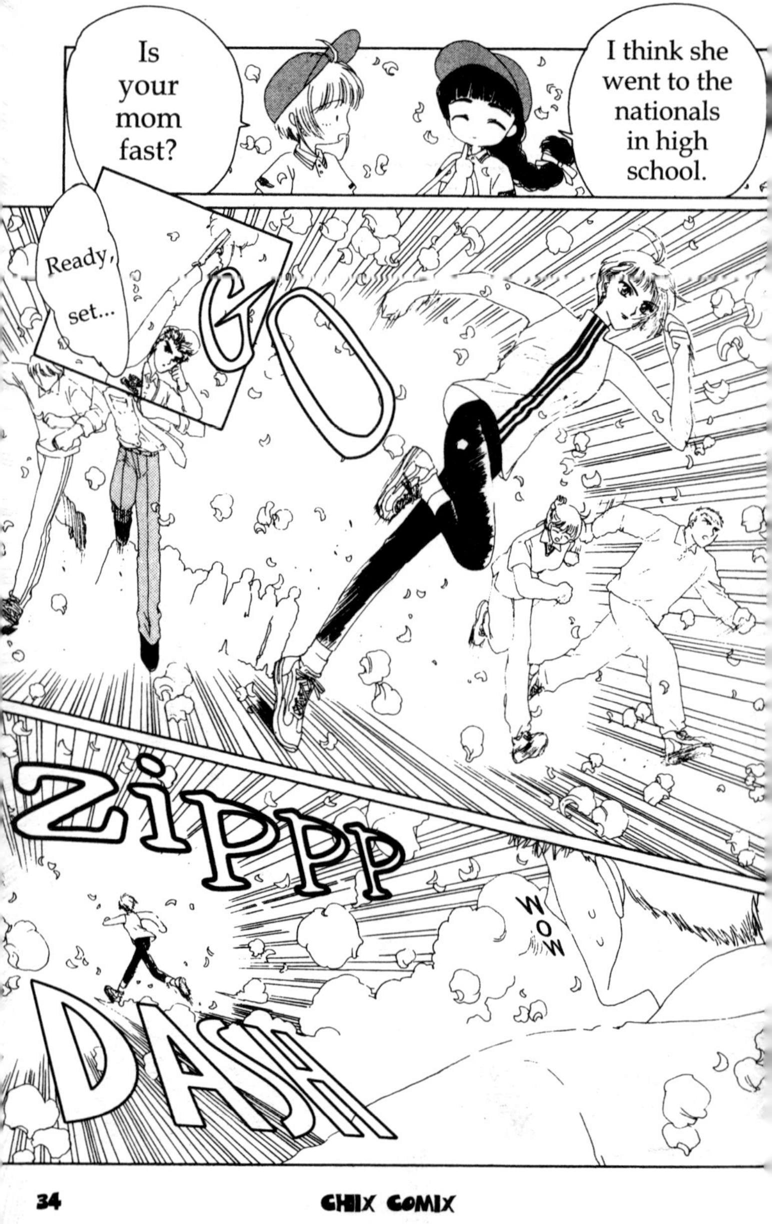

Is your mom fast?
I think she went to the nationals in high school.
Ready, set...
GO
ZiPPP
WOW
DASH

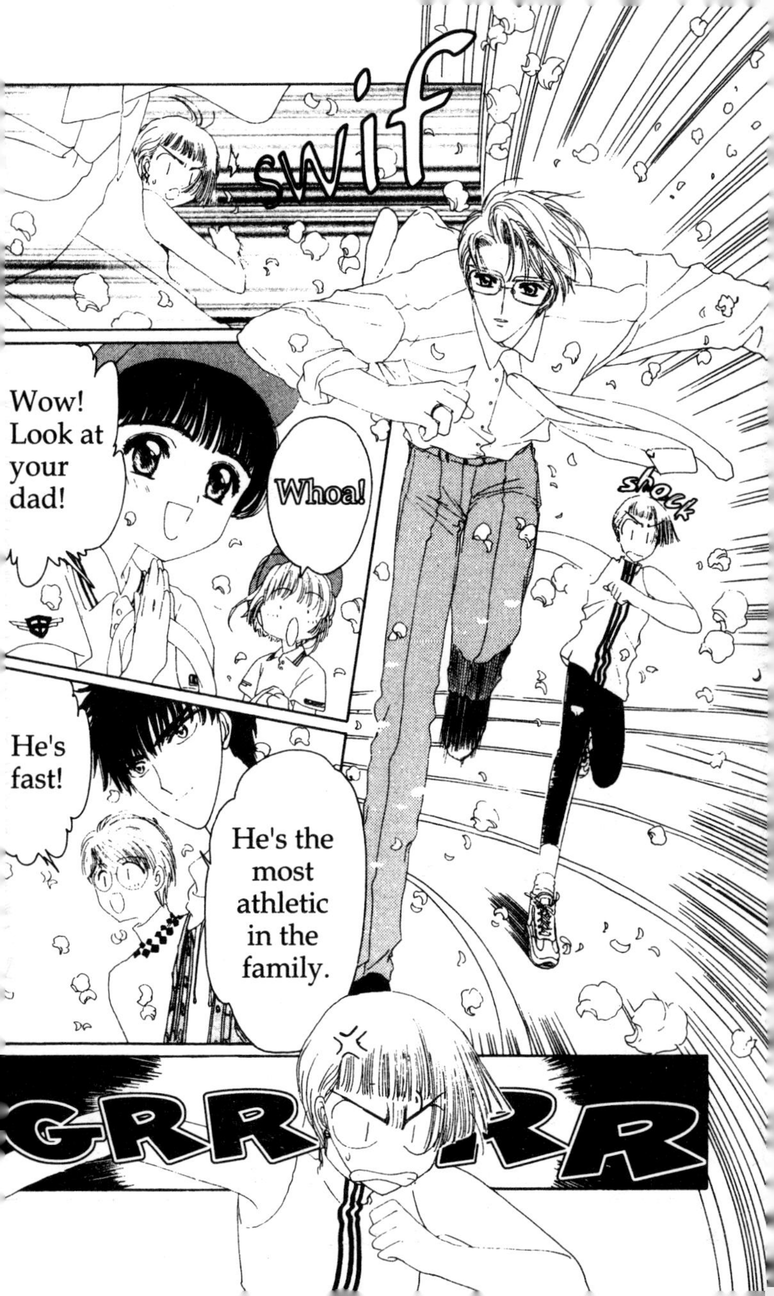
swif
Wow! Look at your dad!
Whoa!
shock
He's fast!
He's the most athletic in the family.
GRRRRR

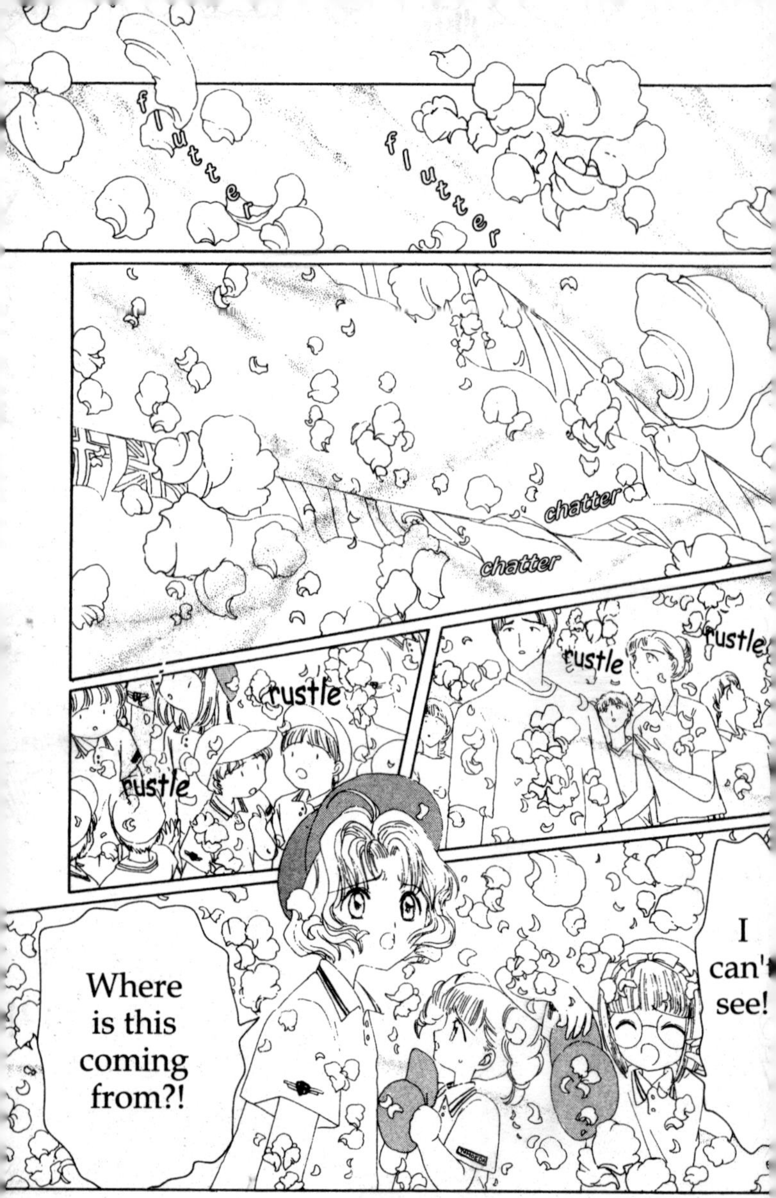
flutter
flutter
chatter
chatter
rustle
rustle
rustle
rustle
Where is this coming from?!
I can't see!

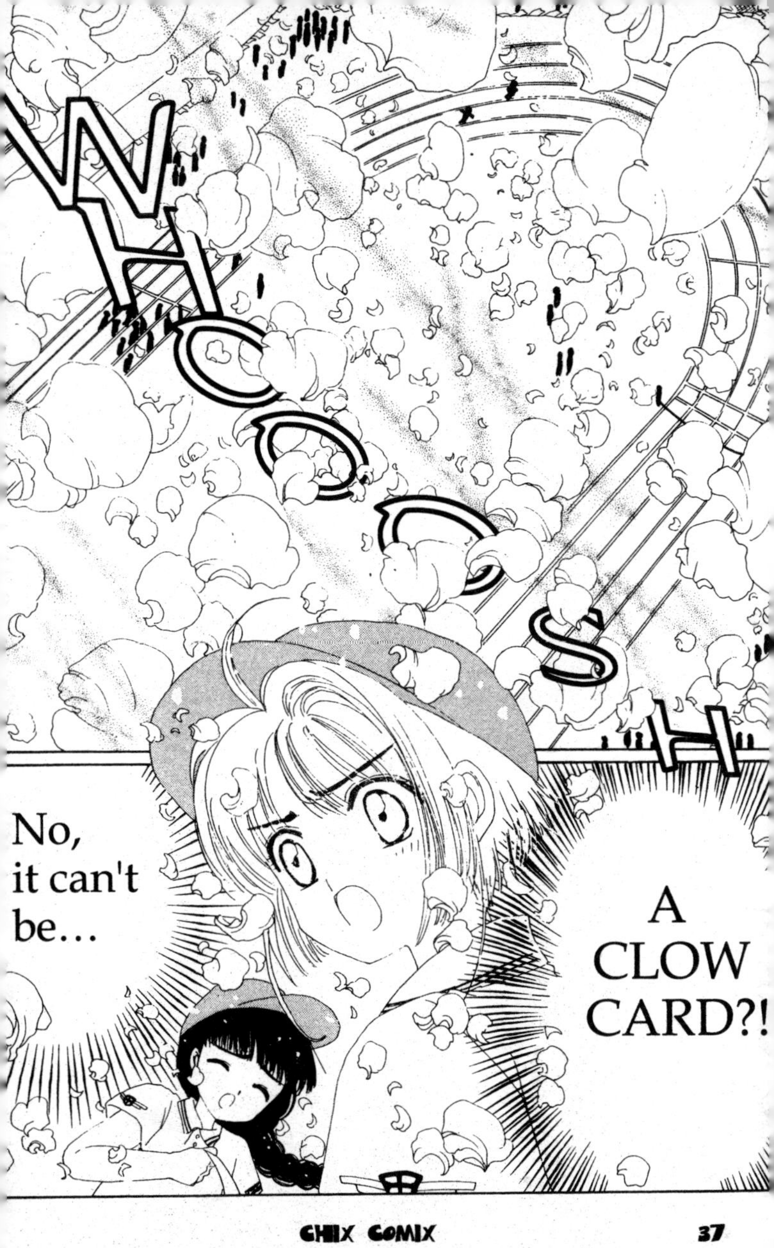
WHOOOSH
No, it can't be…
A CLOW CARD?!

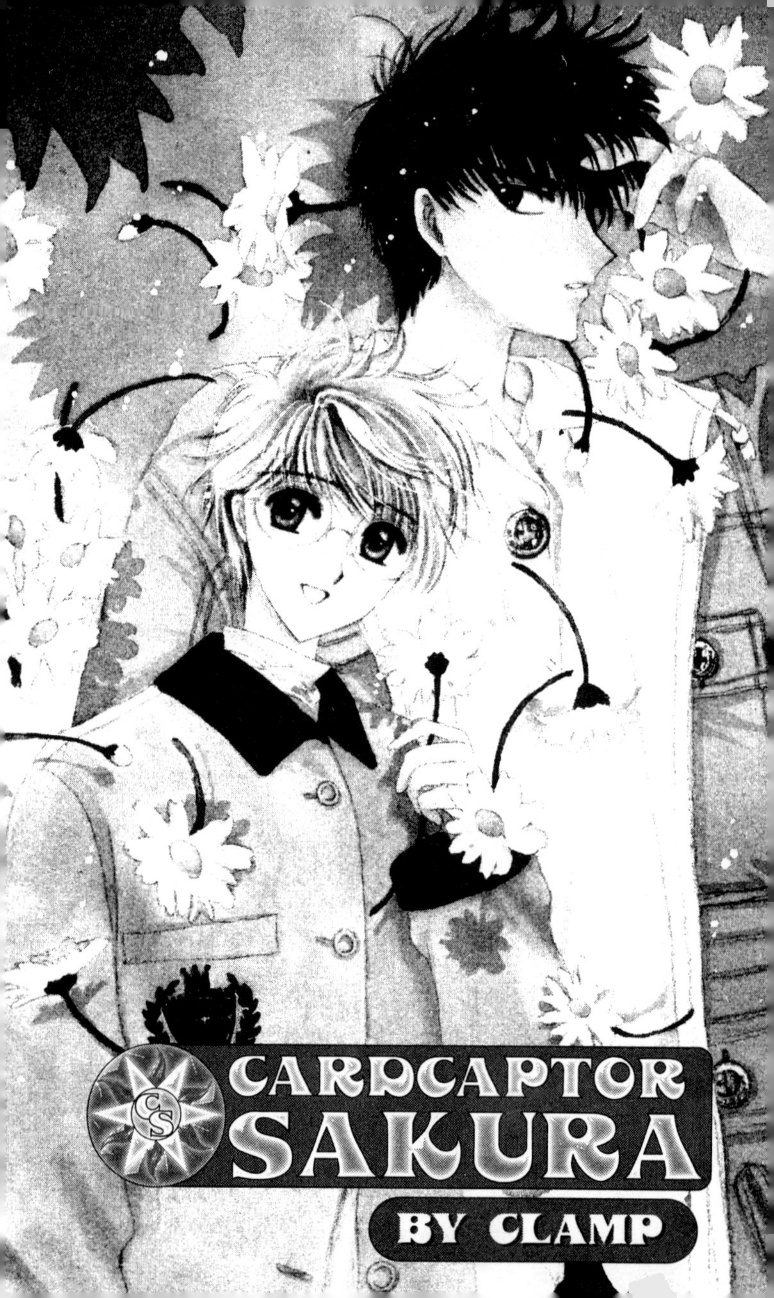
CS
CARDCAPTOR
SAKURA
BY CLAMP

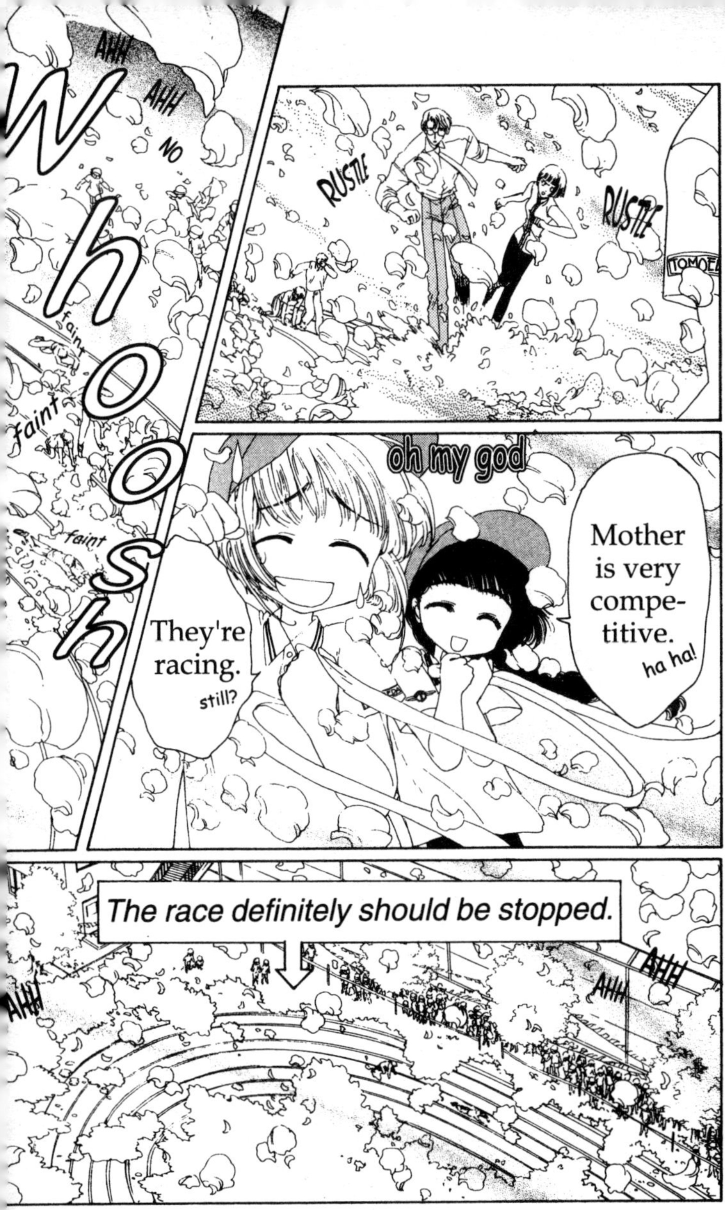
AHH
AHH
NO
Whoosh
faint
faint
faint
RUSTLE
RUSTLE
TOMOEDA
oh my god
They're racing.
still?
Mother is very compe-titive.
ha ha!
The race definitely should be stopped.
AHH
AHH
AHH

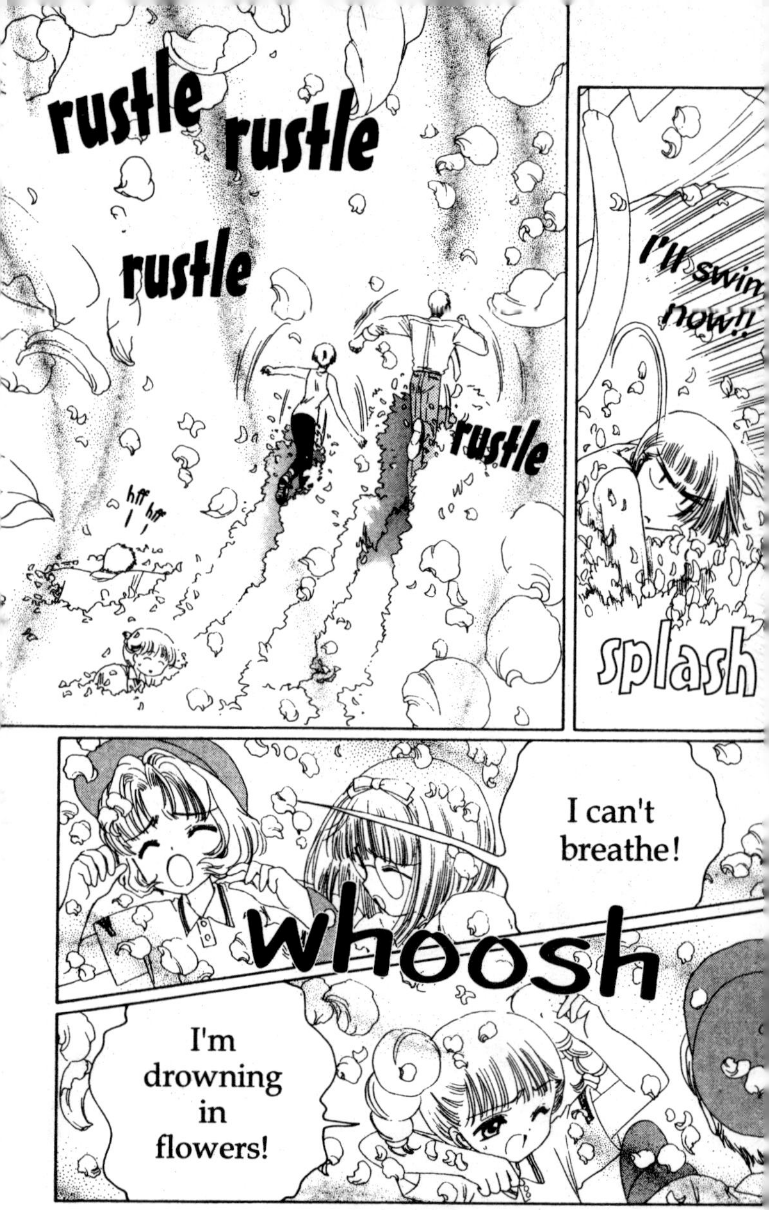
rustle
rustle
rustle
hff hff
rustle
I'll swin now!!
splash
I can't breathe!
whoosh
I'm drowning in flowers!

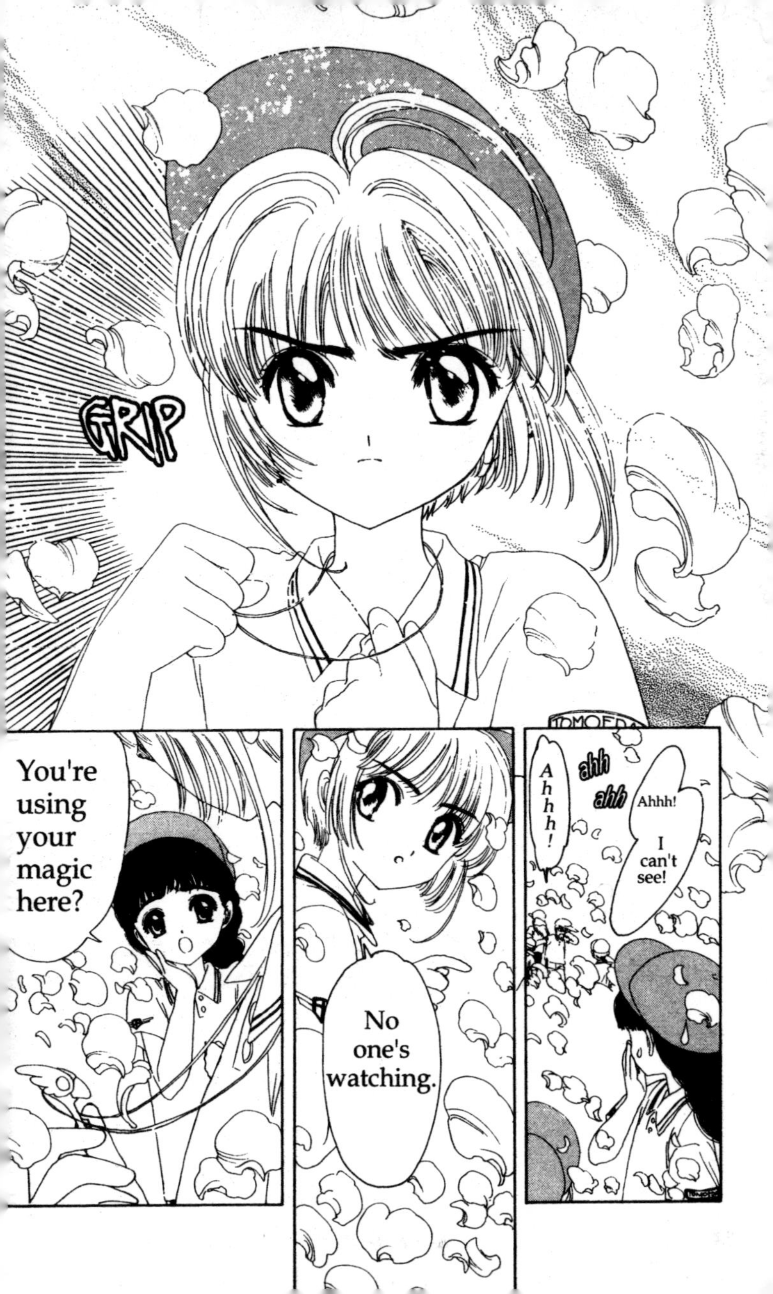
GRIP
You're using your magic here?
No one's watching.
Ahhh!
ahh ahh
Ahhh! I can't see!

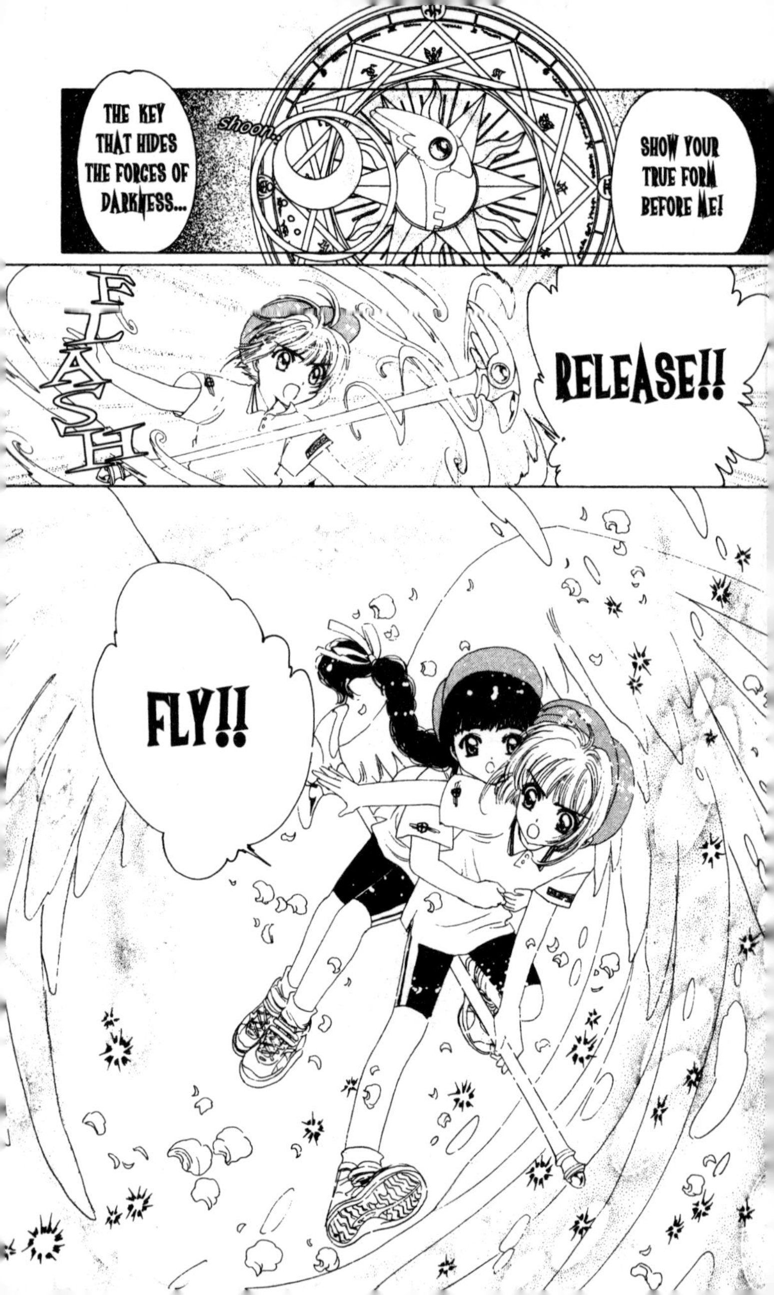
THE KEY THAT HIDES THE FORCES OF DARKNESS...
shoon...
SHOW YOUR TRUE FORM BEFORE ME!
FLASH
RELEASE!!
FLY!!

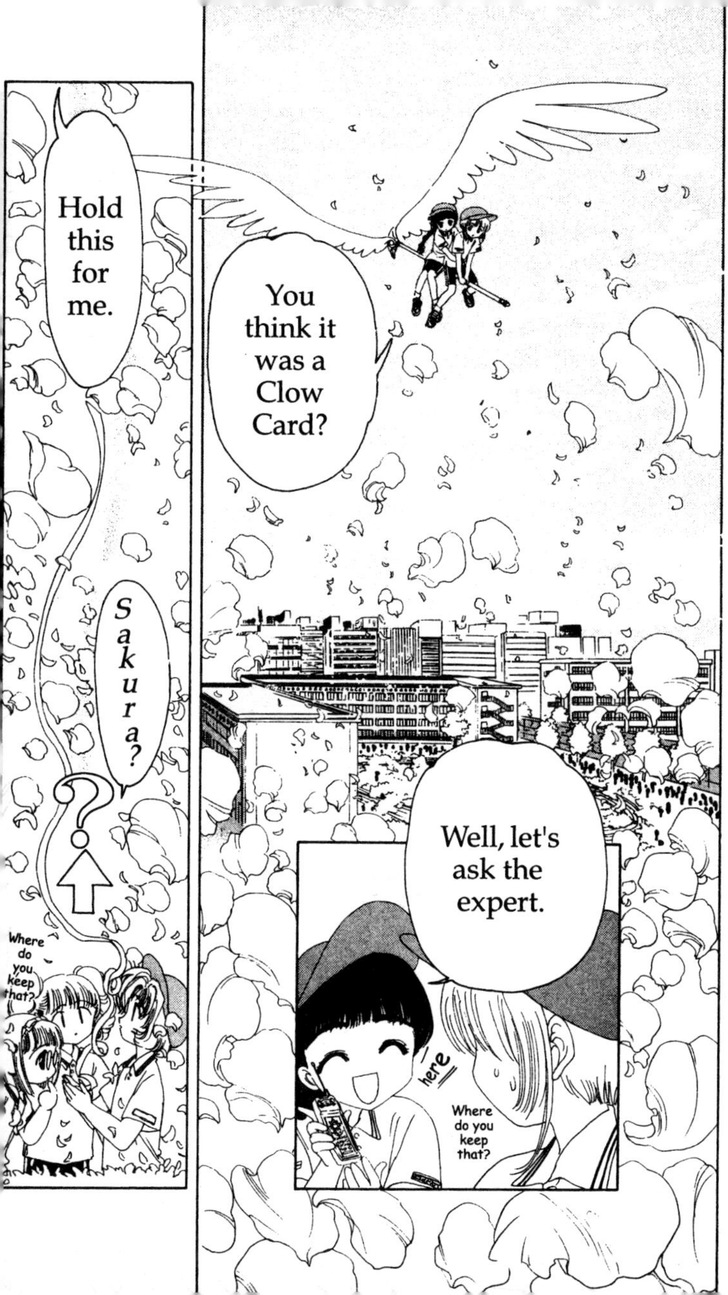
Hold this for me.
Sakura?
Where do you keep that?
You think it was a Clow Card?
Well, let's ask the expert.
here
Where do you keep that?

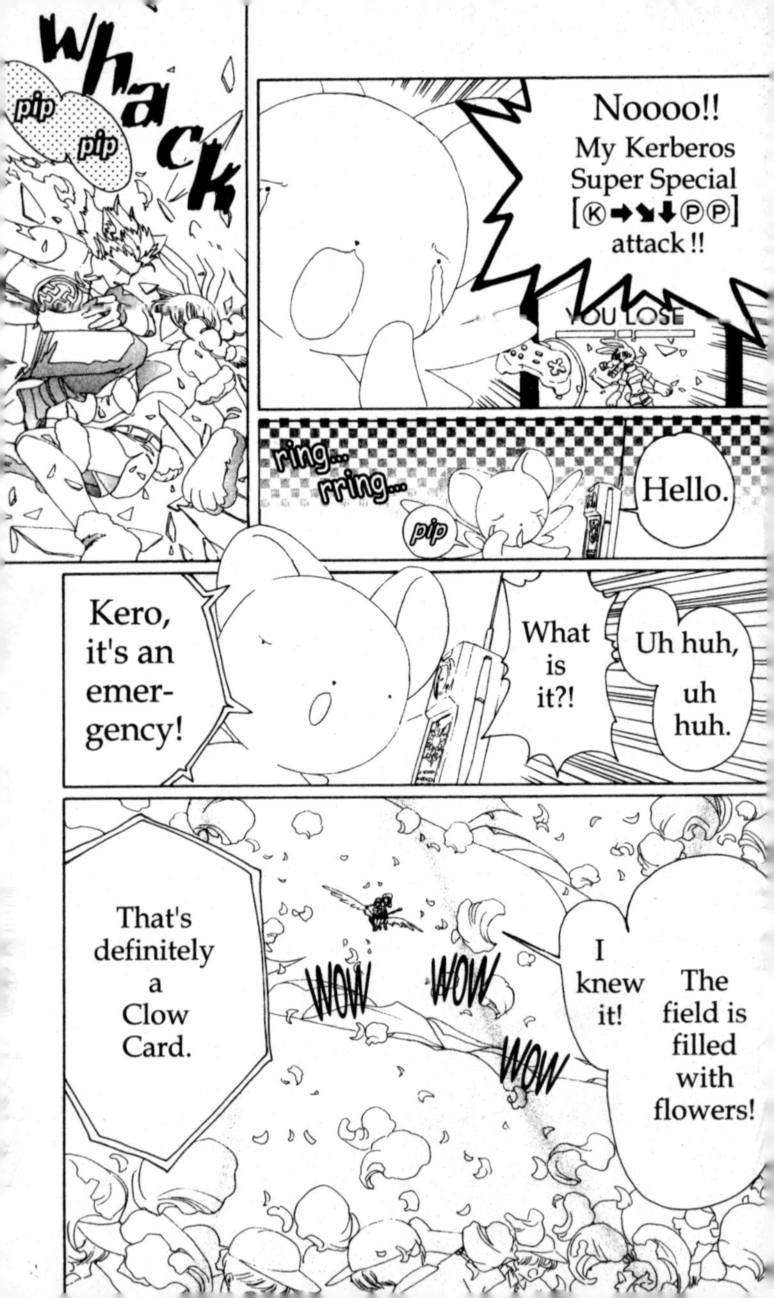
Whack
pip
pip
Noooo!! My Kerberos Super Special [Ⓚ➡↘⬇ⓅⓅ] attack !!
YOU LOSE
ring... rring...
pip
Hello.
Kero, it's an emer-gency!
What is it?!
Uh huh, uh huh.
That's definitely a Clow Card.
WOW
WOW
WOW
I knew it! The field is filled with flowers!

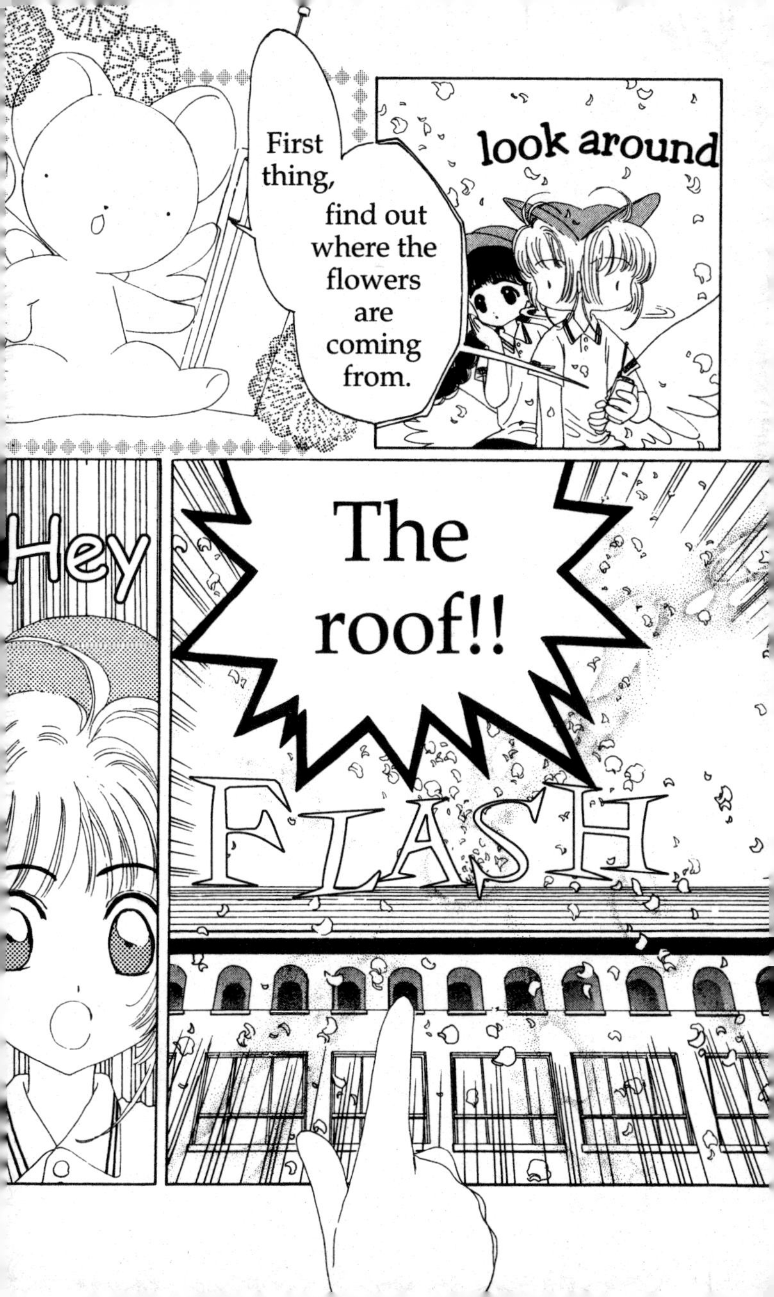
First thing, find out where the flowers are coming from.
look around
Hey
The roof!!
FLASH

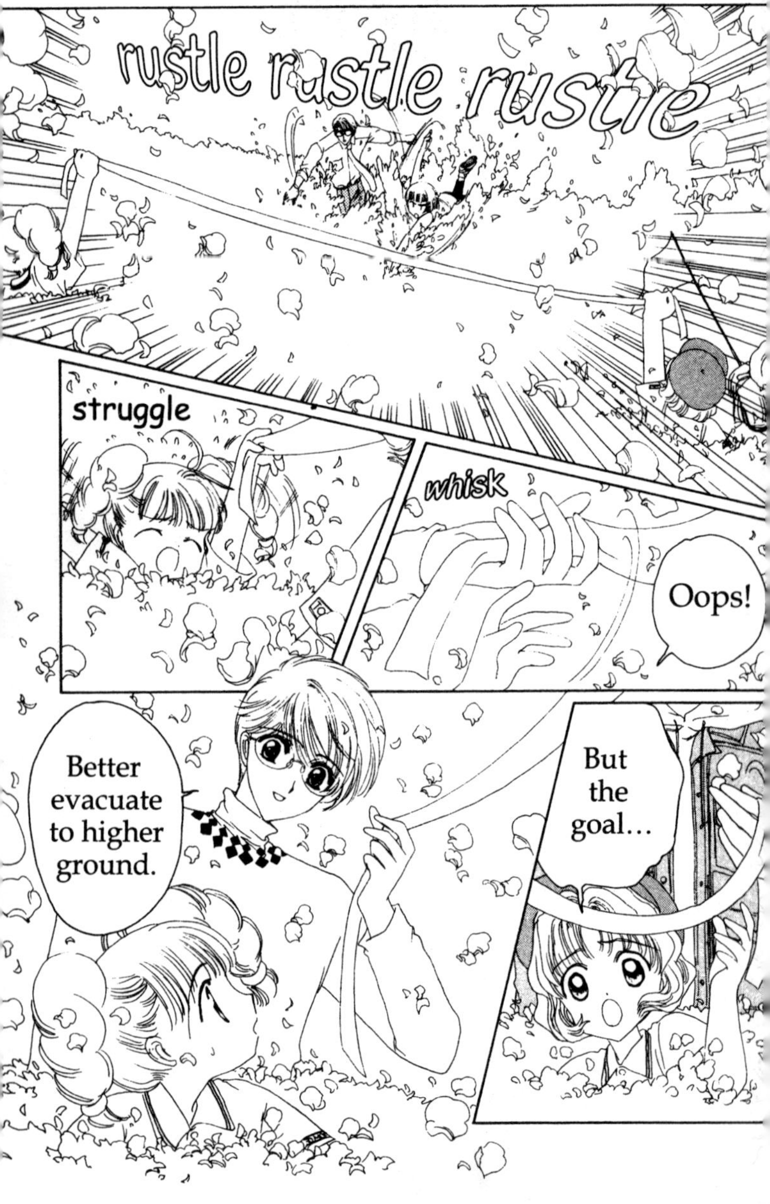
rustle rustle rustle
struggle
whisk
Oops!
Better evacuate to higher ground.
But the goal...

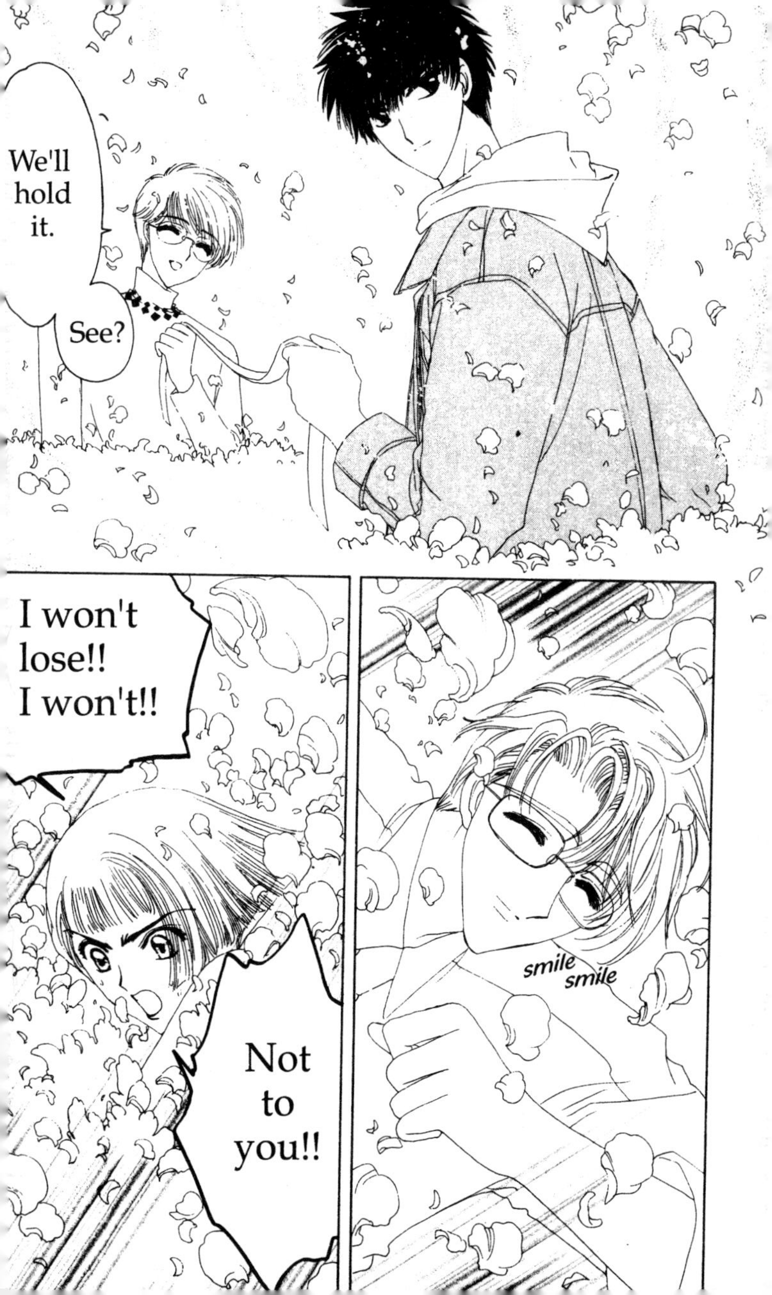
We'll hold it.
See?
I won't lose!! I won't!!
Not to you!!
smile smile

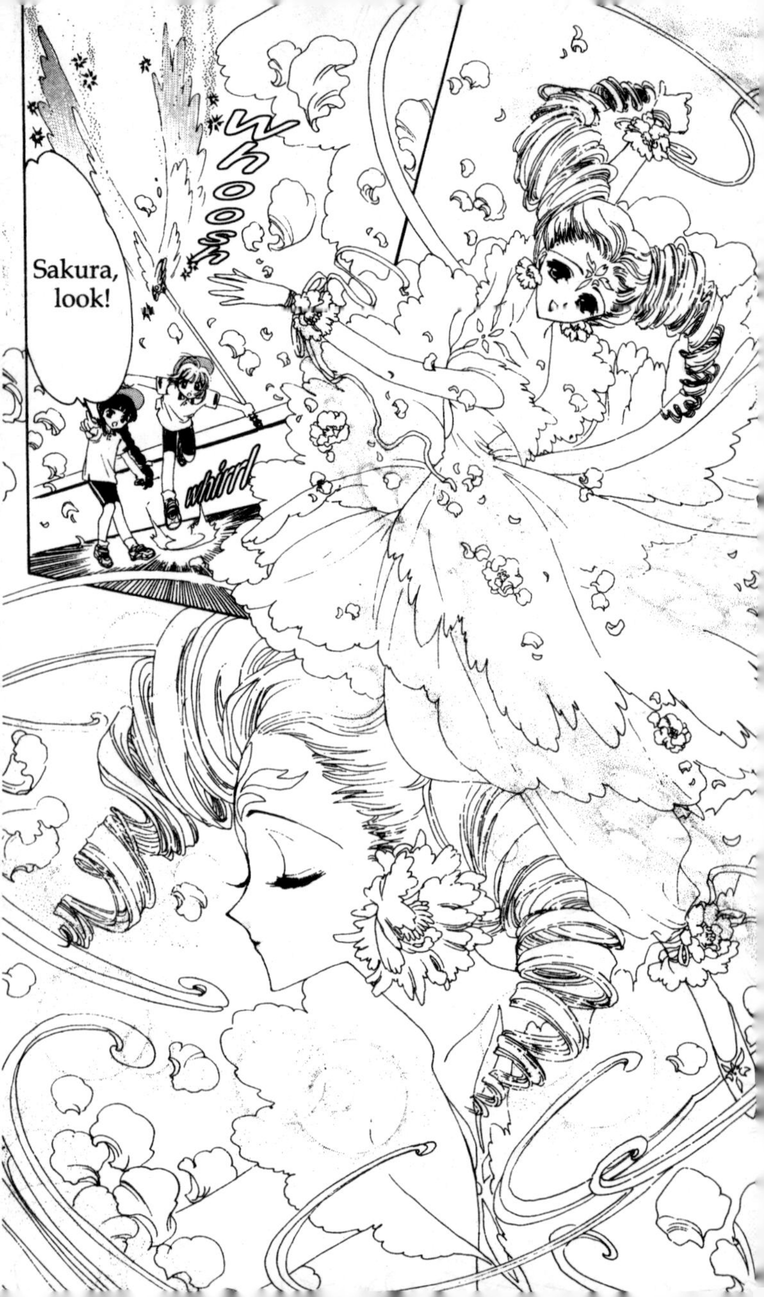
Sakura, look!
whoosh
whirl

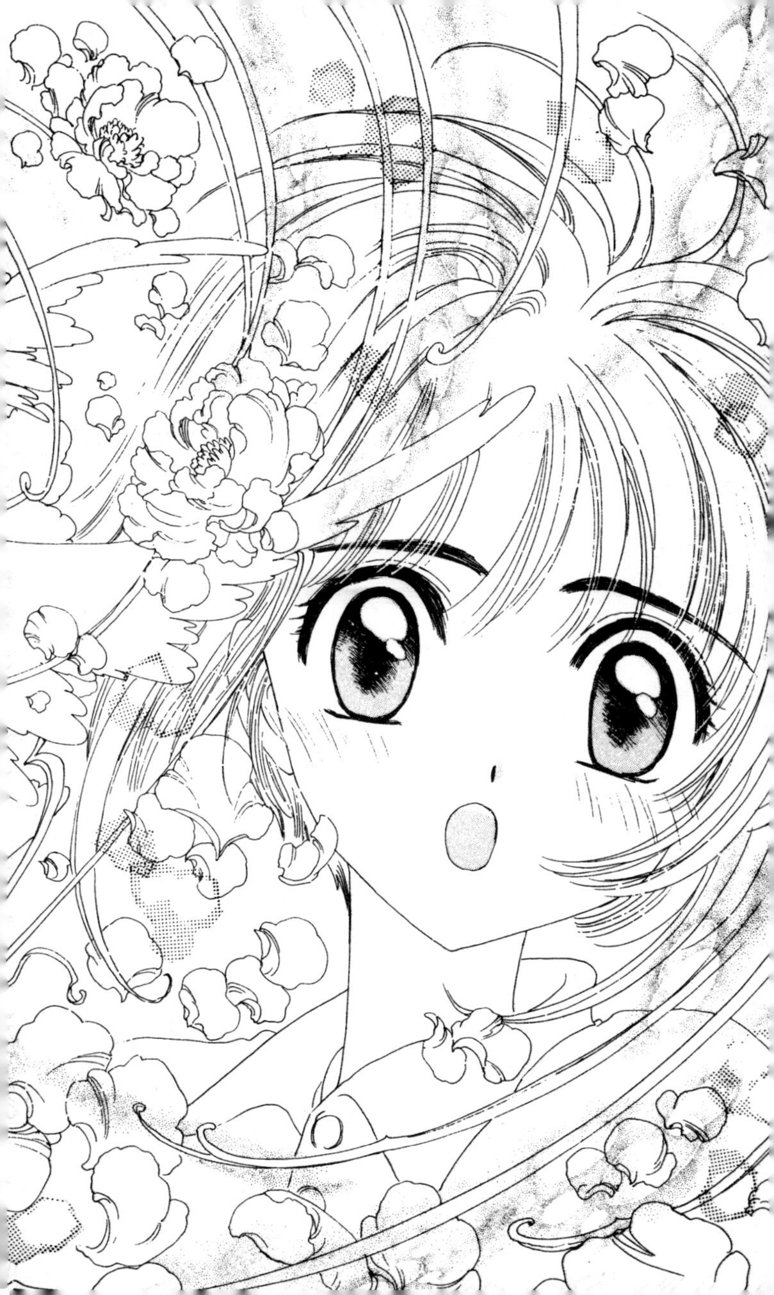

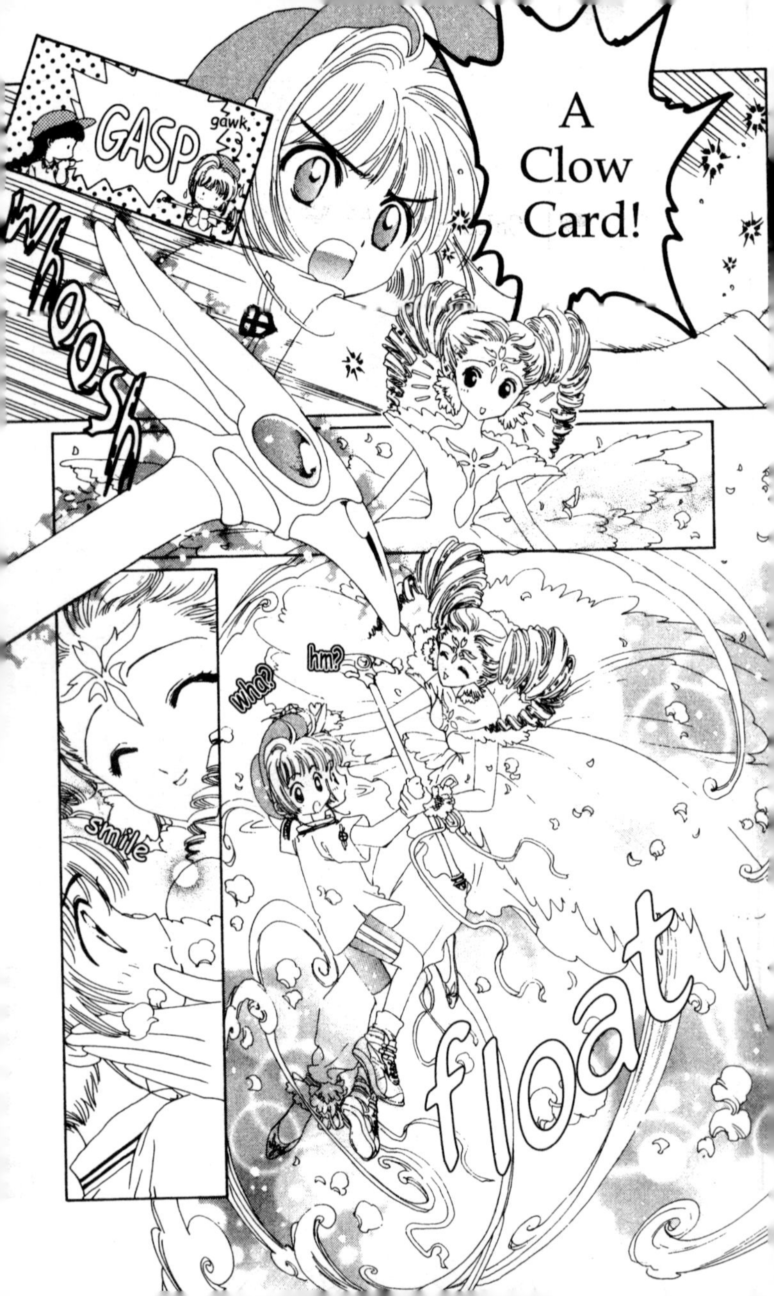
GASP
gawk,
whoosh
A Clow Card!
smile
wha?
hm?
float

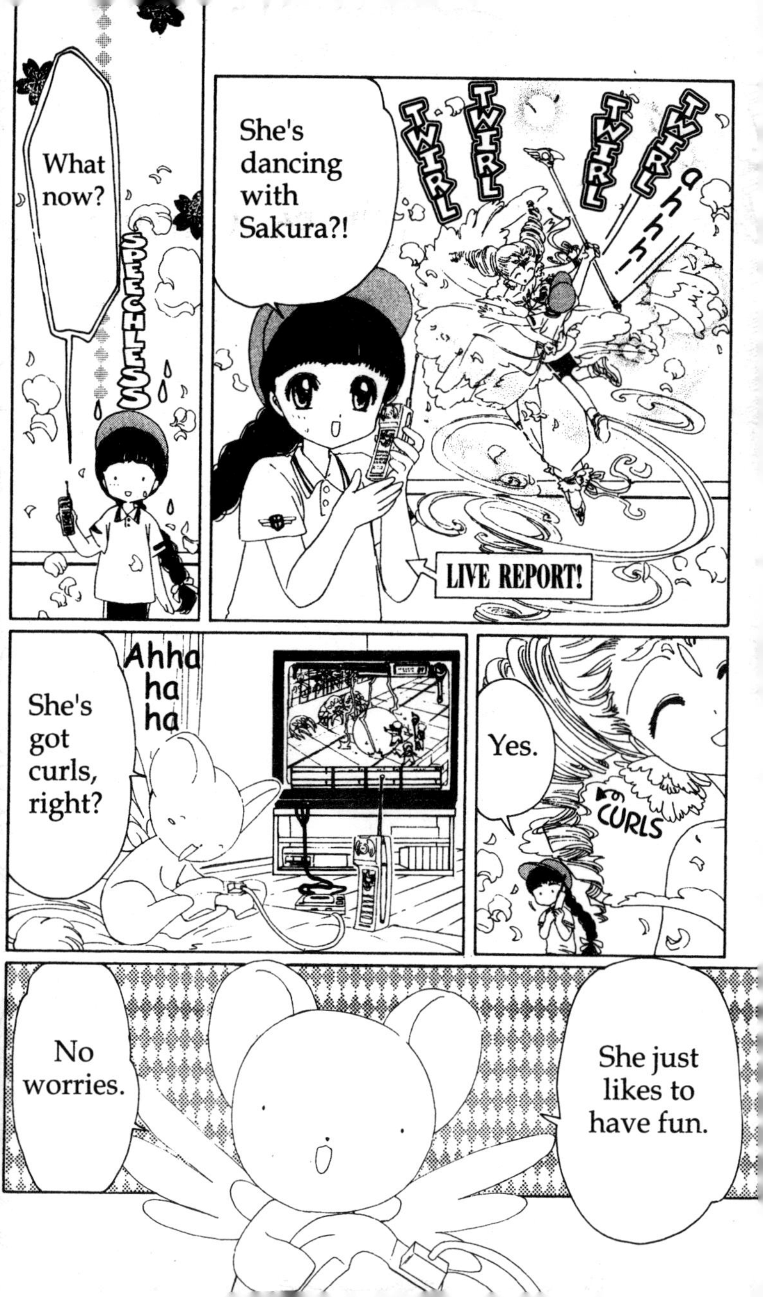
What now?
SPEECHLESS
She's dancing with Sakura?!
TWIRL
TWIRL
TWIRL
TWIRL
ahhhh!
LIVE REPORT!
She's got curls, right?
Ahhahaha
Yes.
CURLS
No worries.
She just likes to have fun.

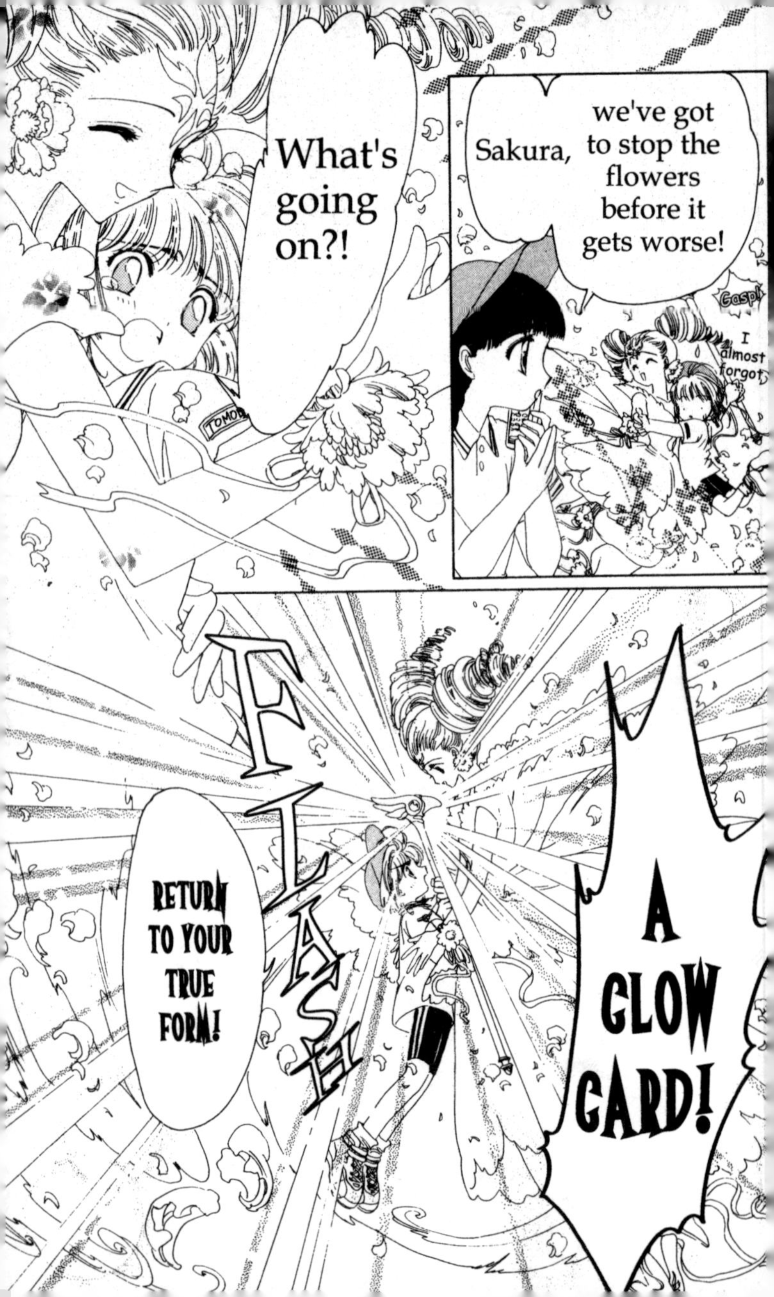
What's going on?!
Sakura, we've got to stop the flowers before it gets worse!
Gasp!
I almost forgot
TOMO
FLASH
RETURN TO YOUR TRUE FORM!
A GLOW CARD!

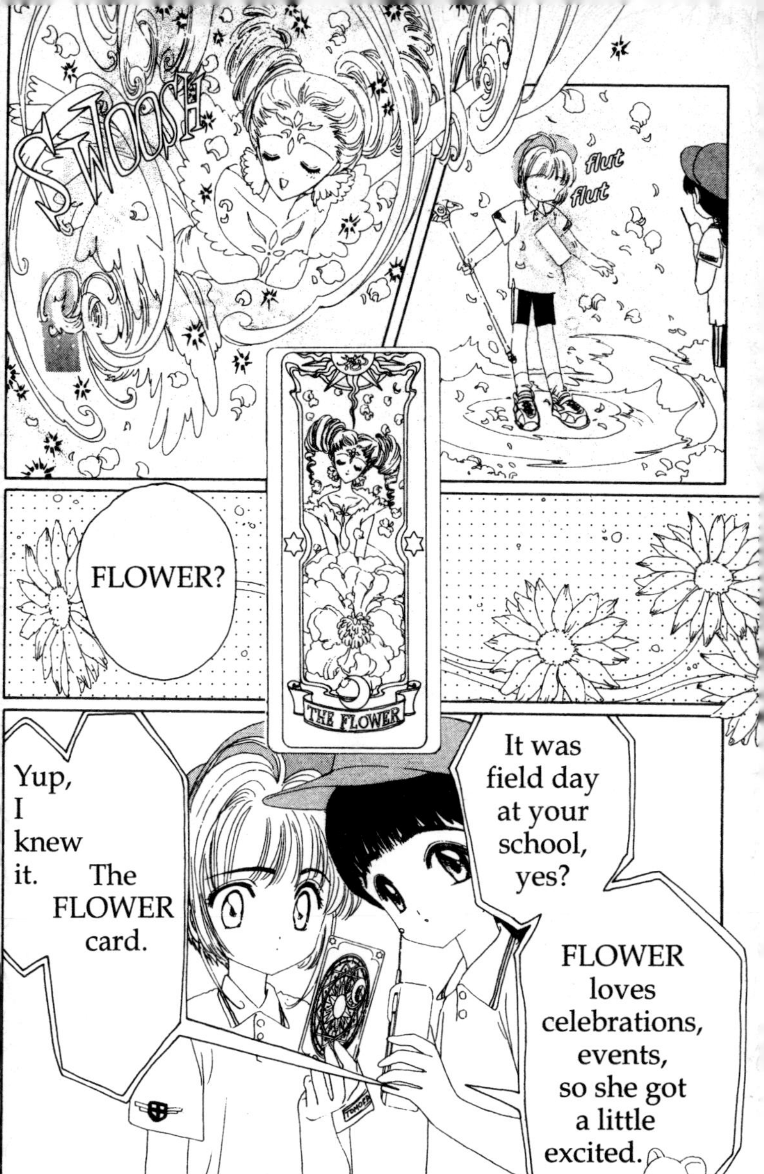
SWOOSH
flut flut
FLOWER?
THE FLOWER
Yup, I knew it. The FLOWER card.
It was field day at your school, yes?
FLOWER loves celebrations, events, so she got a little excited.

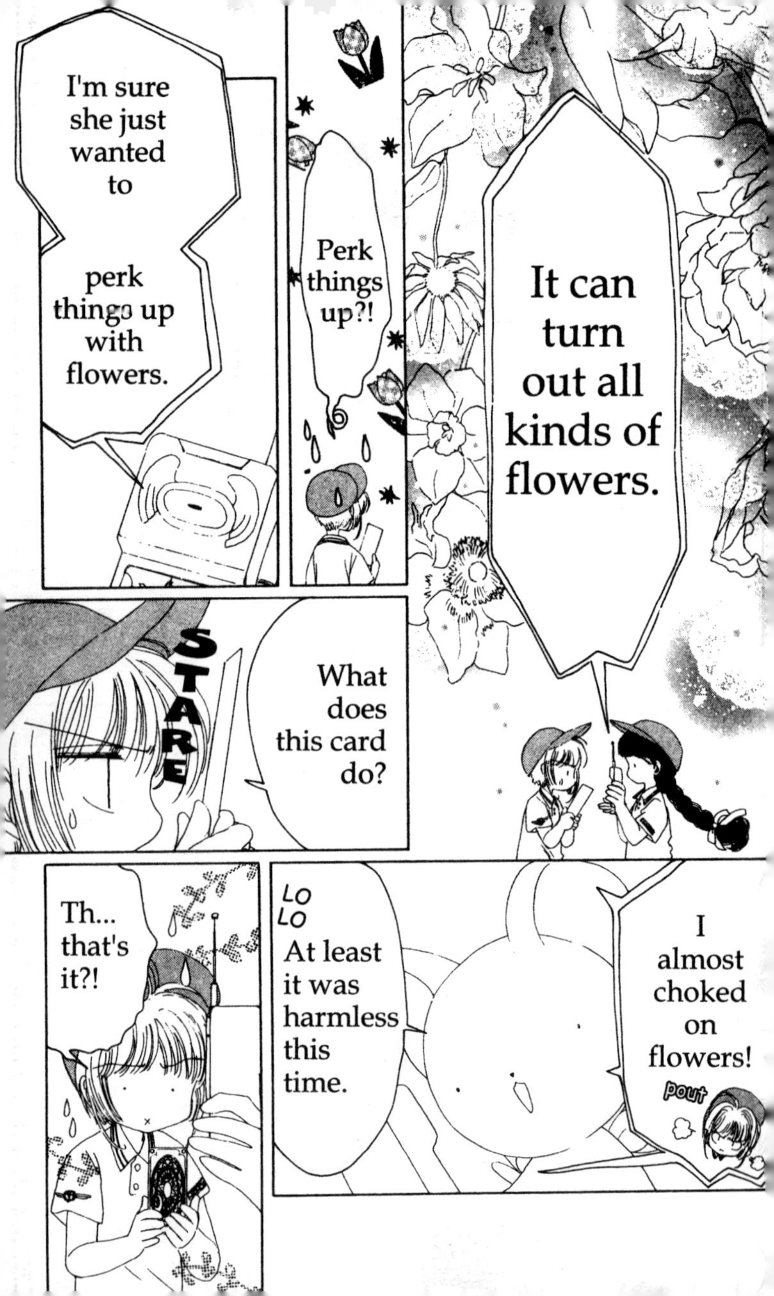

I'm sure she just wanted to
perk things up with flowers.
Perk things up?!
STARE
What does this card do?
It can turn out all kinds of flowers.
Th... that's it?!
LO LO
At least it was harmless this time.
I almost choked on flowers!
pout

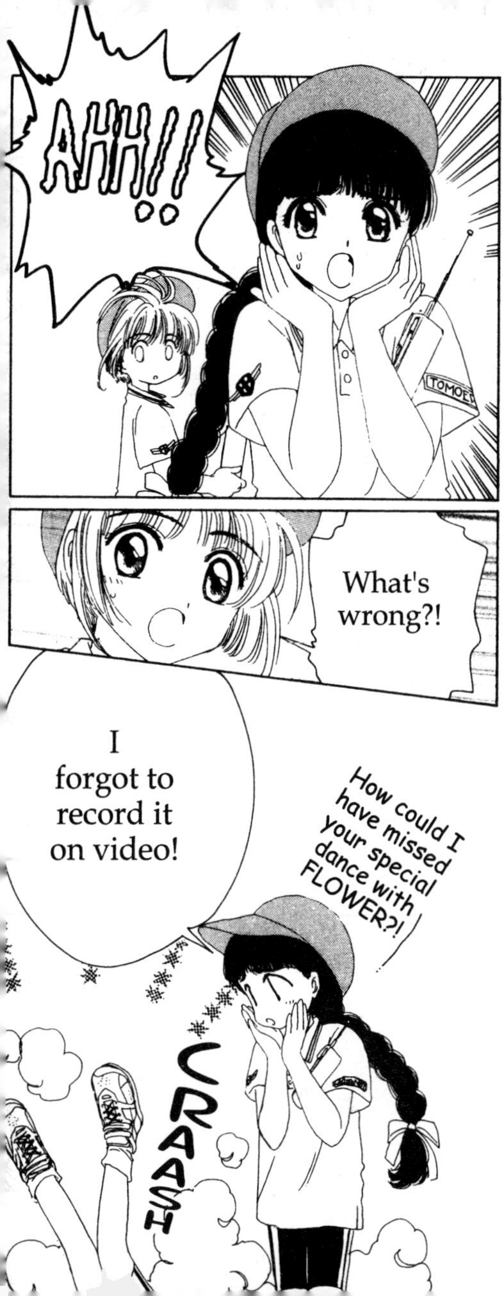
AHH!!
What's wrong?!
I forgot to record it on video!
How could I have missed your special dance with FLOWER?!
CRAASH

6

Li Syaoran

Birthday:
July 13th
Blood Type:
O
Favorite Subject:
Physical Education, Math
Least Favorite Subject:
Japanese
Club Membership:
None
Favorite Color:
Green
Favorite Flower:
Peonies
Favorite Foods
Dim Sum, Chocolate
Least Favorite Foods:
Yam jelly
Favorite Recipe:
None
Wish List:
Magic book written by Clow Reed

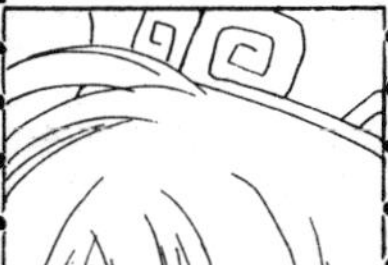

LI SYAORAN

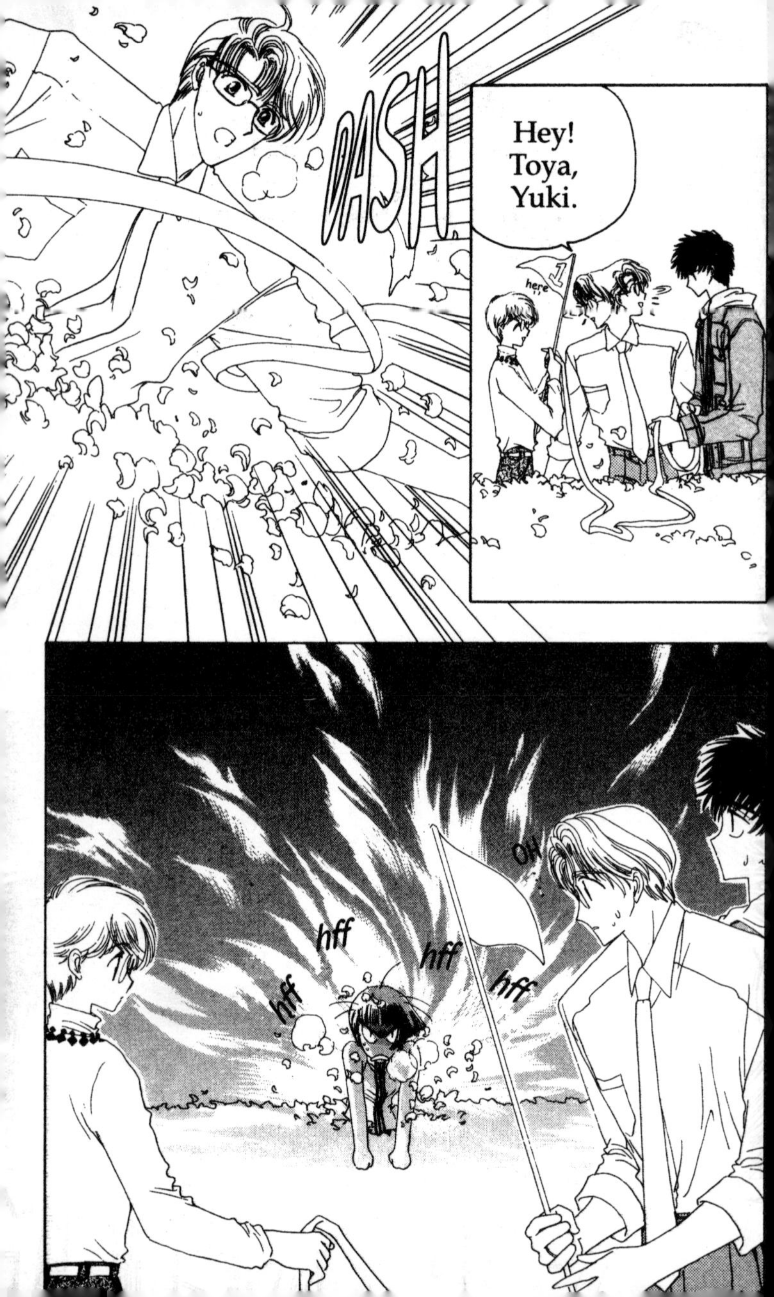
Hey! Toya, Yuki.
here
DASH
OH
hff
hff
hff
hff

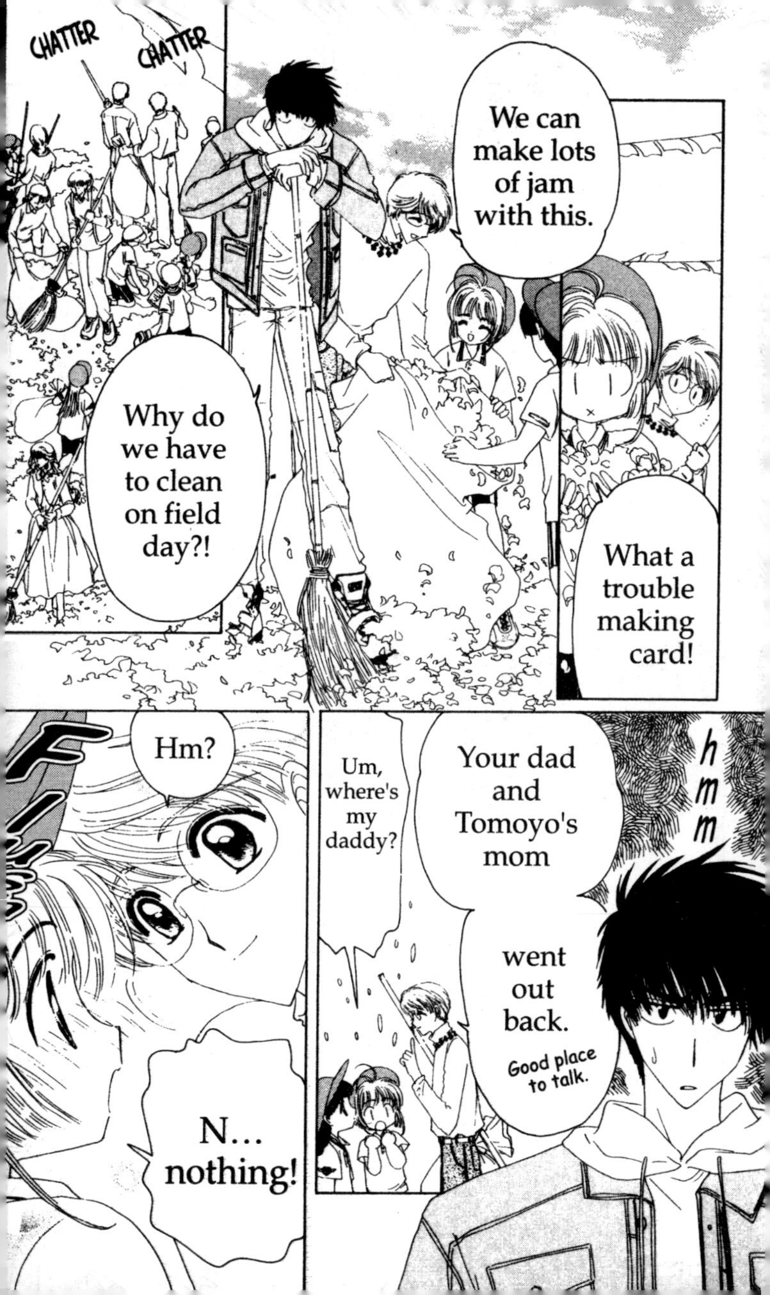
CHATTER
CHATTER
Why do we have to clean on field day?!
We can make lots of jam with this.
What a trouble making card!
Hm?
N... nothing!
Um, where's my daddy?
Your dad and Tomoyo's mom
went out back.
Good place to talk.
hmm

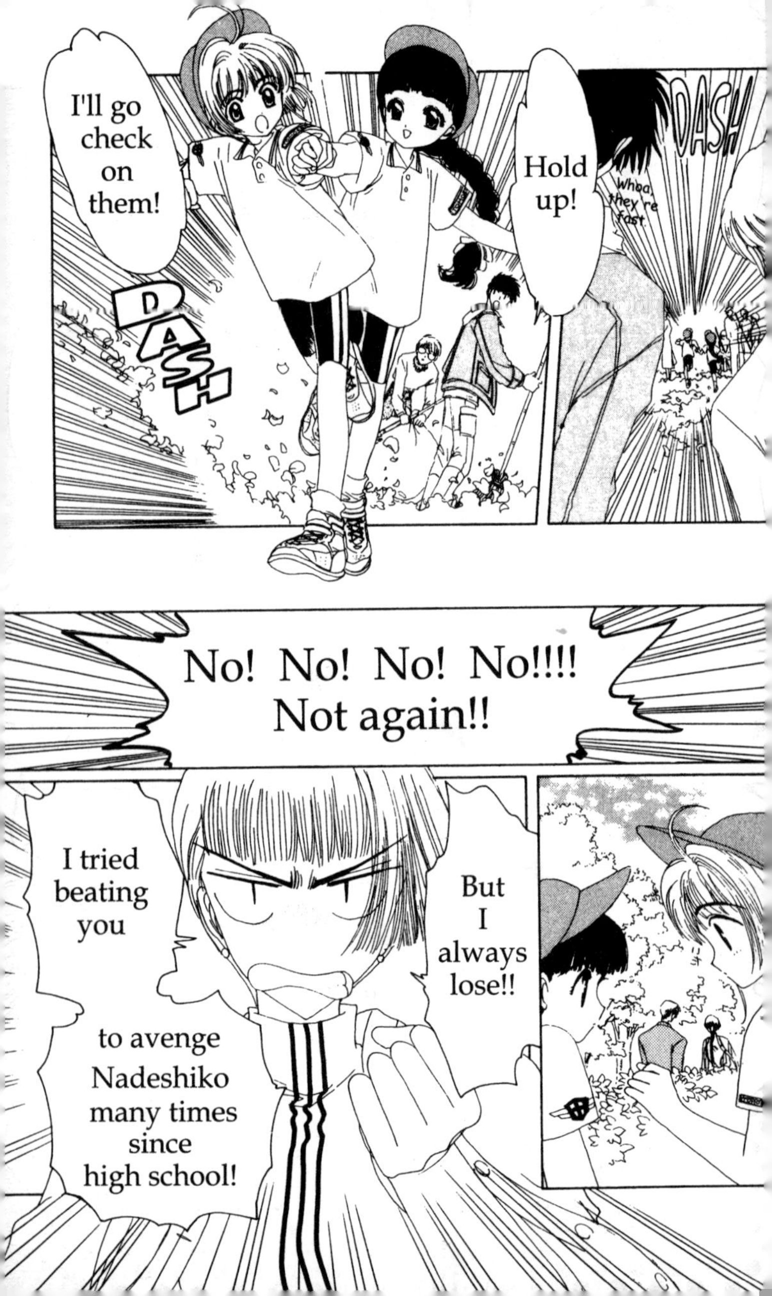

I'll go check on them!
DASH
Hold up!
DASH
Whoa, they're fast.
No! No! No! No!!!! Not again!!
I tried beating you
to avenge Nadeshiko many times since high school!
But I always lose!!

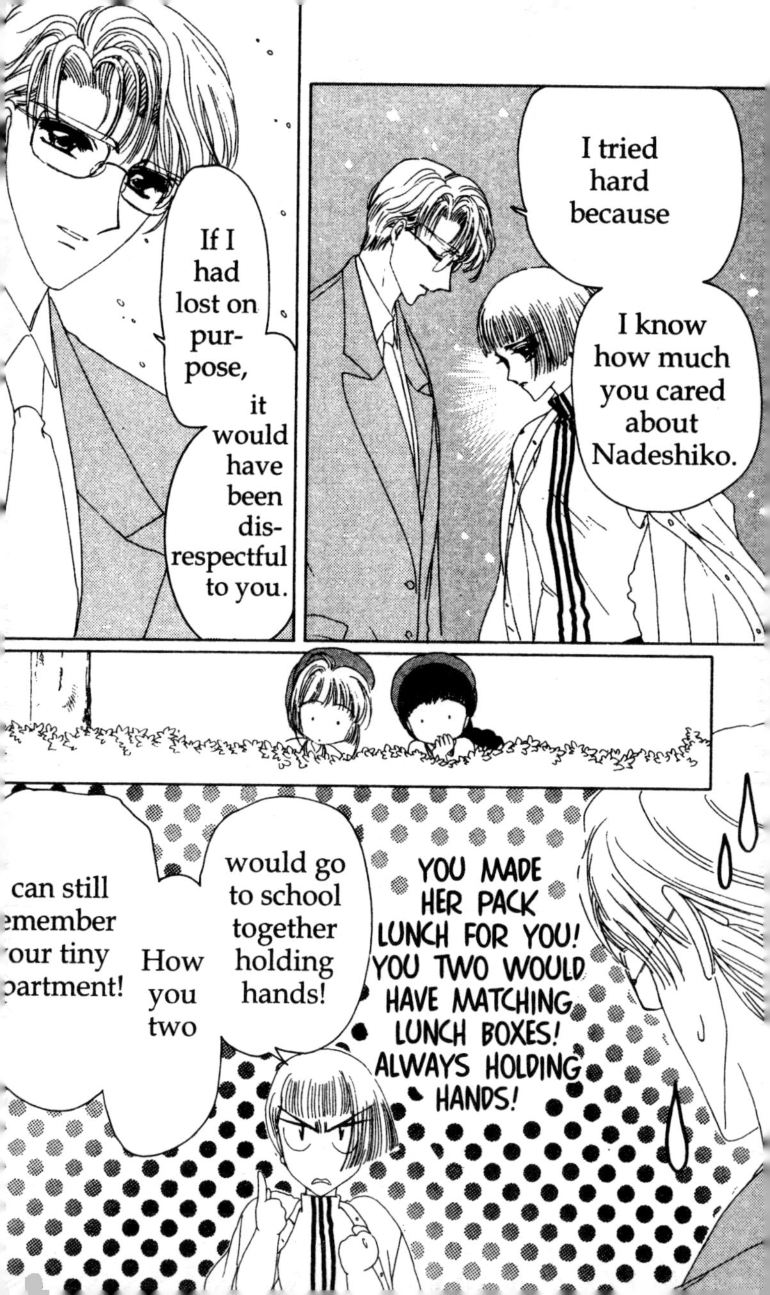

If I had lost on purpose,
it would have been disrespectful to you.
I tried hard because
I know how much you cared about Nadeshiko.
can still emember our tiny partment!
How you two
would go to school together holding hands!
YOU MADE HER PACK LUNCH FOR YOU! YOU TWO WOULD HAVE MATCHING LUNCH BOXES! ALWAYS HOLDING HANDS!

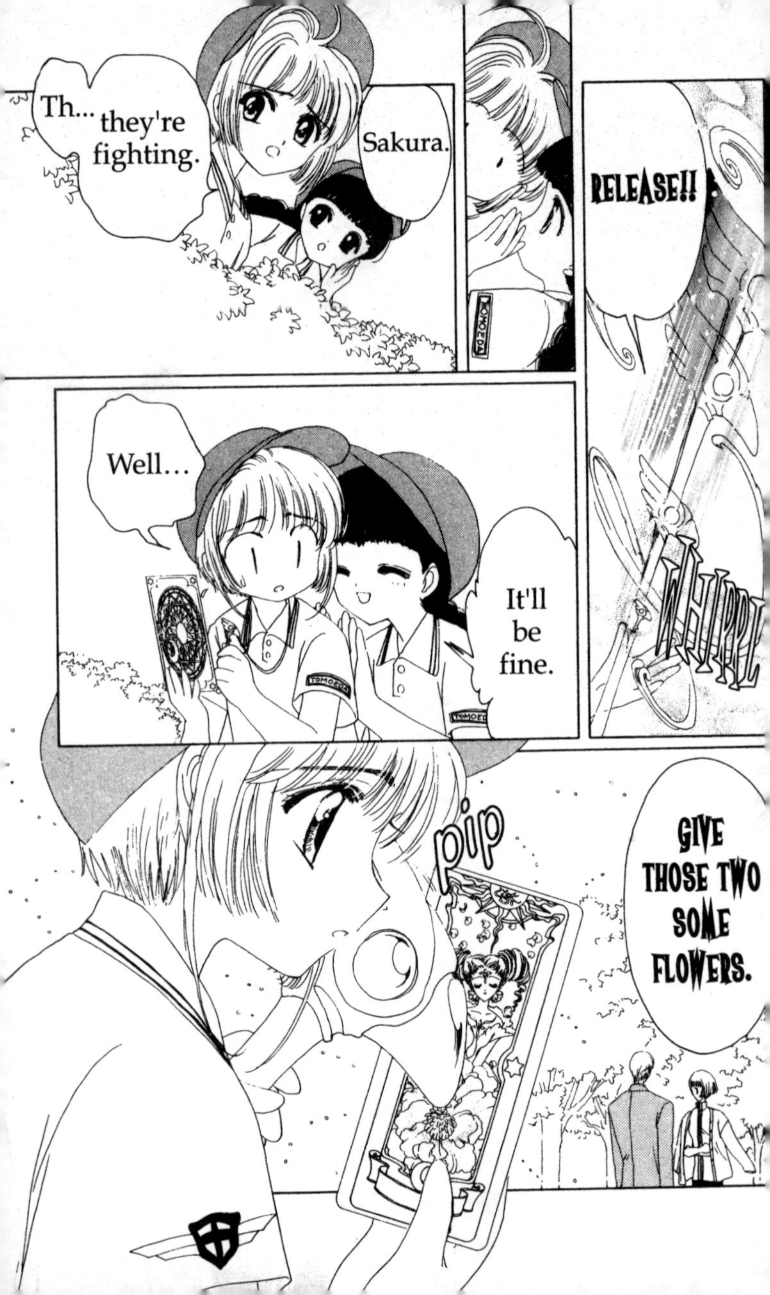
Th... they're fighting.
Sakura.
Well...
It'll be fine.
RELEASE!!
WHIPPL
pip
GIVE THOSE TWO SOME FLOWERS.

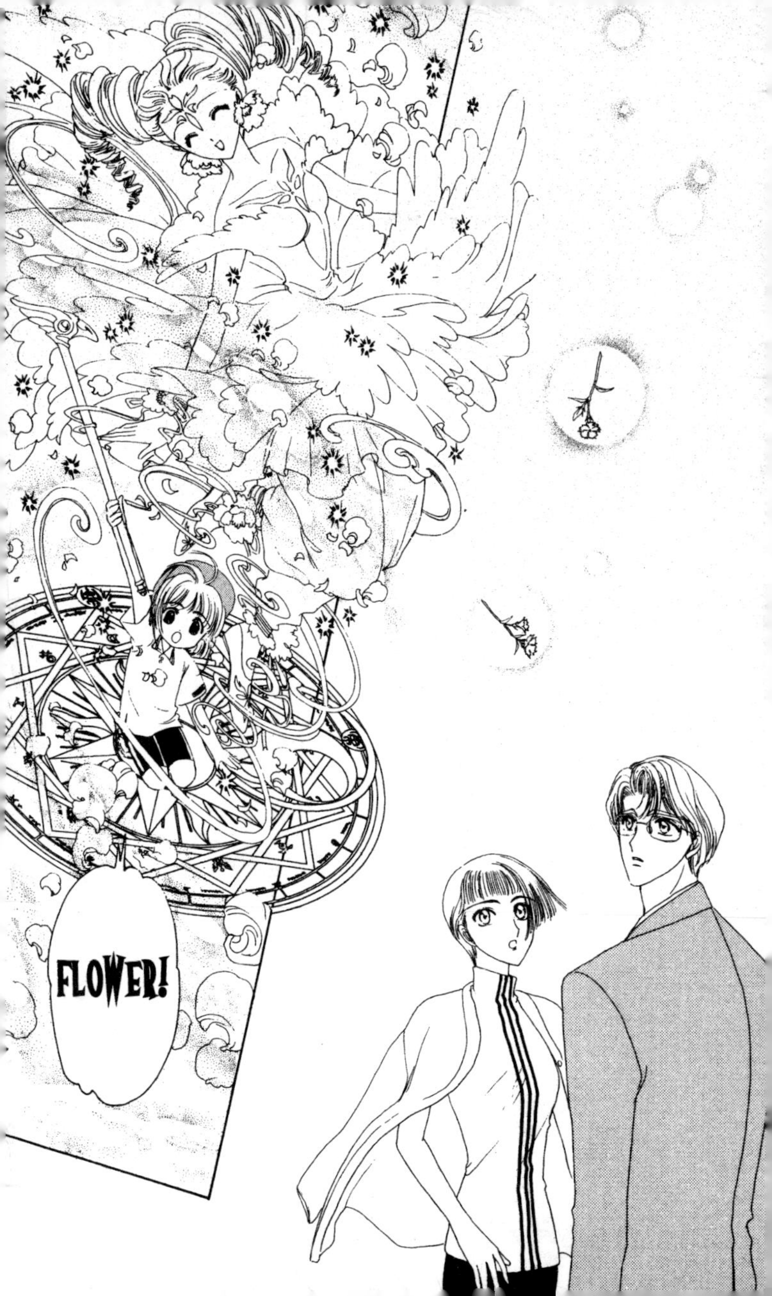
FLOWER!

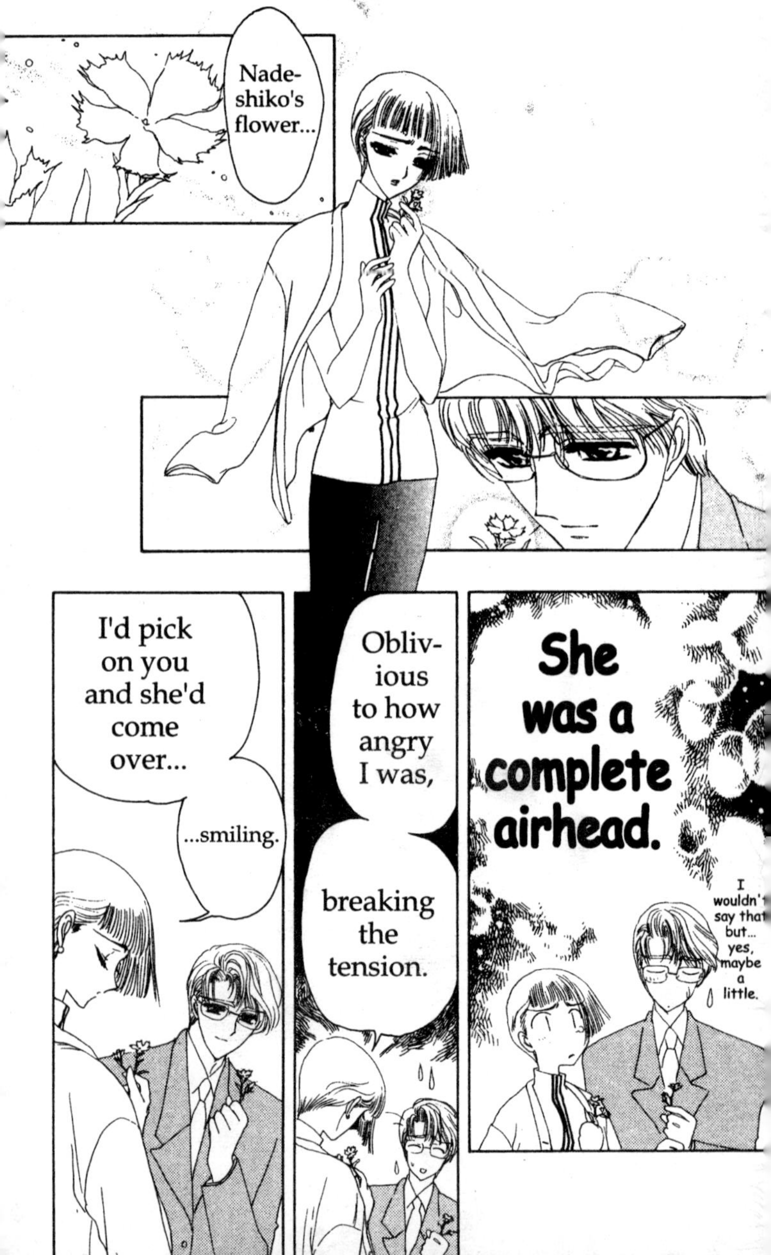
Nade-shiko's flower...
I'd pick on you and she'd come over...
...smiling.
Obliv-ious to how angry I was,
breaking the tension.
She was a complete airhead.
I wouldn't say that but... yes, maybe a little.

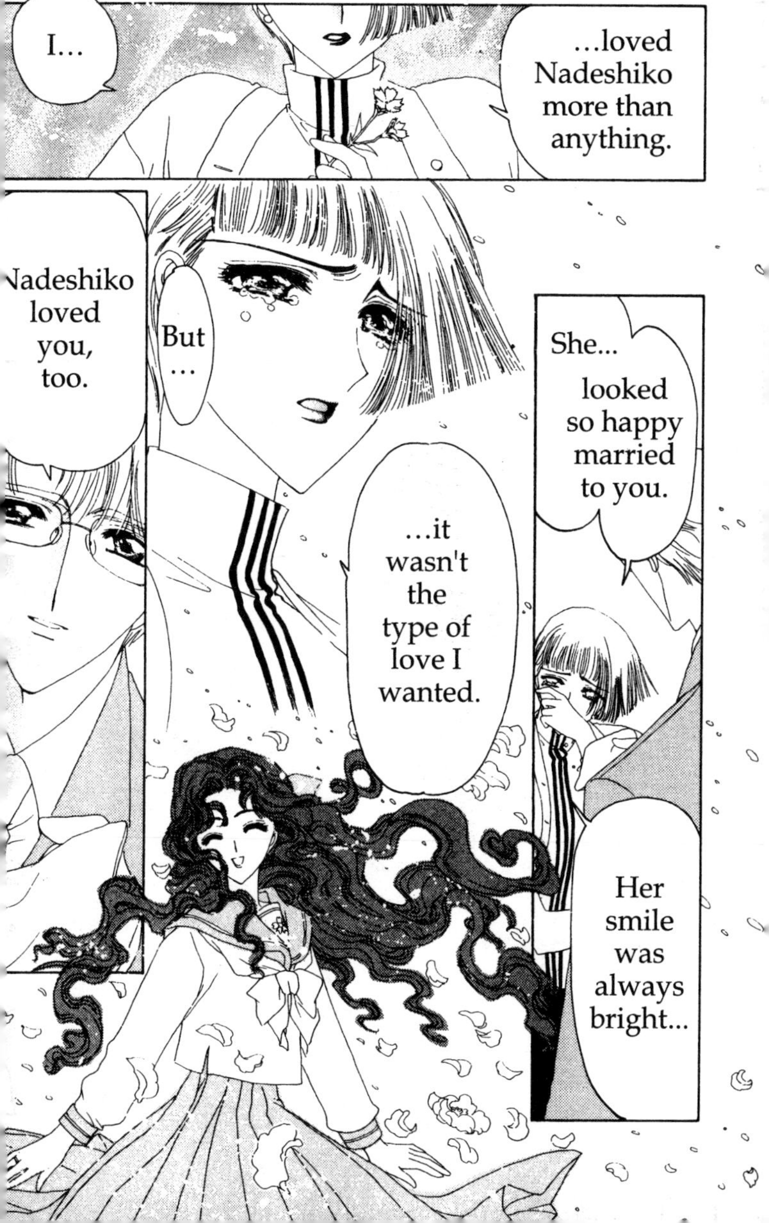
I...
...loved Nadeshiko more than anything.
Nadeshiko loved you, too.
But...
...it wasn't the type of love I wanted.
She...
looked so happy married to you.
Her smile was always bright...

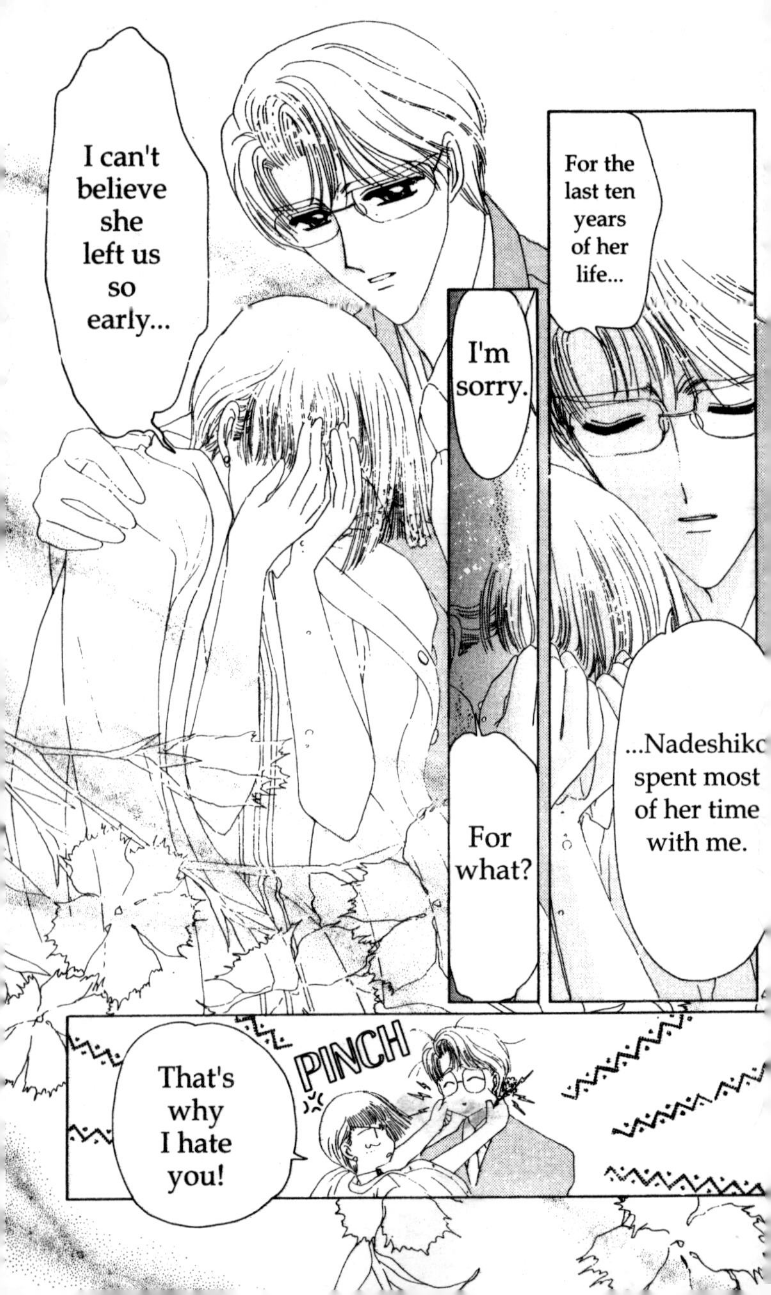
For the last ten years of her life...
...Nadeshiko spent most of her time with me.
I'm sorry.
For what?
I can't believe she left us so early...
PINCH
That's why I hate you!

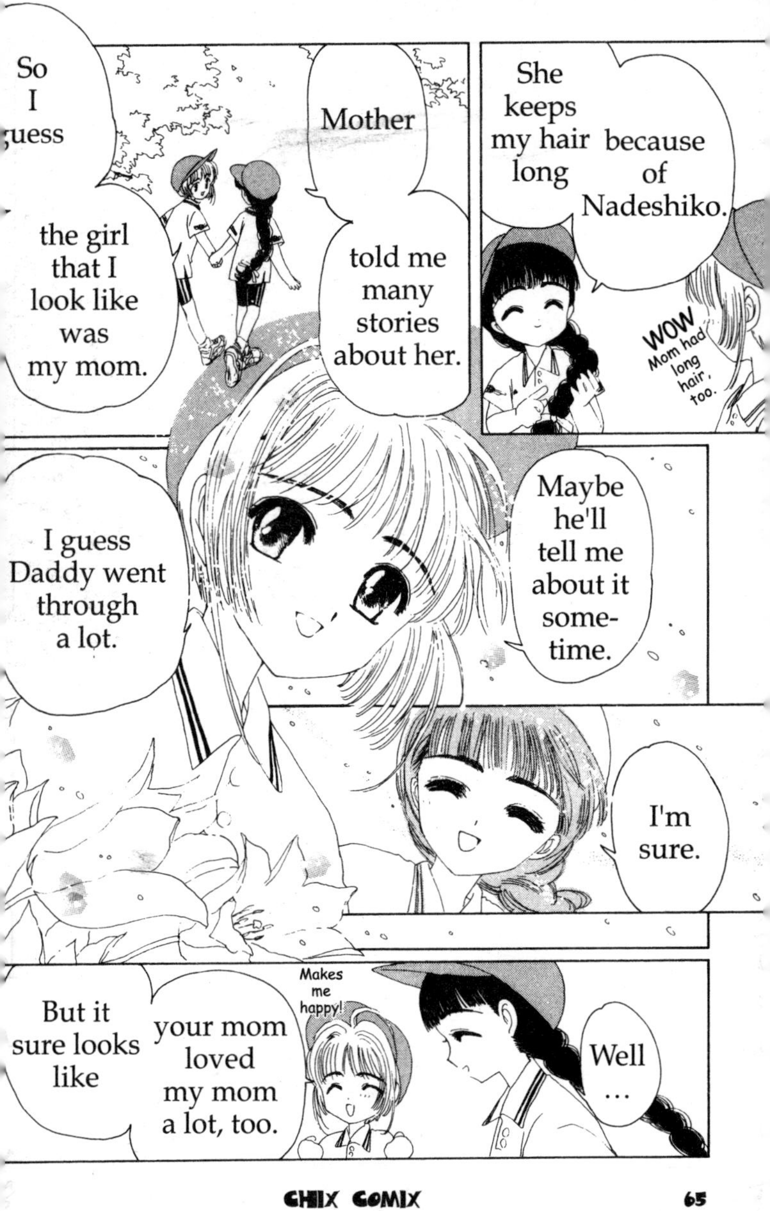
So I guess
the girl that I look like was my mom.
Mother
told me many stories about her.
She keeps my hair long
because of Nadeshiko.
WOW
Mom had long hair, too.
I guess Daddy went through a lot.
Maybe he'll tell me about it some-time.
I'm sure.
But it sure looks like
your mom loved my mom a lot, too.
Makes me happy!
Well ...

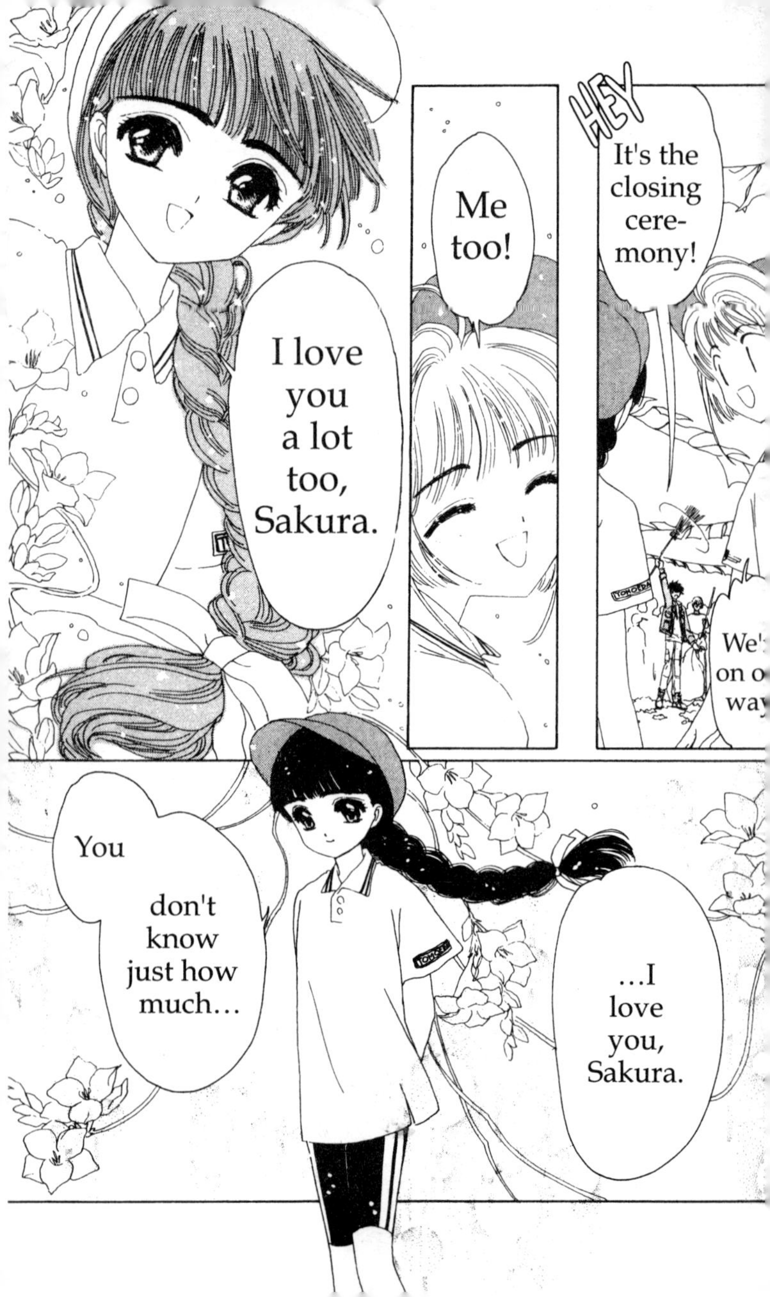

I love you a lot too, Sakura.
Me too!
HEY
It's the closing ceremony!
You don't know just how much…
…I love you, Sakura.

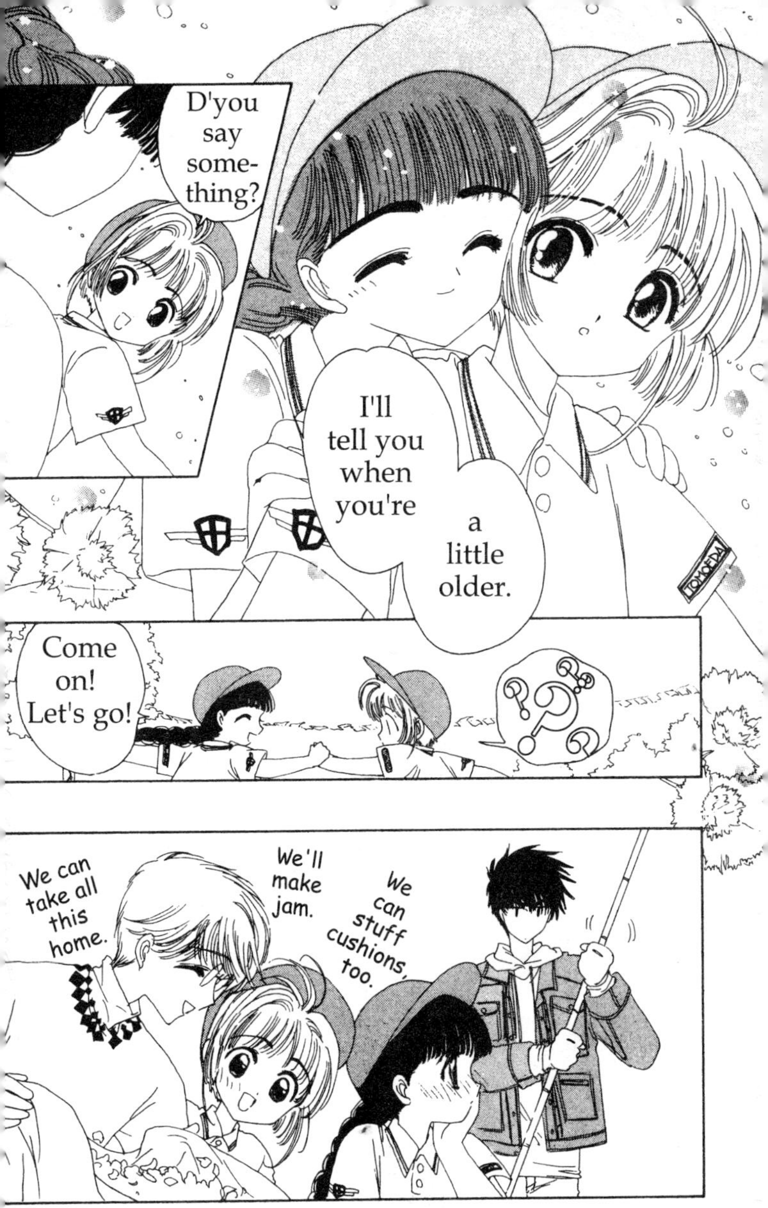
D'you say some-thing?
I'll tell you when you're a little older.
TOMOEDA
Come on! Let's go!
We can take all this home.
We'll make jam.
We can stuff cushions, too.

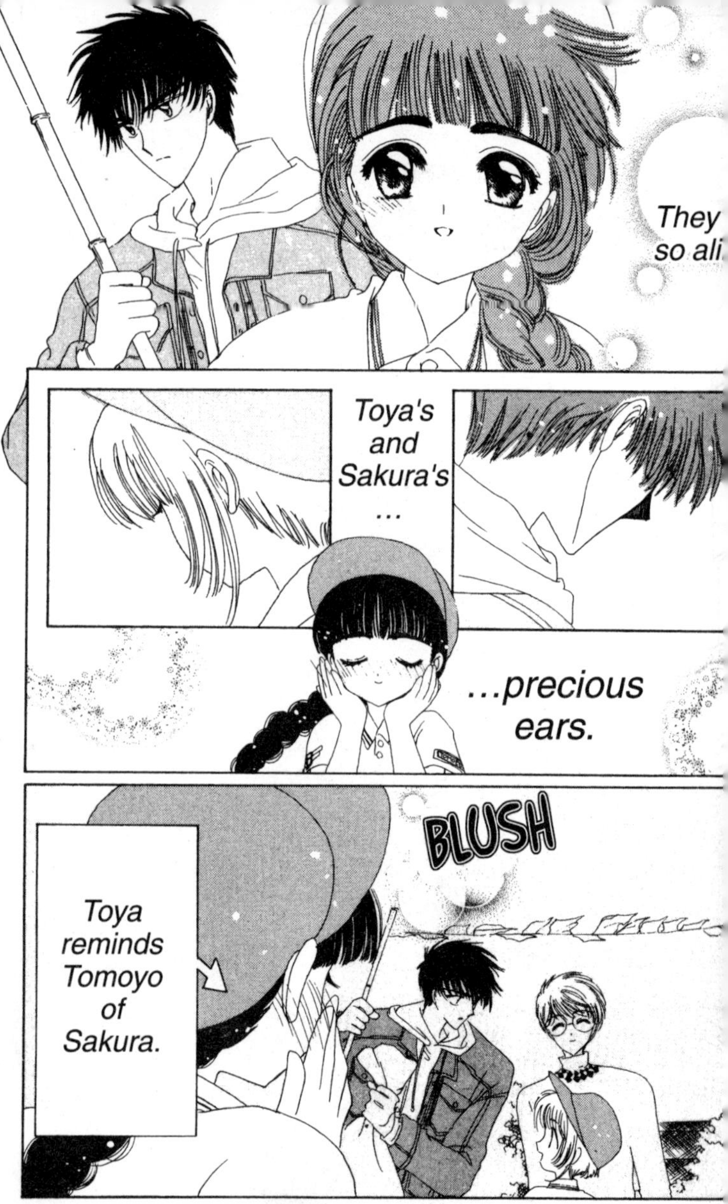
They so ali
Toya's and Sakura's ...
...precious ears.
Toya reminds Tomoyo of Sakura.
BLUSH

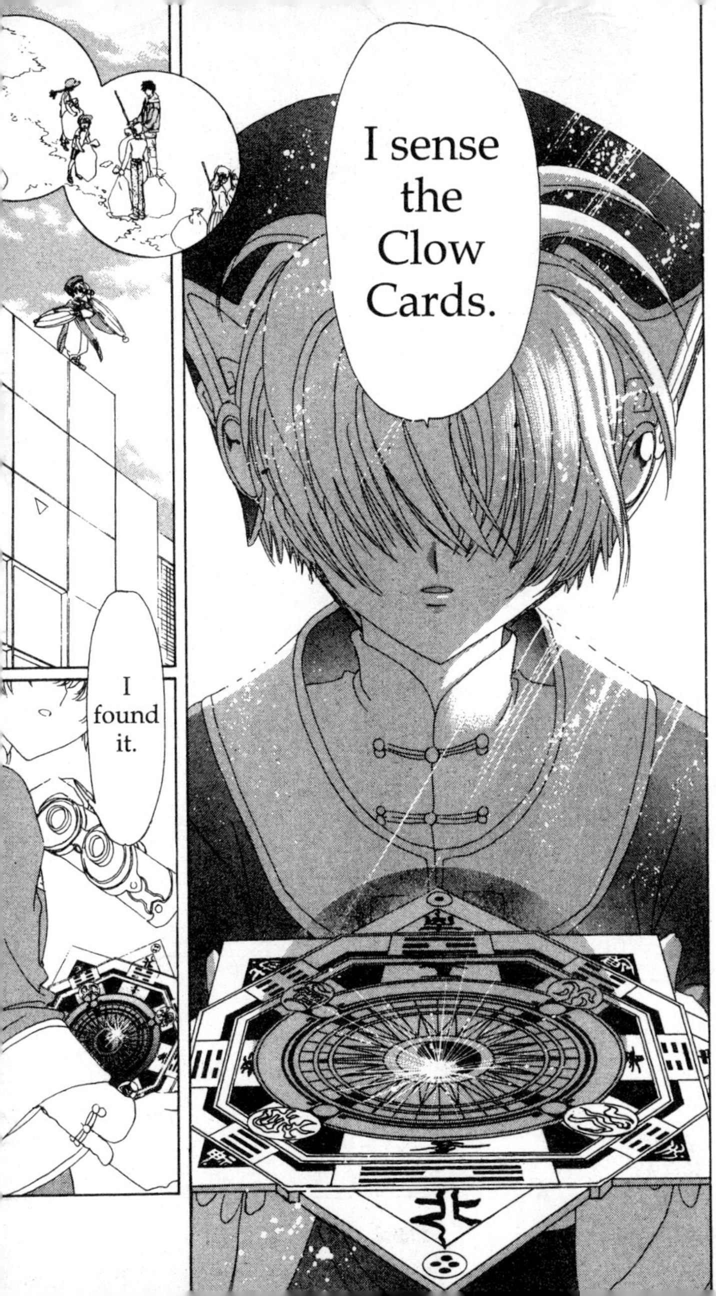
I found it.
I sense the Clow Cards.

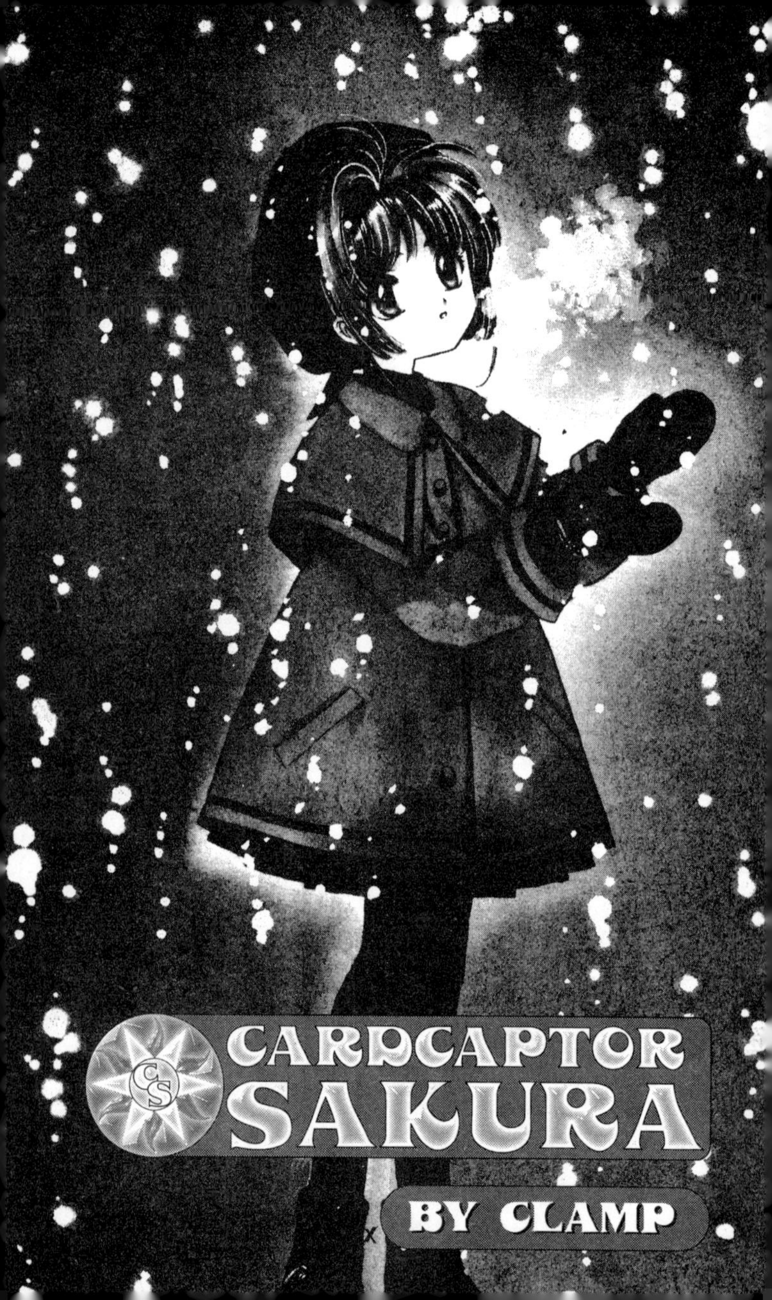
CARDCAPTOR
SAKURA
BY CLAMP

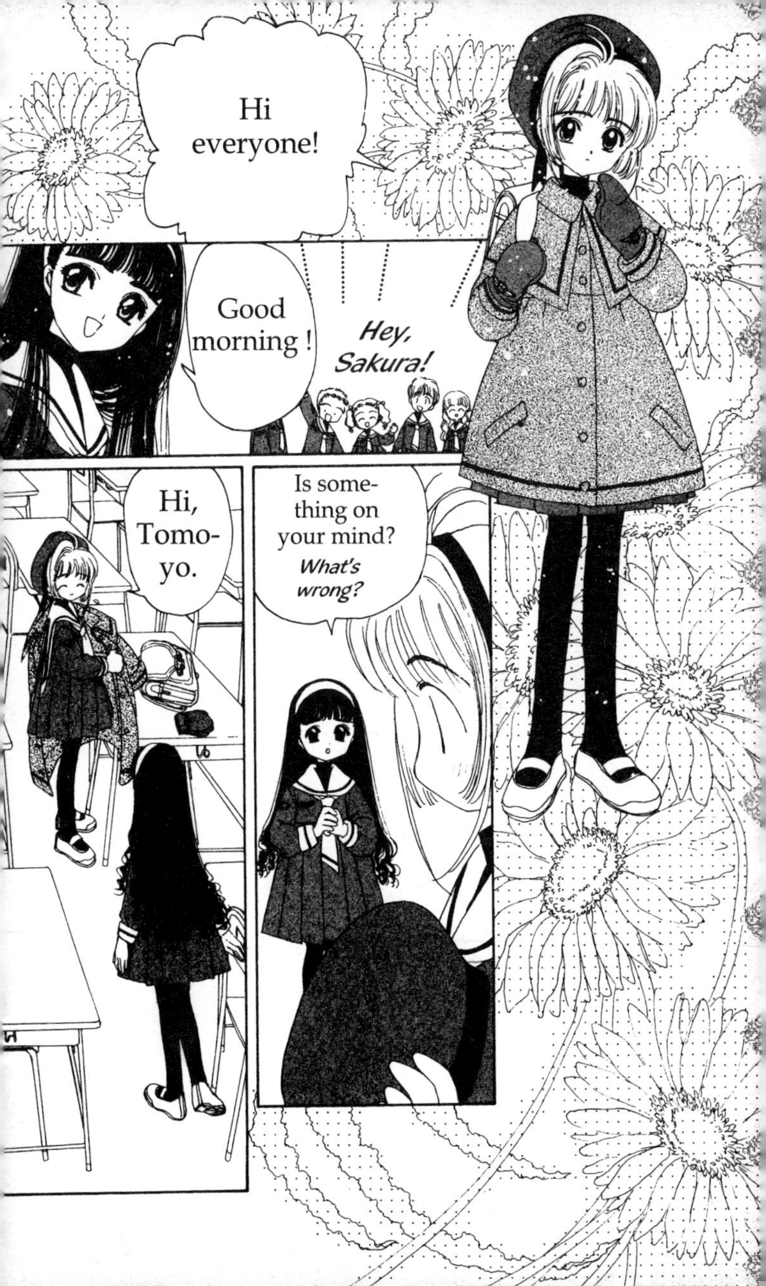

Hi everyone!
Good morning !
Hey, Sakura!
Hi, Tomo-yo.
Is some-thing on your mind?
What's wrong?

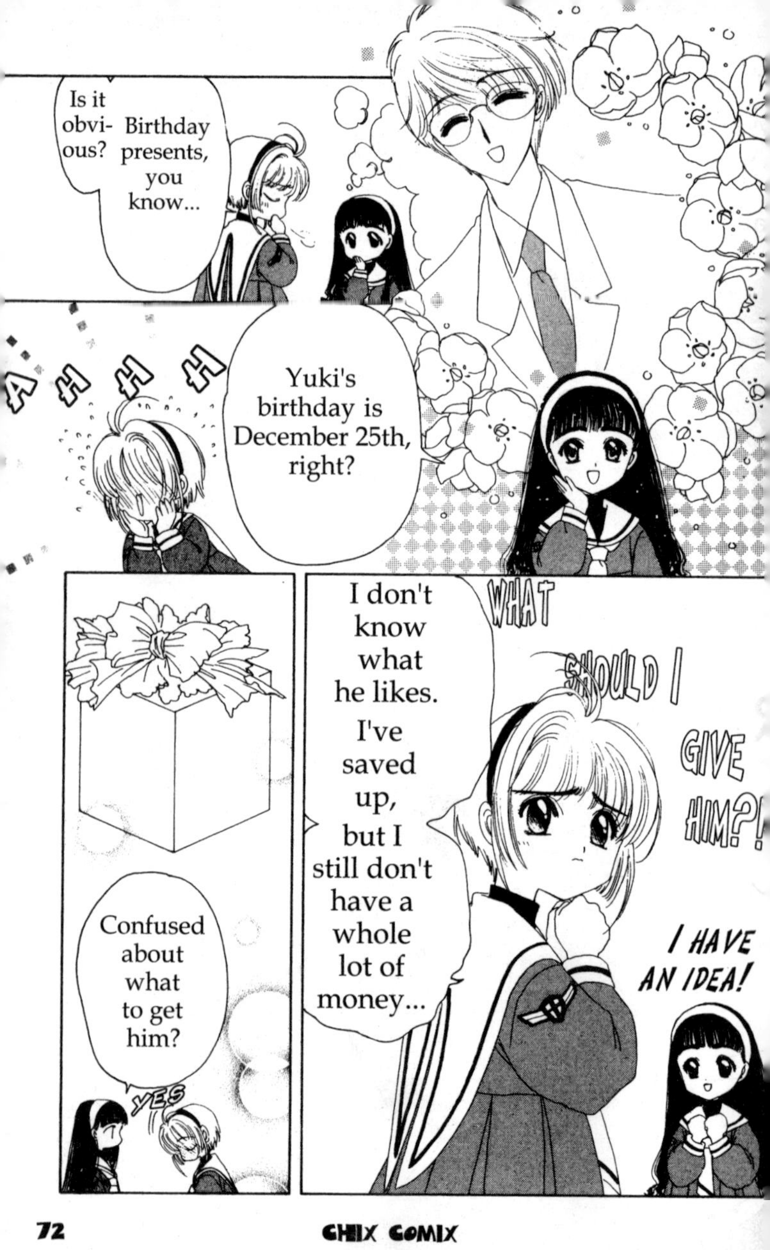

Is it obvi- ous? Birthday presents, you know...
AHHH
Yuki's birthday is December 25th, right?
Confused about what to get him?
YES
I don't know what he likes. I've saved up, but I still don't have a whole lot of money...
WHAT SHOULD I GIVE HIM?!
I HAVE AN IDEA!

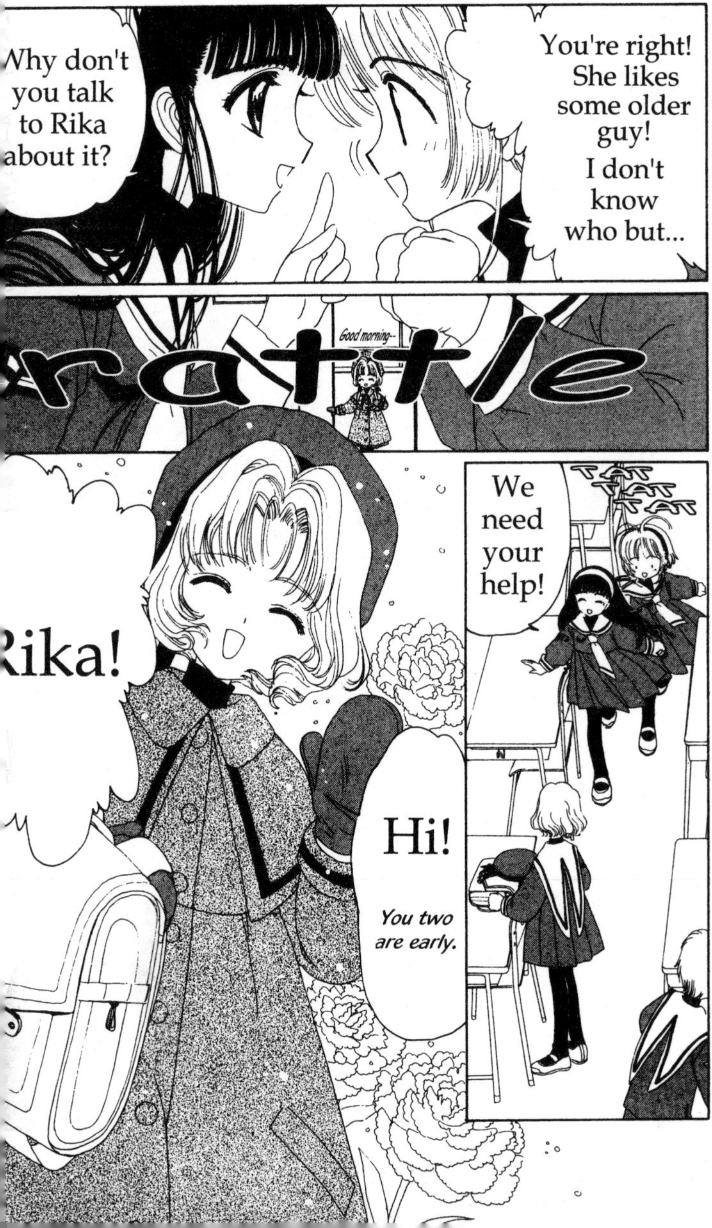

Why don't you talk to Rika about it?
You're right! She likes some older guy! I don't know who but...
rattle
Good morning--
Rika!
Hi!
You two are early.
TAT TAT TAT
We need your help!

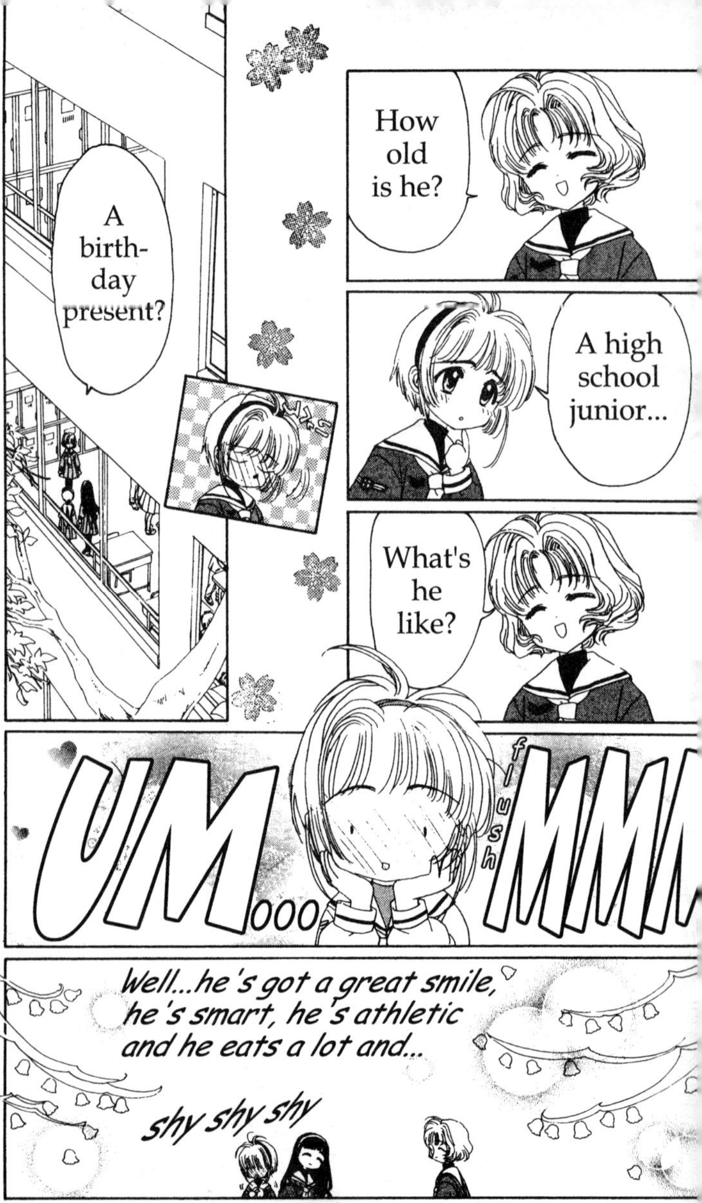
A birth-day present?
How old is he?
A high school junior...
What's he like?
UMooo
f—ush
MMM
Well...he's got a great smile, he's smart, he's athletic and he eats a lot and...
shy shy shy

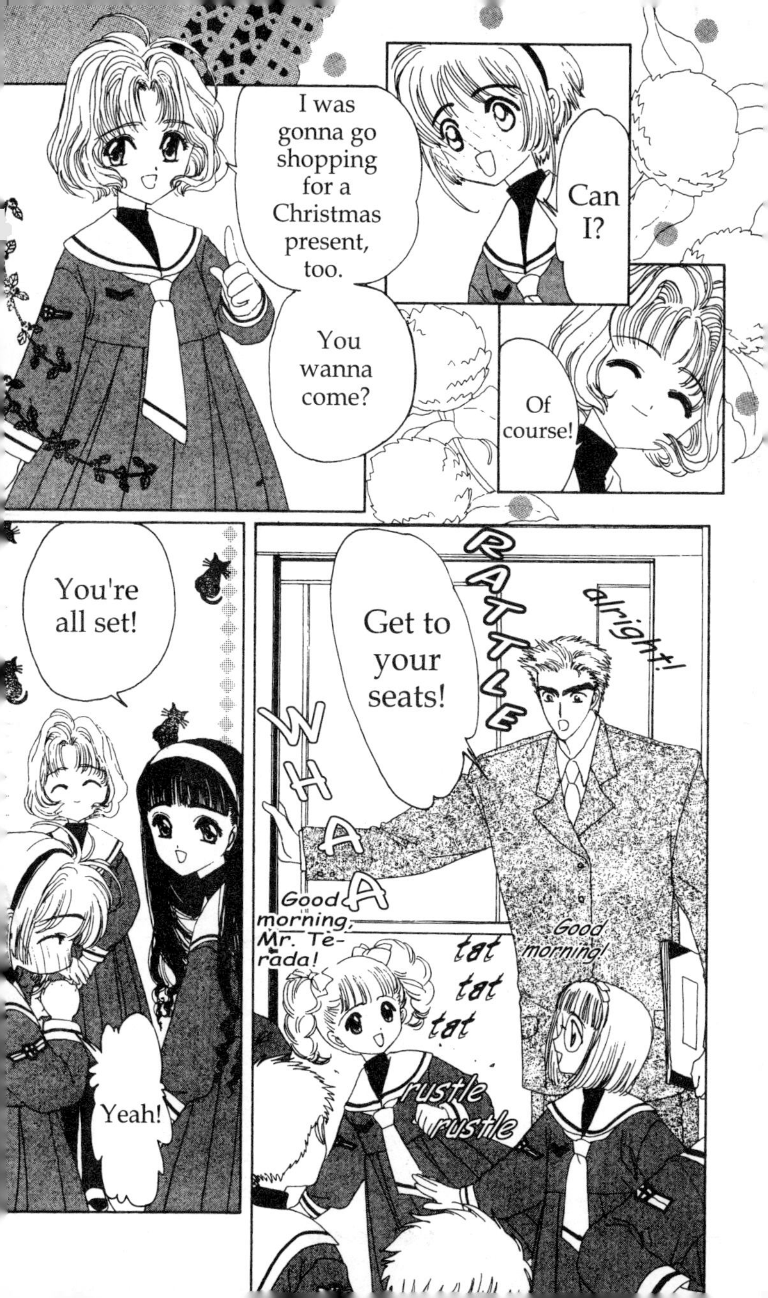
I was gonna go shopping for a Christmas present, too.
You wanna come?
Can I?
Of course!
You're all set!
Yeah!
RATTLE
Get to your seats!
alright!
WHAA
Good morning, Mr. Te-rada!
tat tat tat
Good morning!
rustle rustle

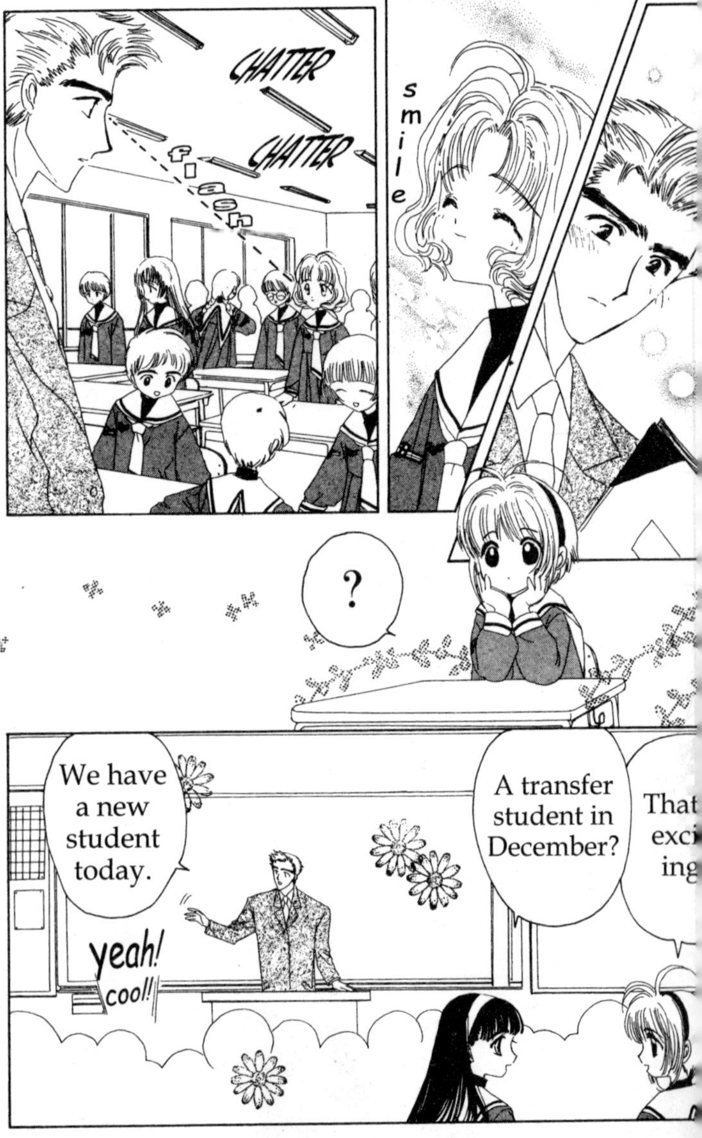
CHATTER
CHATTER
flash
smile
?
We have a new student today.
yeah!
cool!
A transfer student in December?
That exci ing

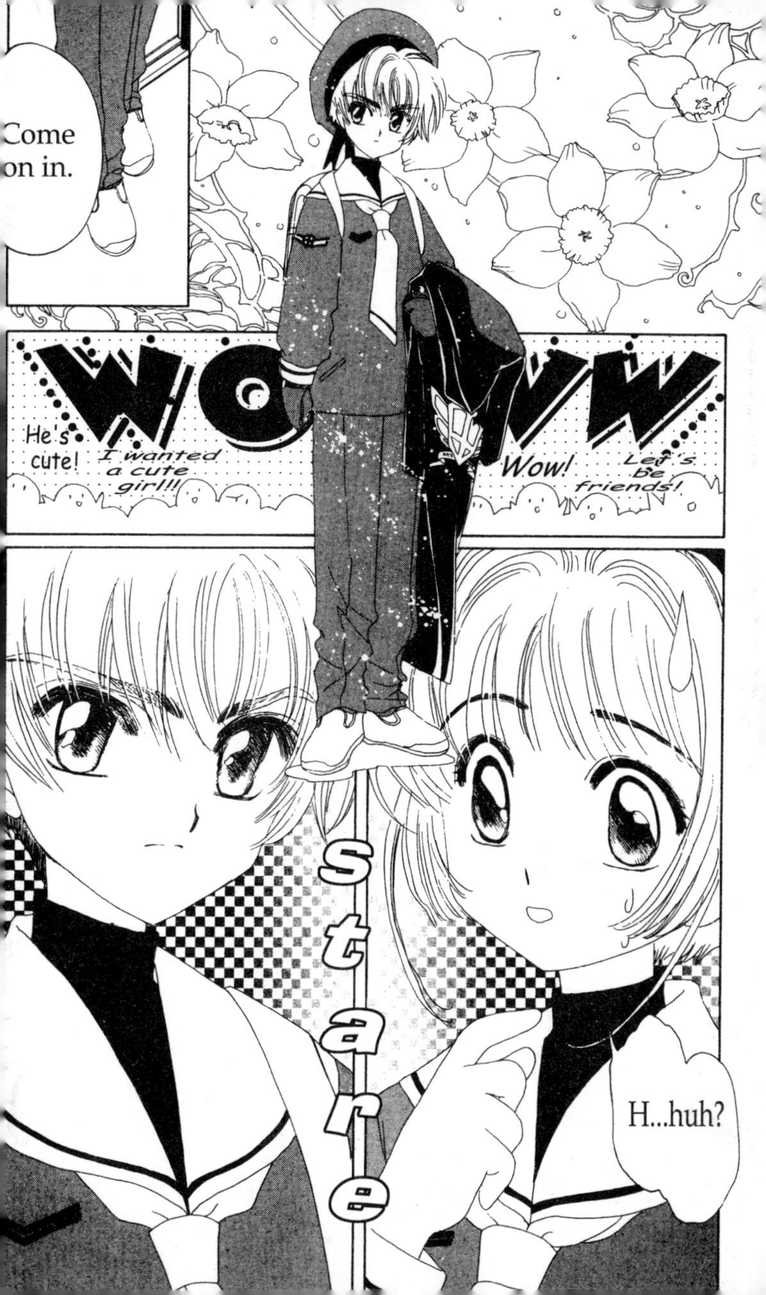

Come on in.
WOW
He's cute!
I wanted a cute girl!!
Wow!
Let's be friends!
stare
H...huh?

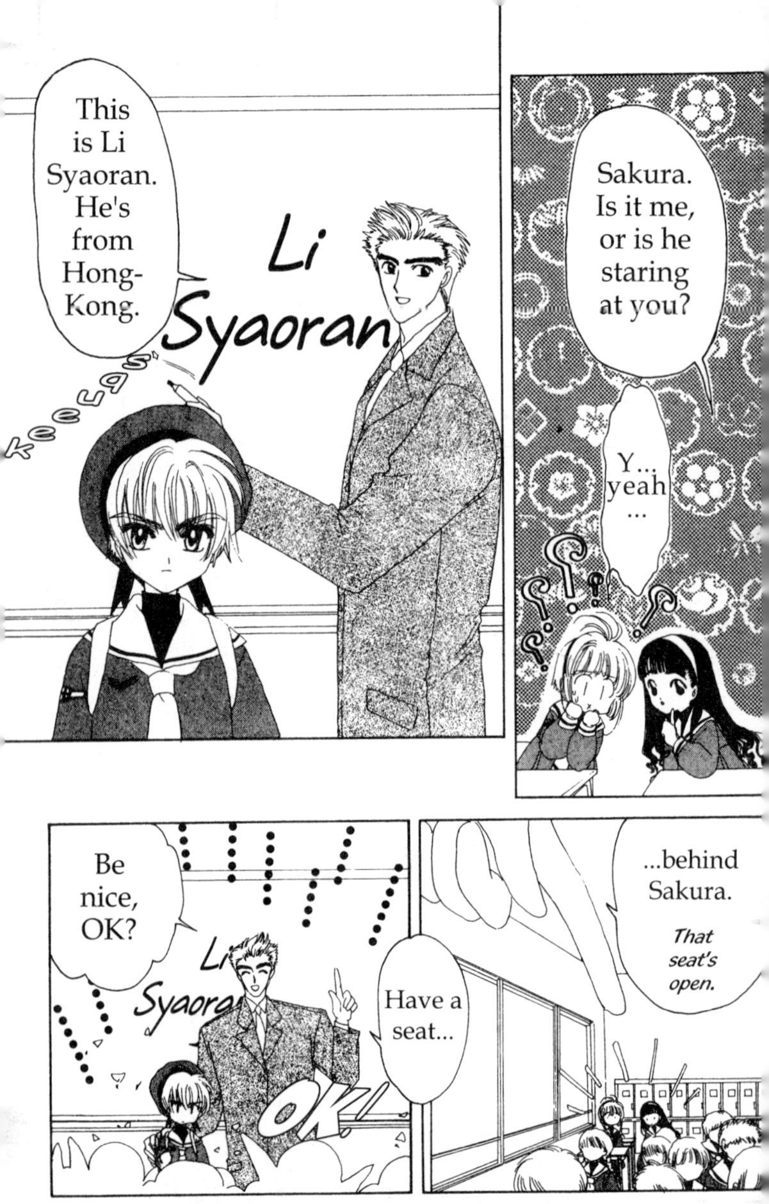

This is Li Syaoran. He's from Hong-Kong.
Li Syaoran
Sakura. Is it me, or is he staring at you?
Y... yeah...
Be nice, OK?
Li Syaoran
Have a seat...
OK!
...behind Sakura.
That seat's open.

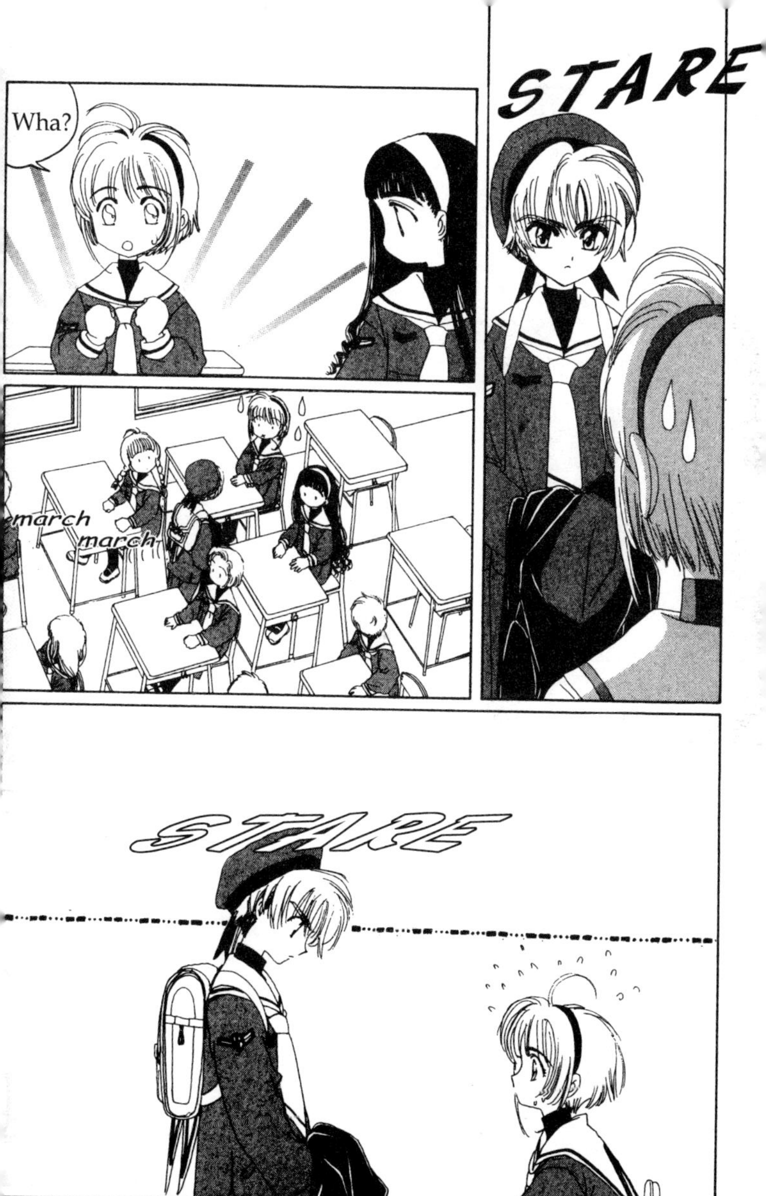
Wha?
march
march
STARE
STARE

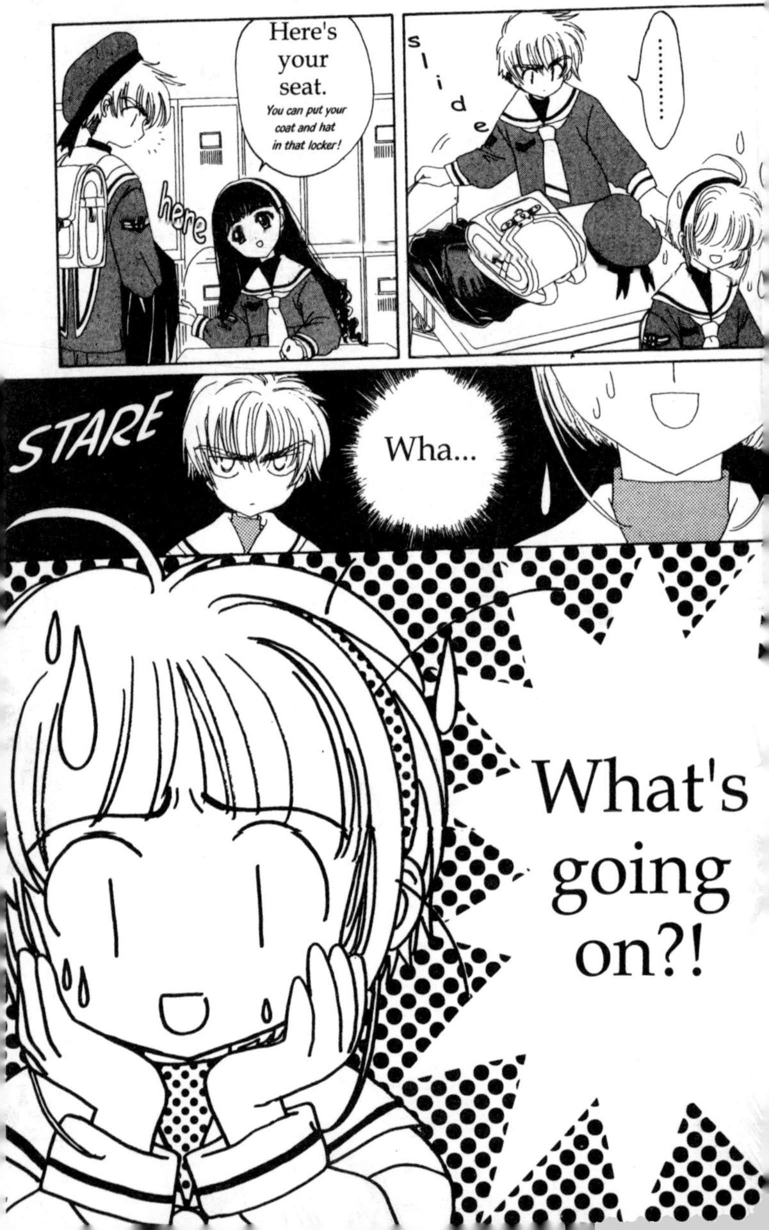

Here's your seat.
You can put your coat and hat in that locker!
here
slide
....
STARE
Wha...
What's going on?!

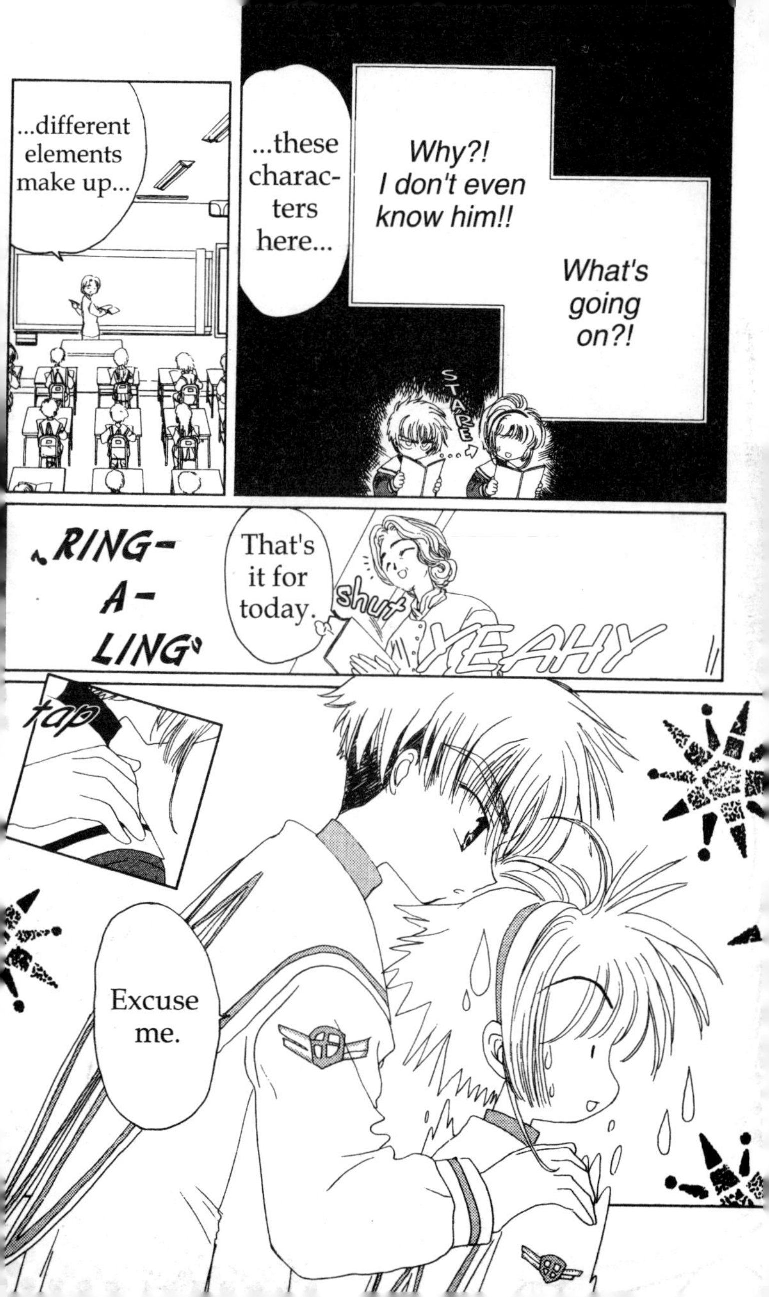

...different elements make up...
...these charac-ters here...
Why?! I don't even know him!!
What's going on?!
STARE
RING-A-LING
That's it for today.
shut
YEAHY
tap
Excuse me.

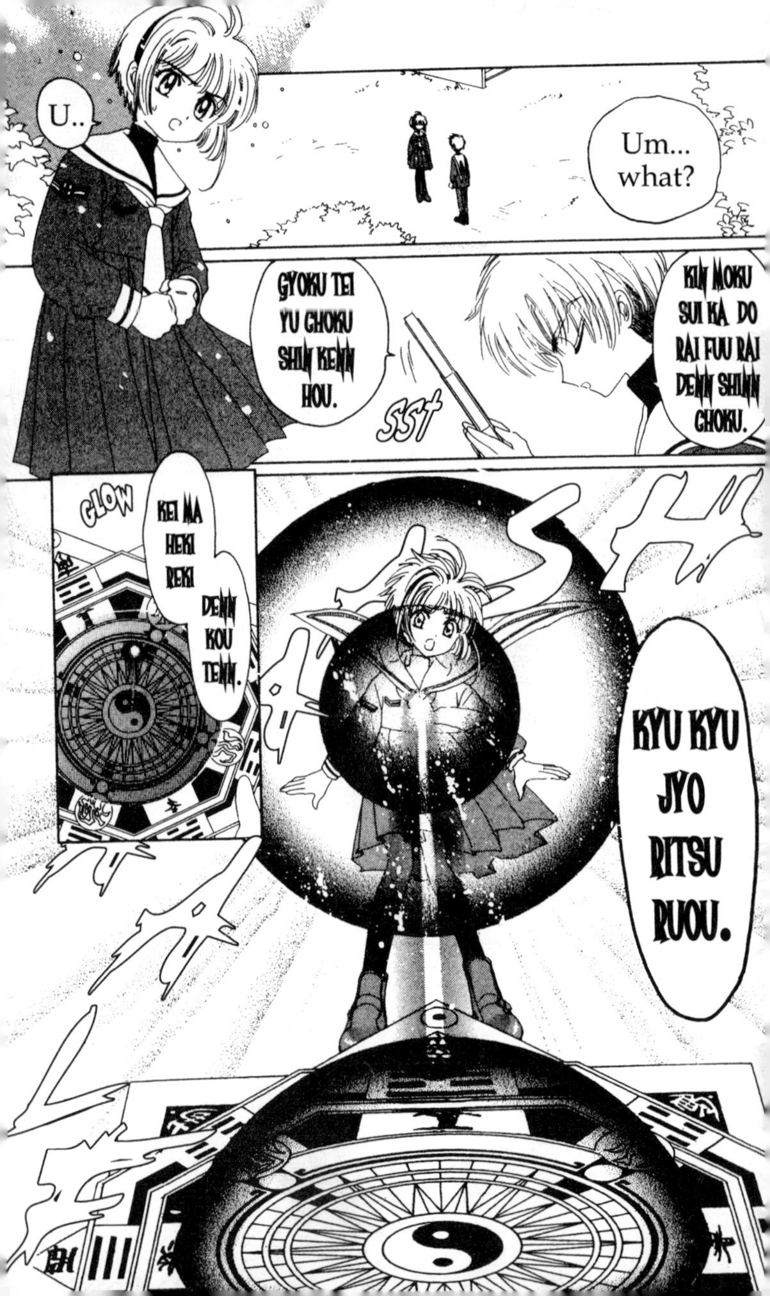
U..
Um... what?
GYOKU TEI YU CHOKU SHIN KENN HOU.
SST
KIN MOKU SUI KA DO RAI FUU RAI DENN SHINN CHOKU.
GLOW
KEI MA HEKI REKI DENN KOU TENN.
KYU KYU JYO RITSU RUOU.

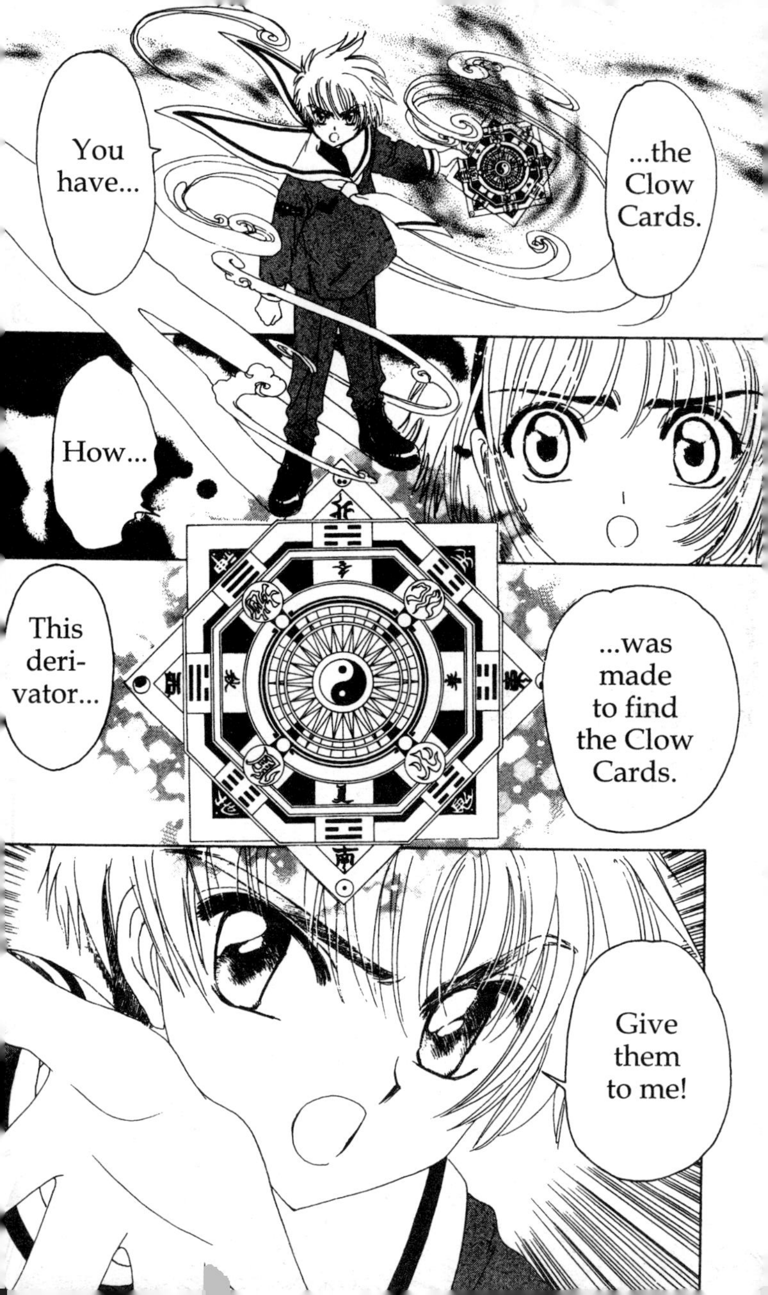
You have...
...the Clow Cards.
How...
This deri-vator...
...was made to find the Clow Cards.
Give them to me!

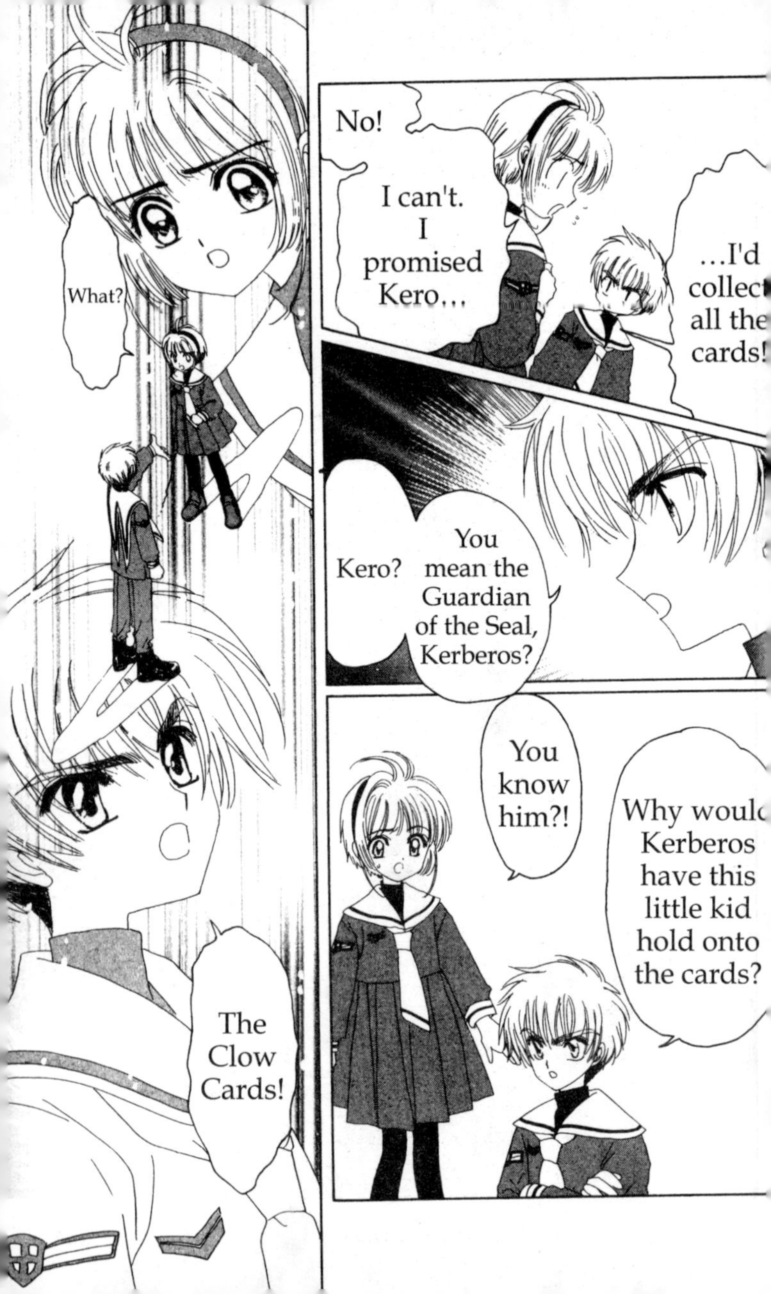
What?
The Clow Cards!
No!
I can't. I promised Kero...
...I'd collect all the cards!
Kero?
You mean the Guardian of the Seal, Kerberos?
You know him?!
Why would Kerberos have this little kid hold onto the cards?

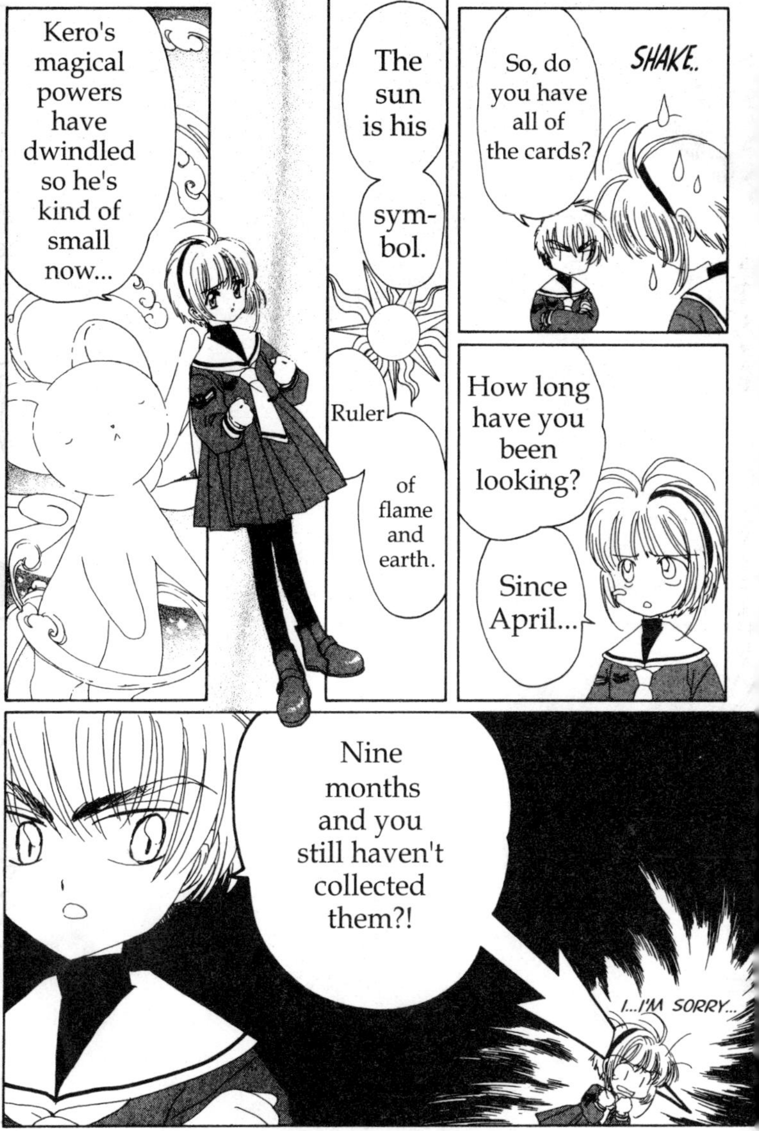
Kero's magical powers have dwindled so he's kind of small now...
The sun is his symbol.
Ruler of flame and earth.
So, do you have all of the cards?
SHAKE..
How long have you been looking?
Since April...
Nine months and you still haven't collected them?!
I...I'M SORRY...

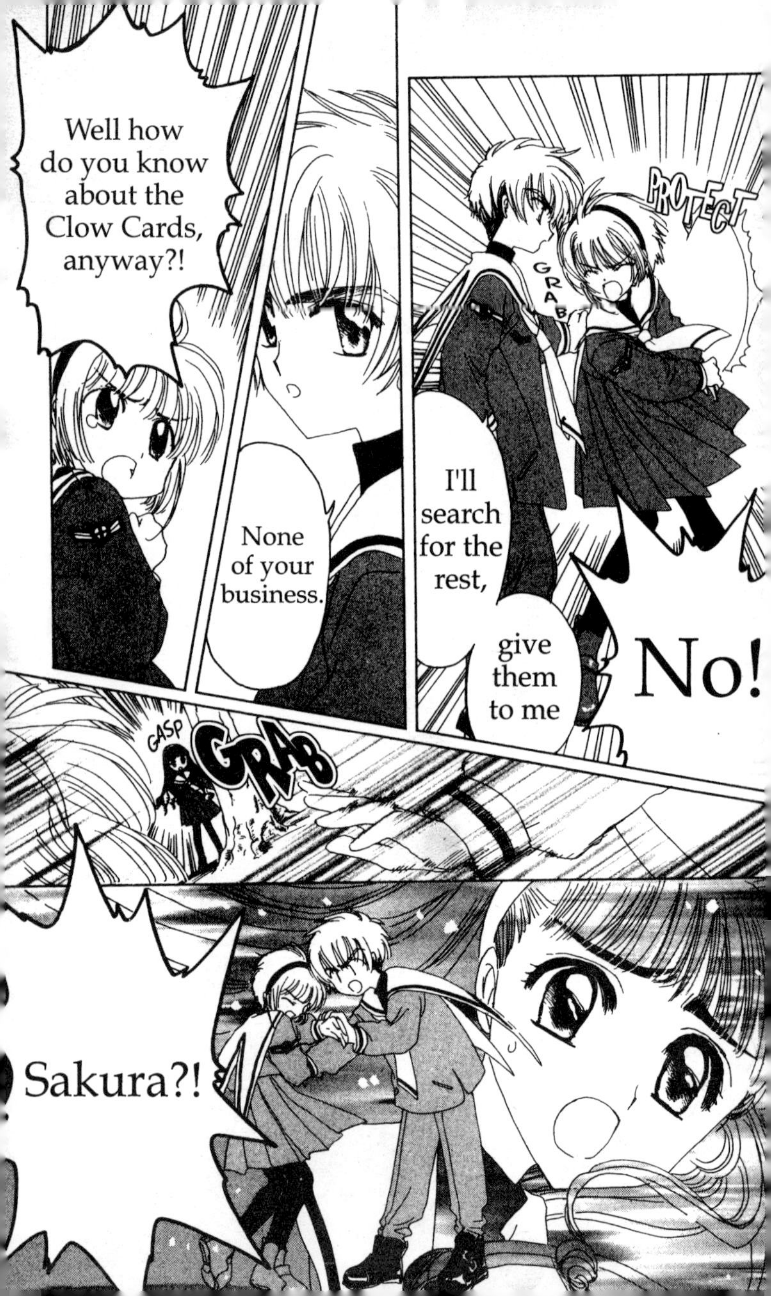
Well how do you know about the Clow Cards, anyway?!
None of your business.
PROTECT
GRAB
I'll search for the rest,
give them to me
No!
GASP
GRAB
Sakura?!

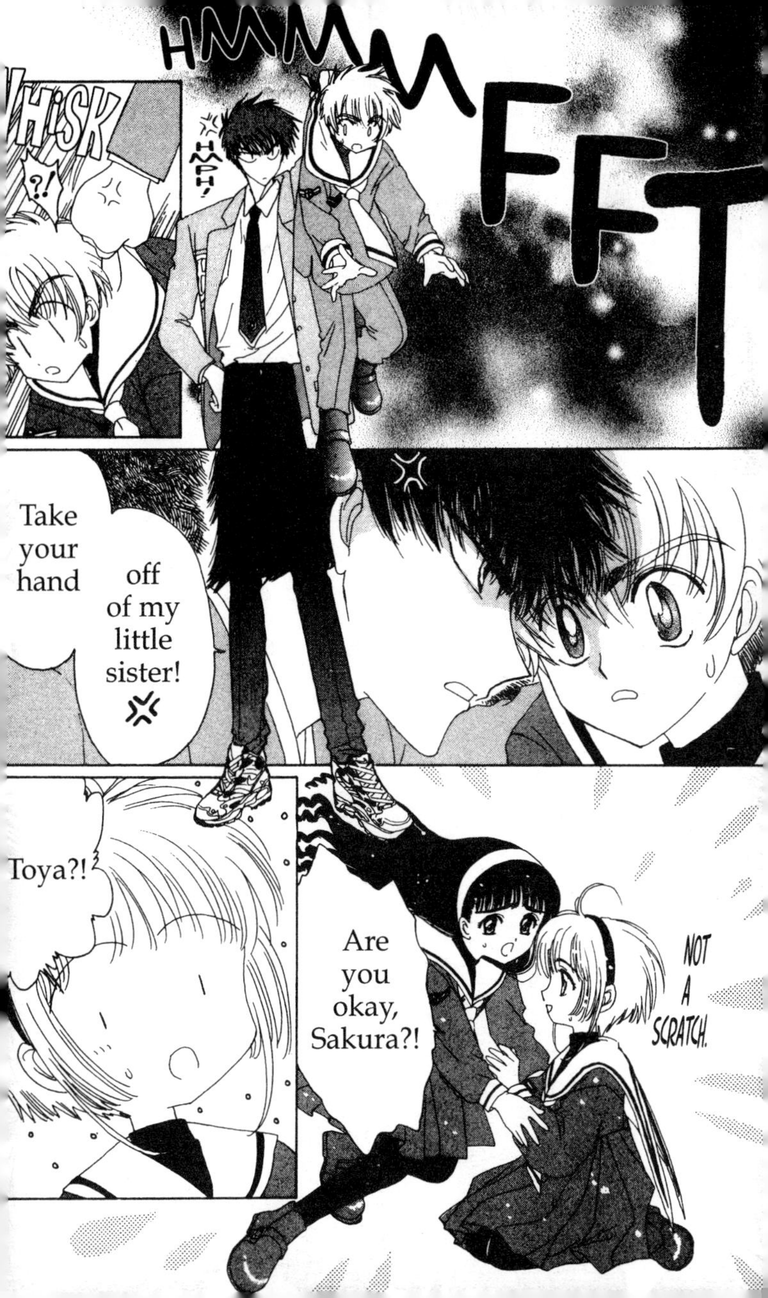

HMMMM
FFFT
WHISK
?!
HMPH!
Take your hand
off of my little sister!
Toya?!
Are you okay, Sakura?!
NOT A SCRATCH.

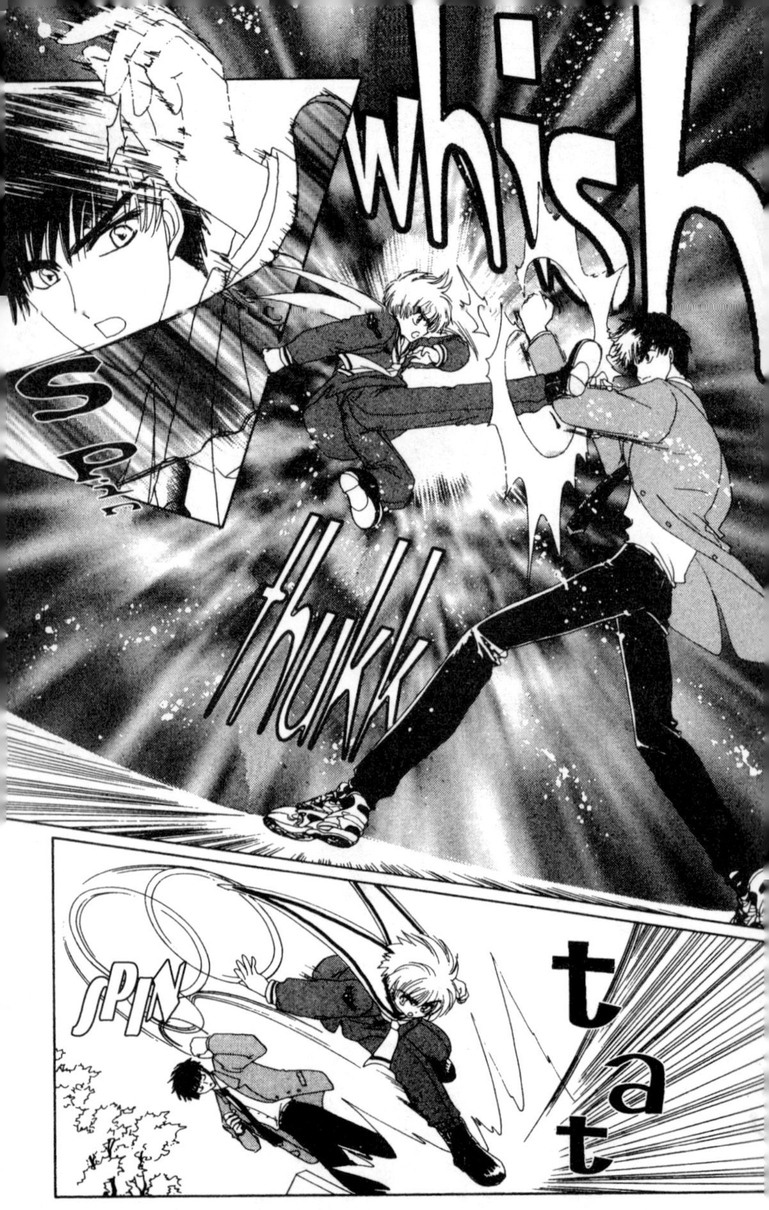
whish
thukk
SPIN
tat

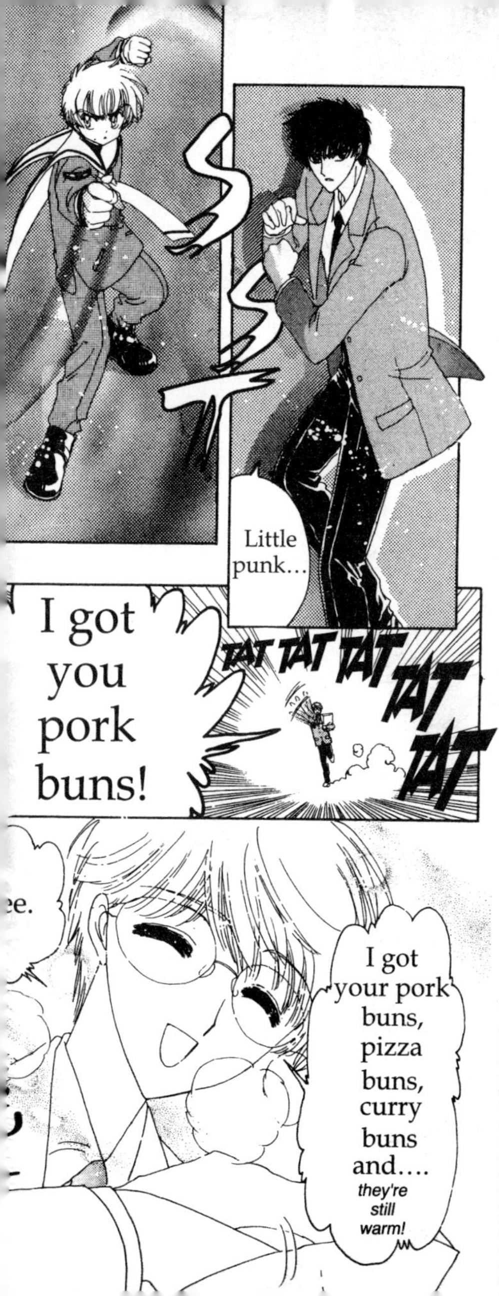

Little punk....
I got you pork buns!
TAT TAT TAT TAT TAT TAT
ee.
I got your pork buns, pizza buns, curry buns and.... they're still warm!

Fujitaka Kinomoto

Birthday
January 3rd
Occupation
University Professor
Favorite Foods
Sweets, noodles
Least Favorite Foods
None
Favorite Pastime
Video Games
Favorite Colors
White, Ivory, Brown
Favorite Flowers
Nadeshiko,
Peach, Sakura
Favorite Recipes
Sweets
Special Skills
Remembering people's faces and names
Hobby
Cooking
Wish List
Nothing

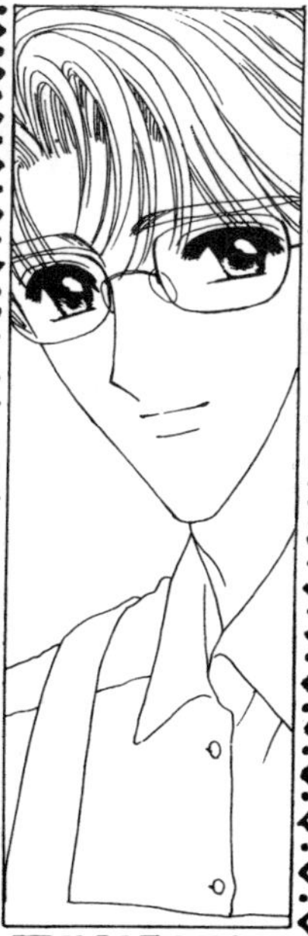

FUJITAKA KINOMOTO

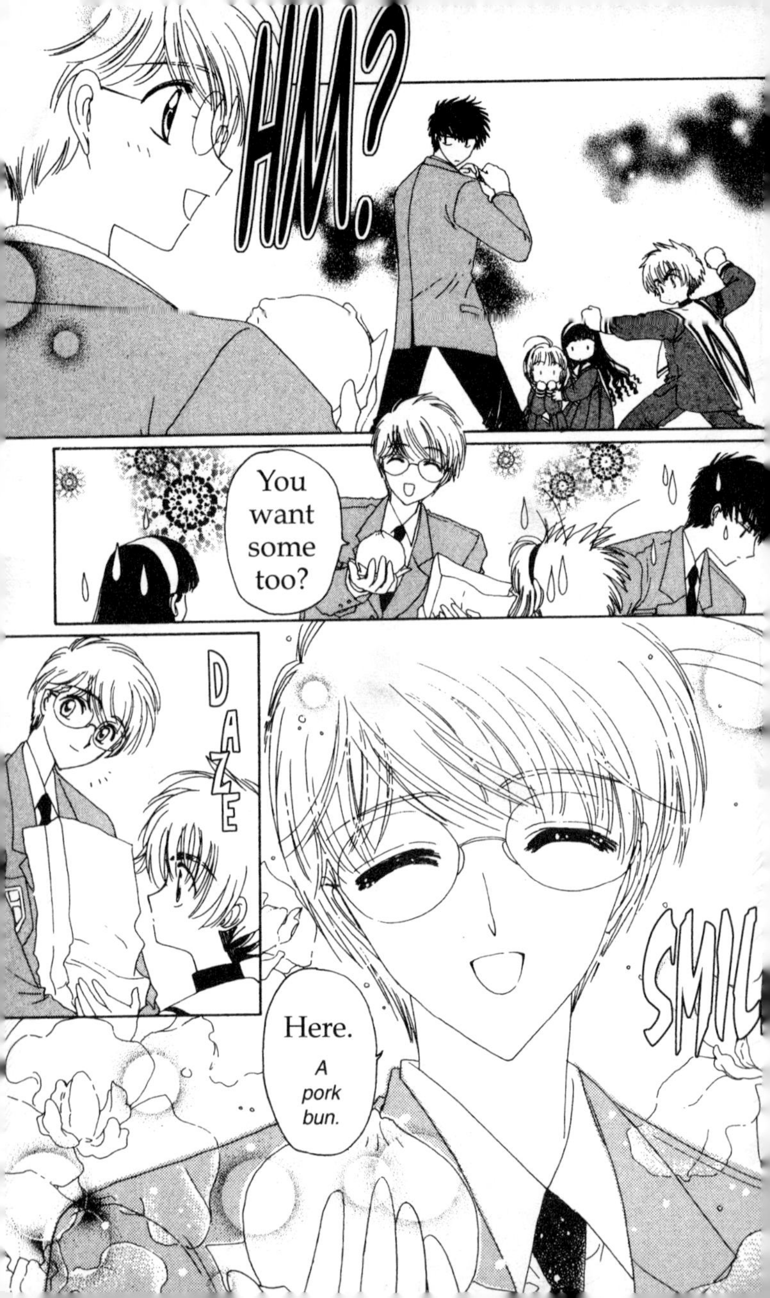
HM?
You want some too?
DAZE
Here.
A pork bun.
SMIL

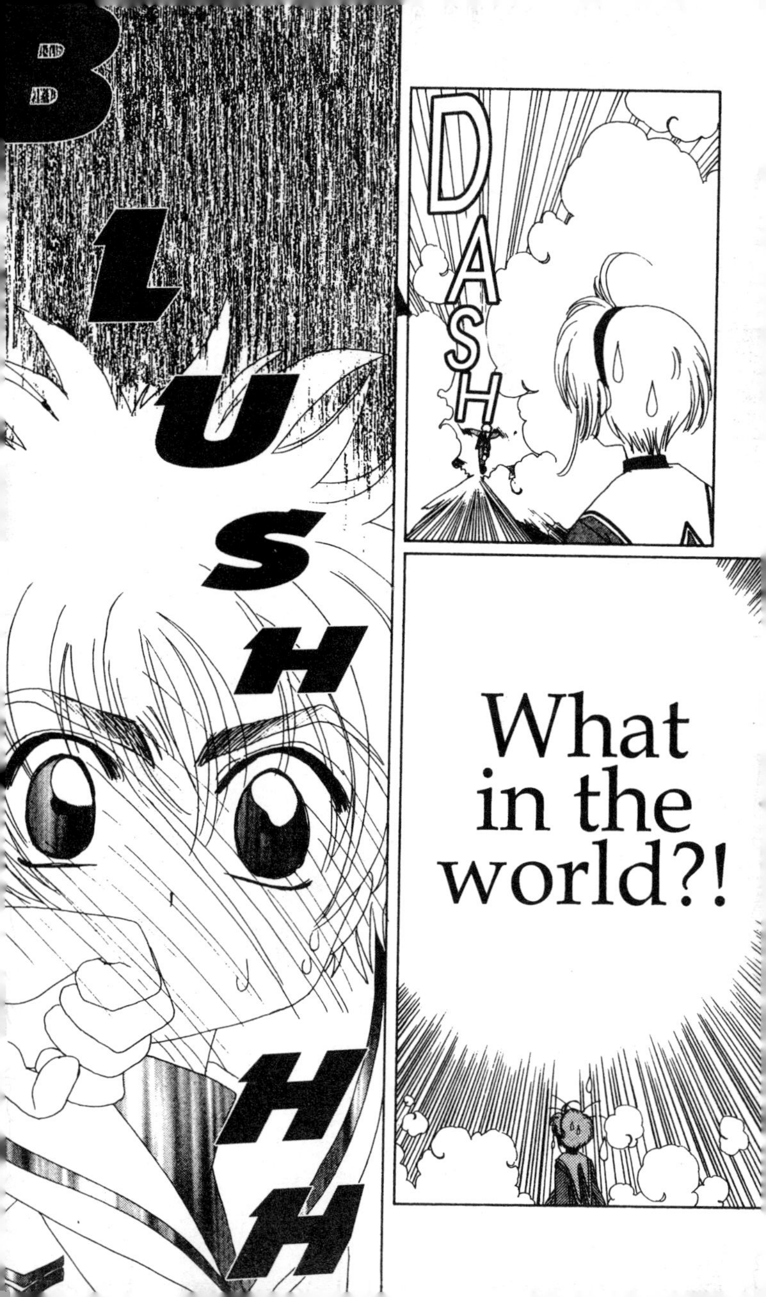
BLUSHHHH
DASH
What in the world?!

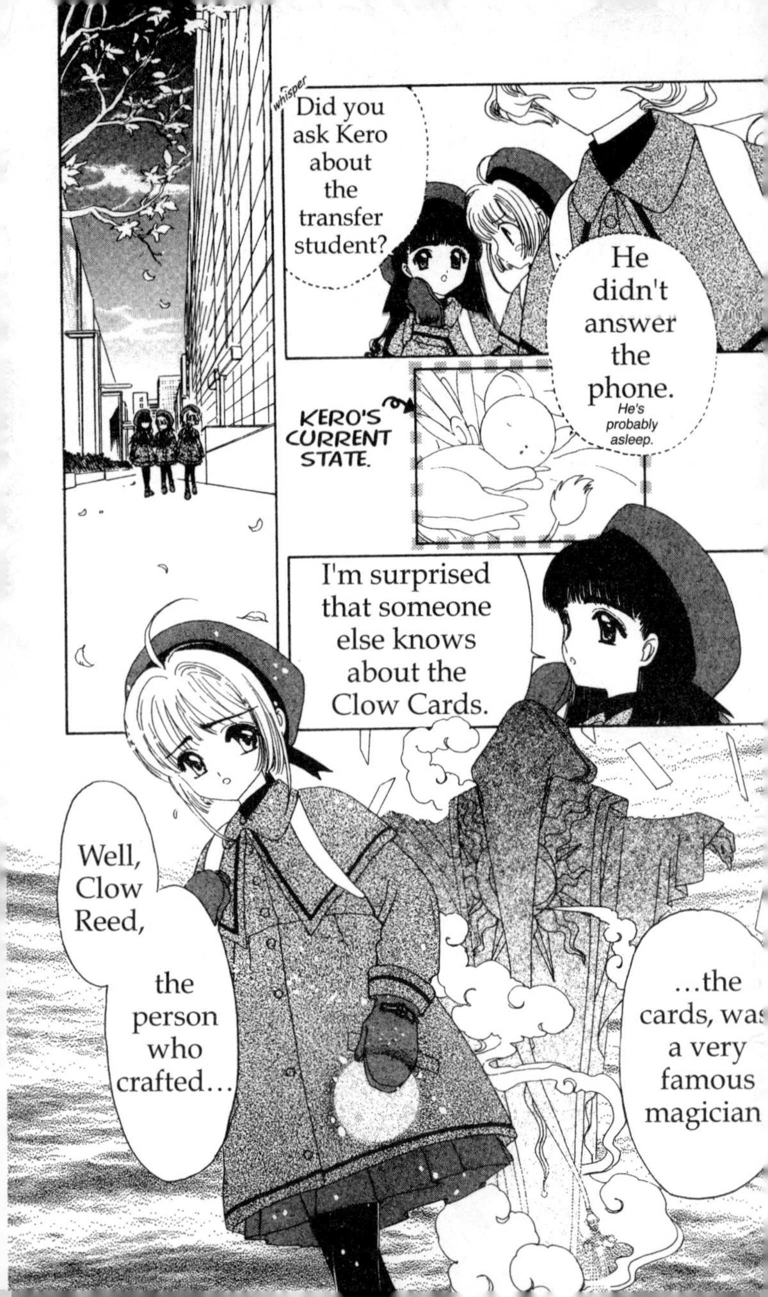
whisper
Did you ask Kero about the transfer student?
He didn't answer the phone.
He's probably asleep.
KERO'S CURRENT STATE.
I'm surprised that someone else knows about the Clow Cards.
Well, Clow Reed,
the person who crafted...
...the cards, was a very famous magician

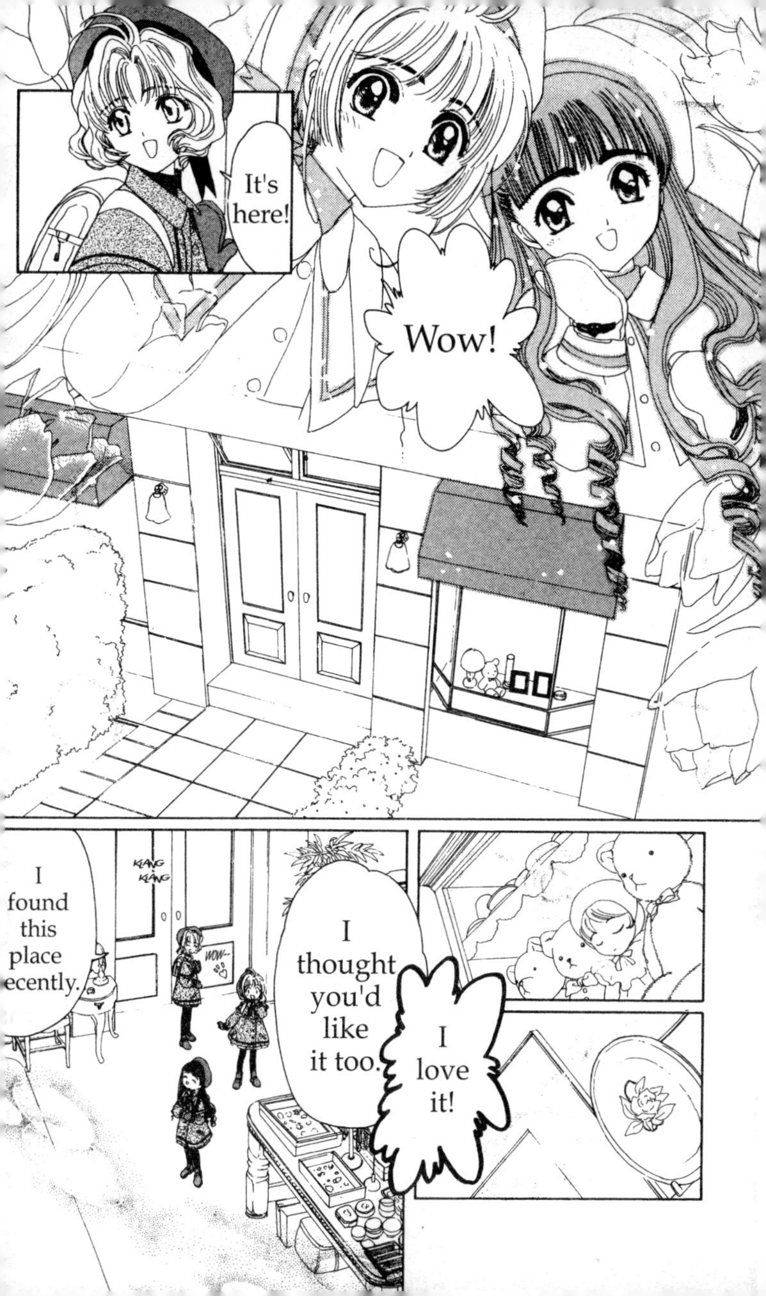
It's here!
Wow!
I found this place ecently.
KLANG KLANG
WOW...
I thought you'd like it too.
I love it!

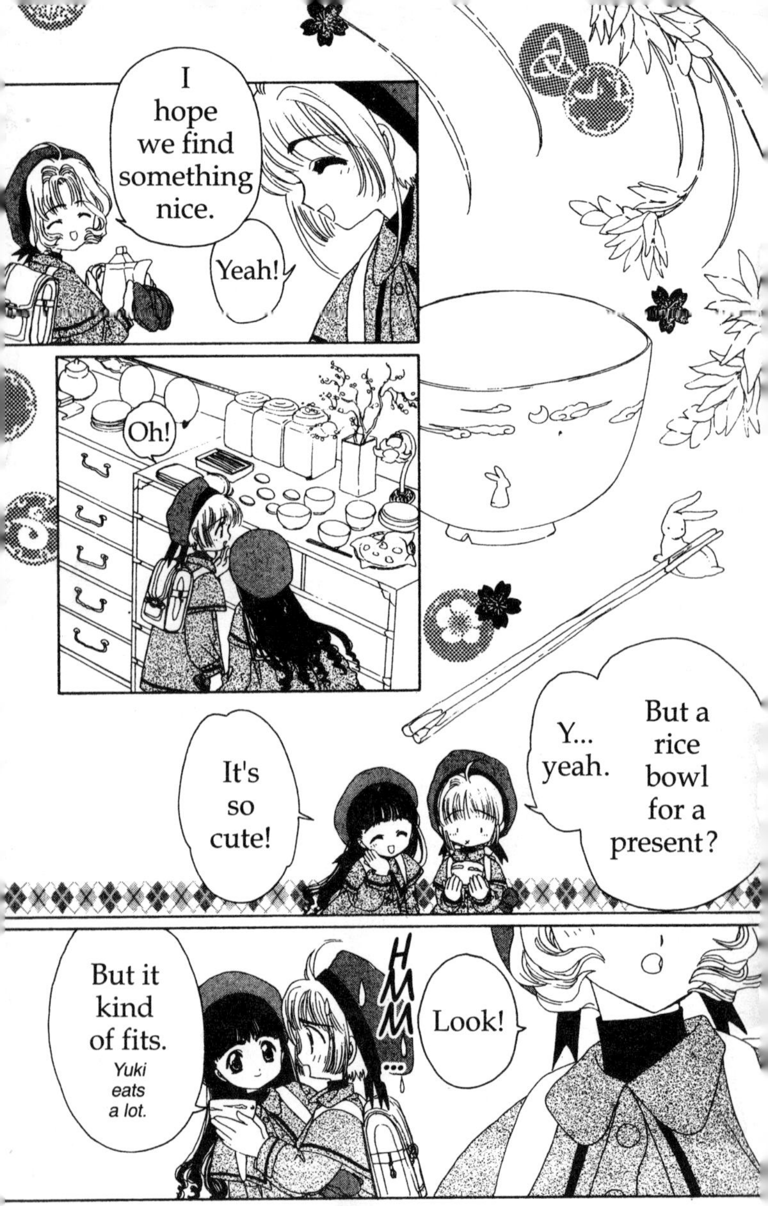

I hope we find something nice.
Yeah!
Oh!
It's so cute!
Y... yeah.
But a rice bowl for a present?
But it kind of fits.
Yuki eats a lot.
HMM...
Look!

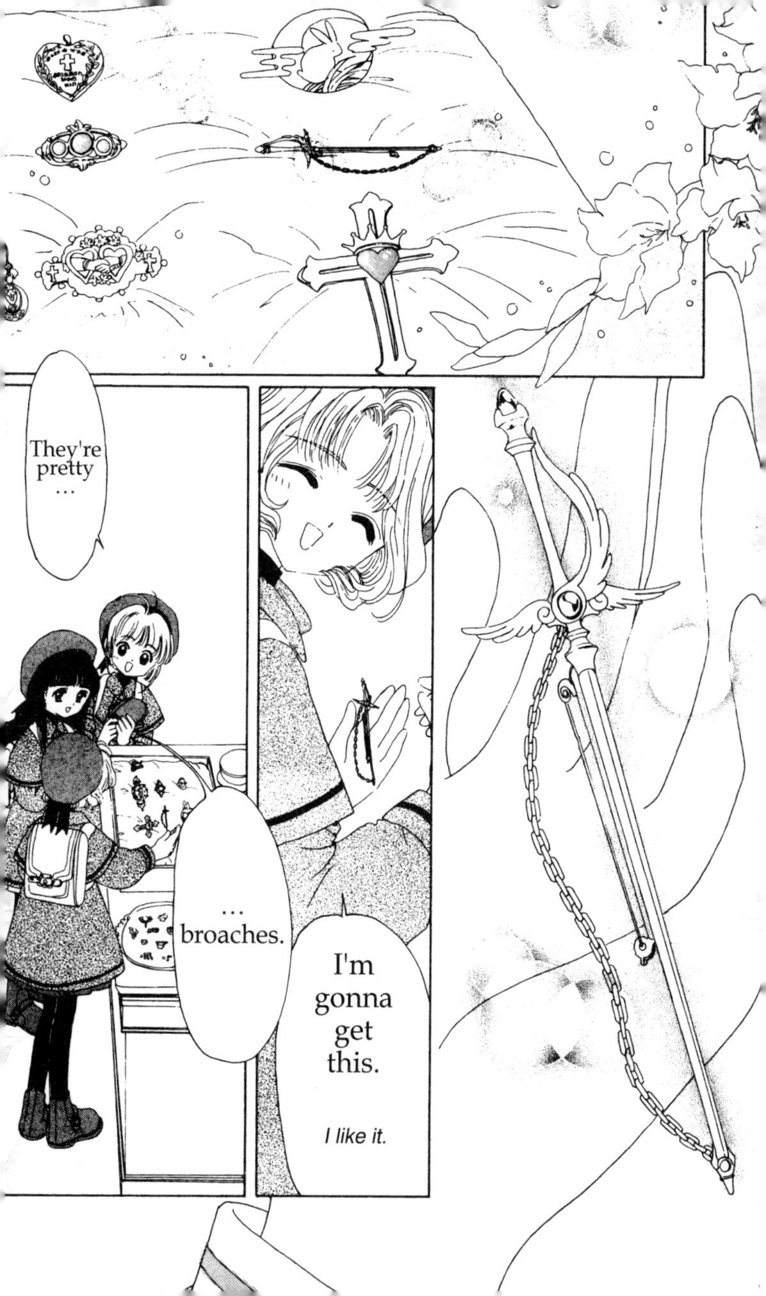
They're pretty ...
... broaches.
I'm gonna get this.
I like it.

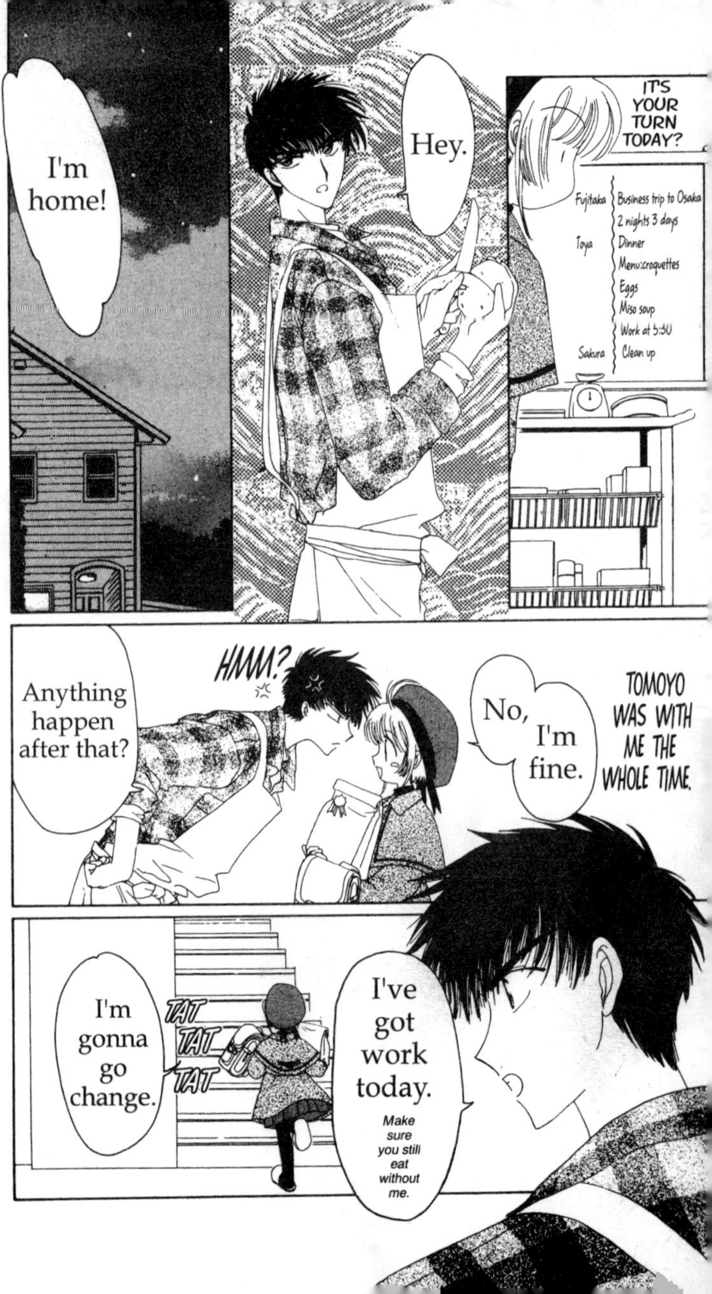

I'm home!
Hey.
IT'S YOUR TURN TODAY?
Fujitaka
Business trip to Osaka
2 nights 3 days
Toya
Dinner
Menu:croquettes
Eggs
Miso soup
Work at 5:30
Sakura
Clean up
Anything happen after that?
HMM?
No, I'm fine.
TOMOYO WAS WITH ME THE WHOLE TIME.
I'm gonna go change.
TAT
TAT
TAT
I've got work today.
Make sure you still eat without me.

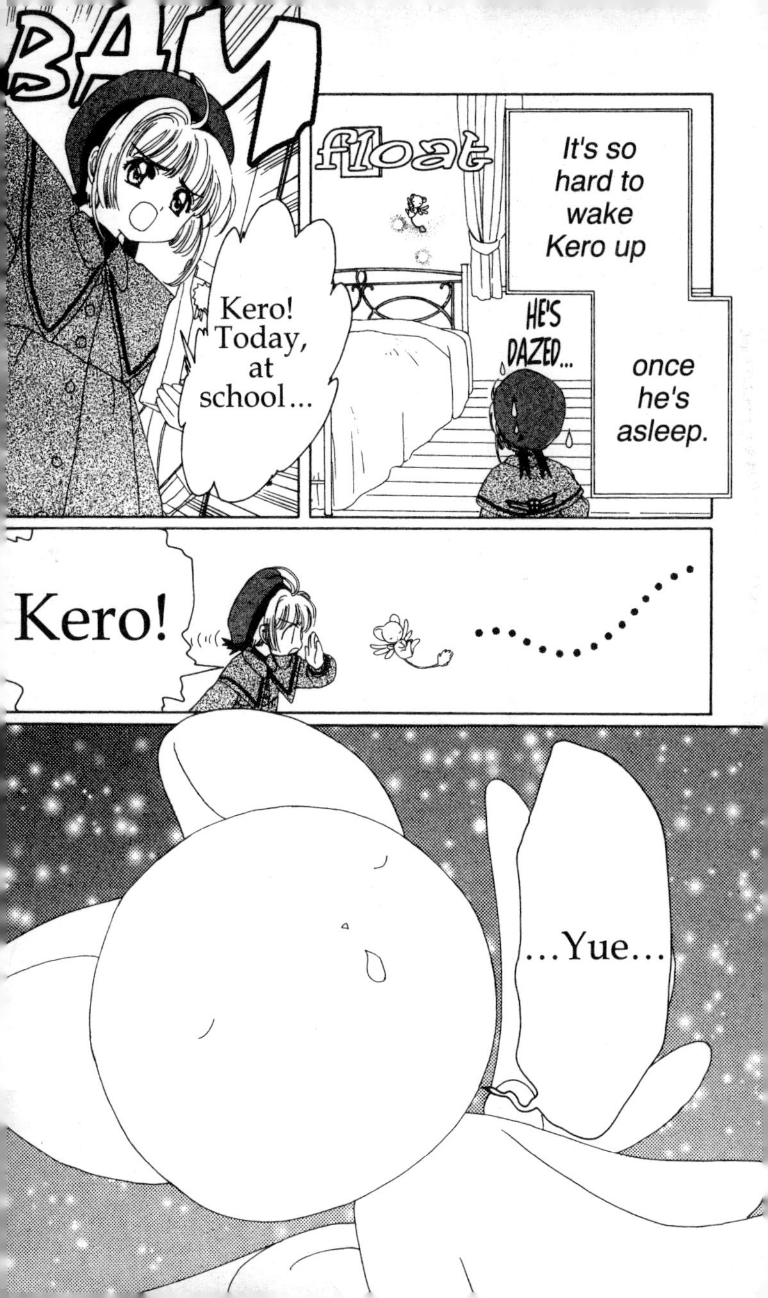
BAM
Kero! Today, at school...
float
It's so hard to wake Kero up
HE'S DAZED...
once he's asleep.
Kero!
....
...Yue...

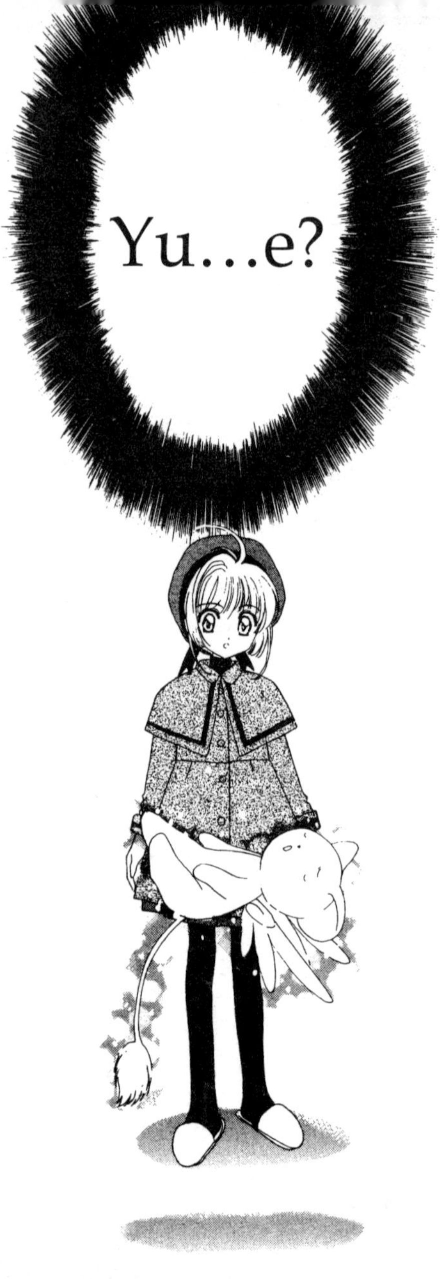
Yu...e?

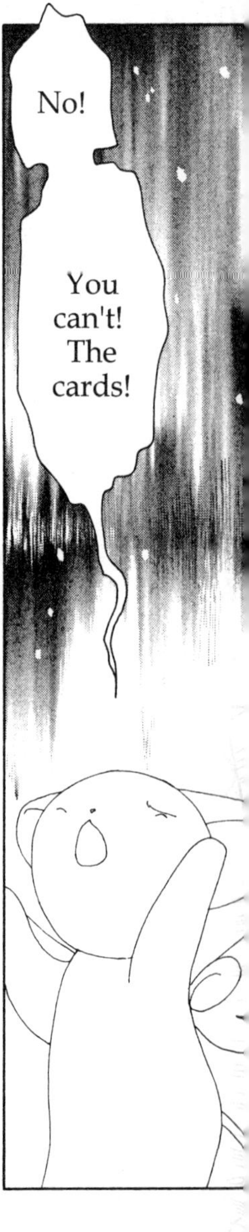
No!
You can't! The cards!

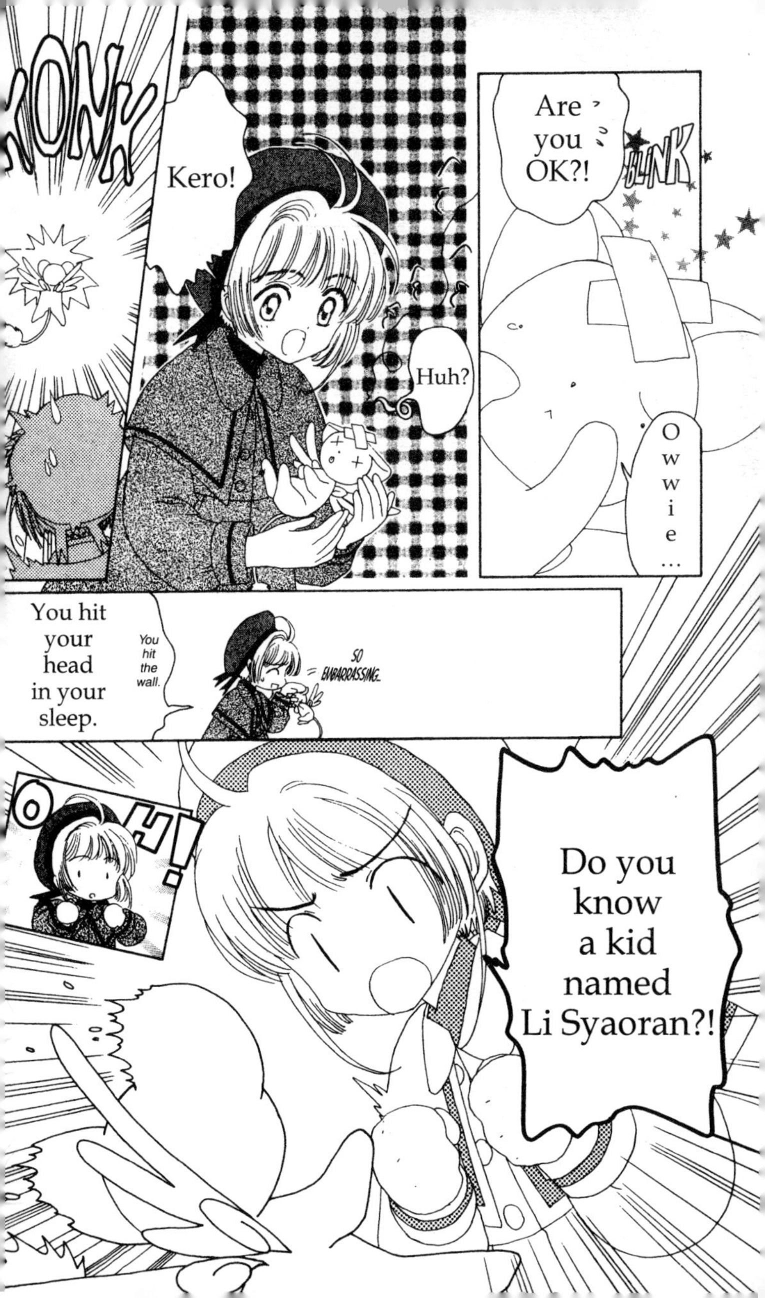
KONK
Kero!
Huh?
Are you OK?!
BLINK
Owwie...
You hit your head in your sleep.
You hit the wall.
SO EMBARRASSING...
OH!
Do you know a kid named Li Syaoran?!

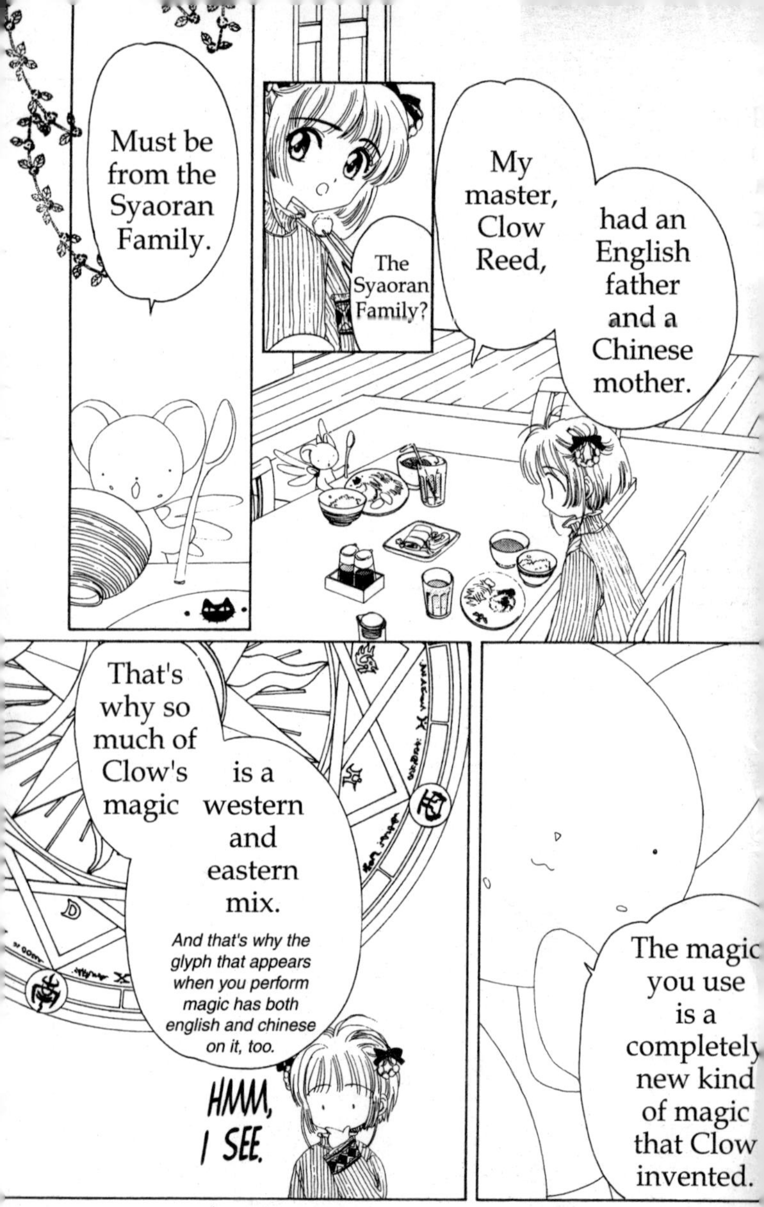
Must be from the Syaoran Family.
The Syaoran Family?
My master, Clow Reed,
had an English father and a Chinese mother.
That's why so much of Clow's magic
is a western and eastern mix.
And that's why the glyph that appears when you perform magic has both english and chinese on it, too.
HMM, I SEE.
The magic you use is a completely new kind of magic that Clow invented.

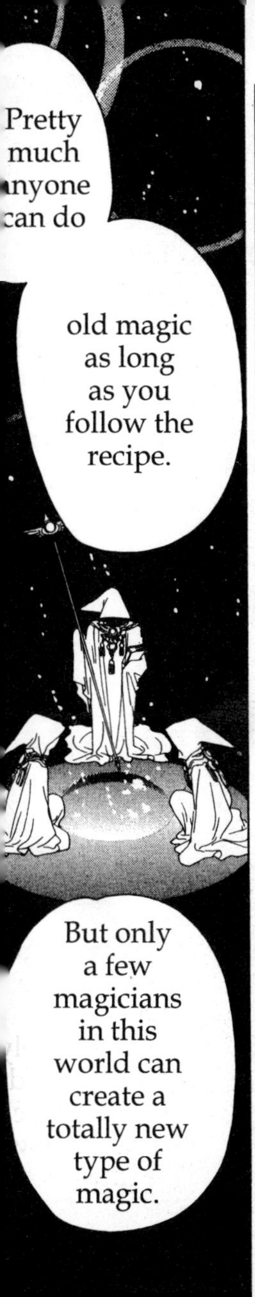
Pretty much nyone can do
old magic as long as you follow the recipe.
But only a few magicians in this world can create a totally new type of magic.

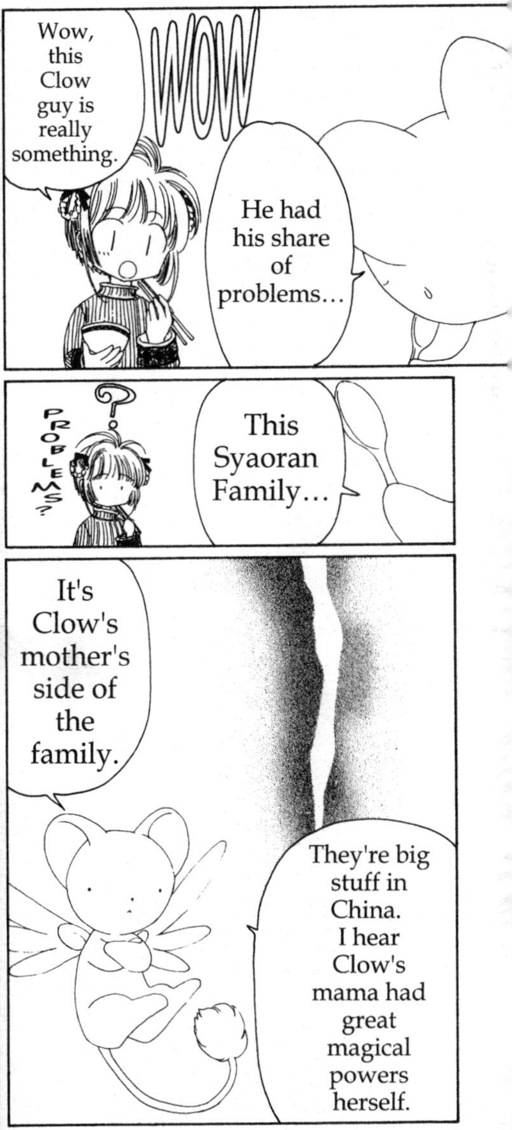
Wow, this Clow guy is really something.
WOW
He had his share of problems...
PROBLEMS?
This Syaoran Family...
It's Clow's mother's side of the family.
They're big stuff in China. I hear Clow's mama had great magical powers herself.

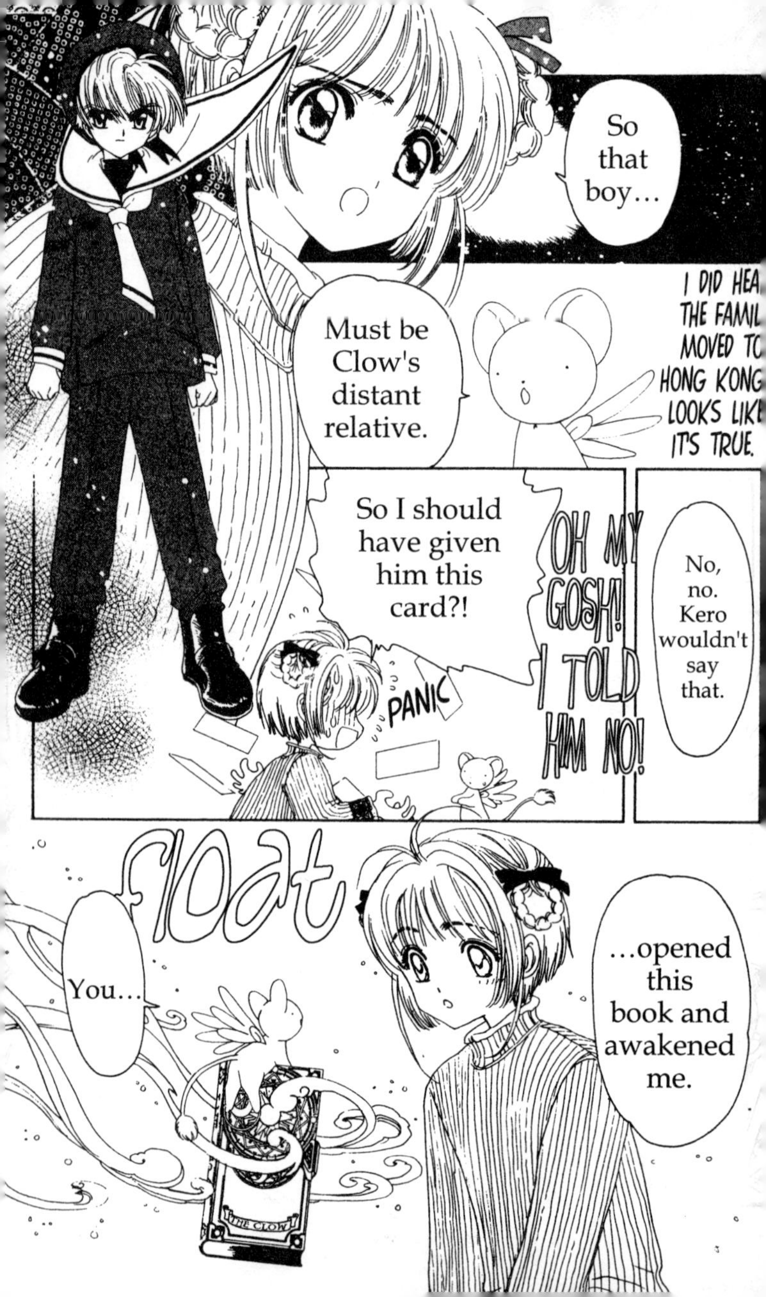
So that boy...
Must be Clow's distant relative.
I DID HEA
THE FAMIL
MOVED TO
HONG KONG
LOOKS LIK
IT'S TRUE.
So I should have given him this card?!
PANIC
OH MY GOSH! I TOLD HIM NO!
No, no. Kero wouldn't say that.
FLOAT
You...
...opened this book and awakened me.
THE CLOW

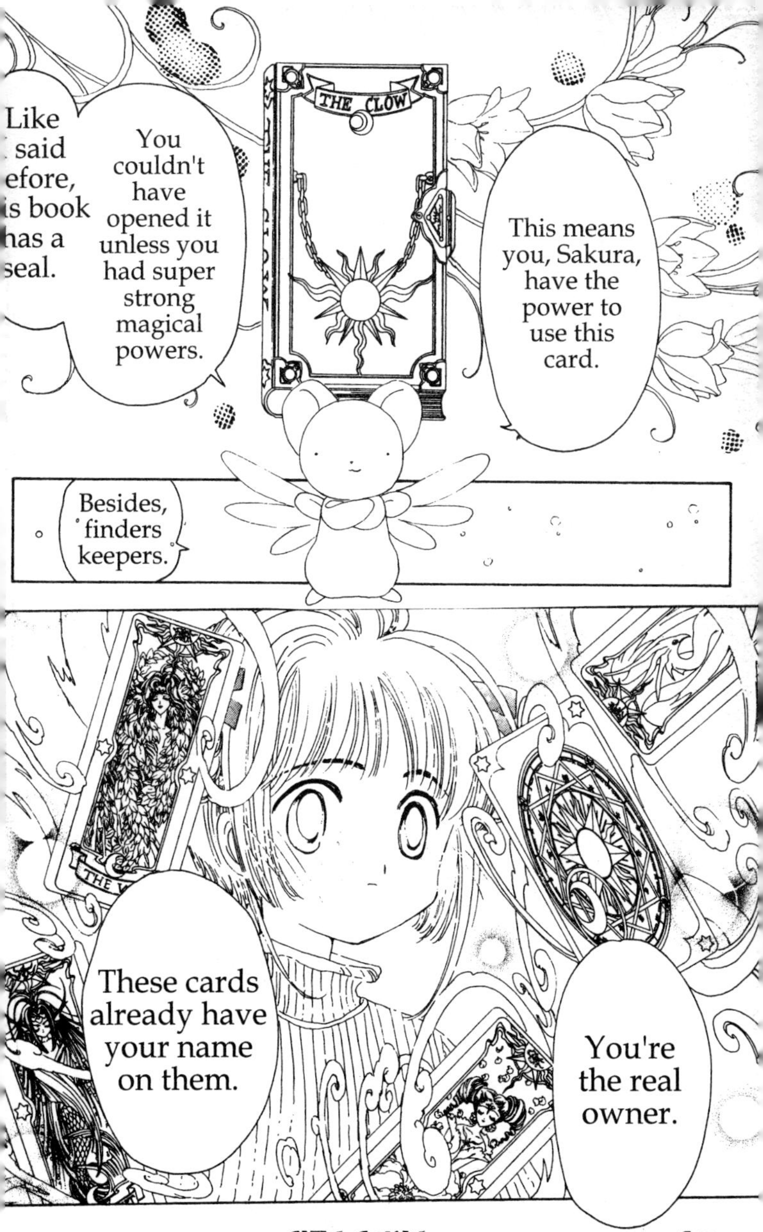
Like
said
efore,
s book
has a
seal.
You couldn't have opened it unless you had super strong magical powers.
THE CLOW
This means you, Sakura, have the power to use this card.
Besides, finders keepers.
These cards already have your name on them.
You're the real owner.

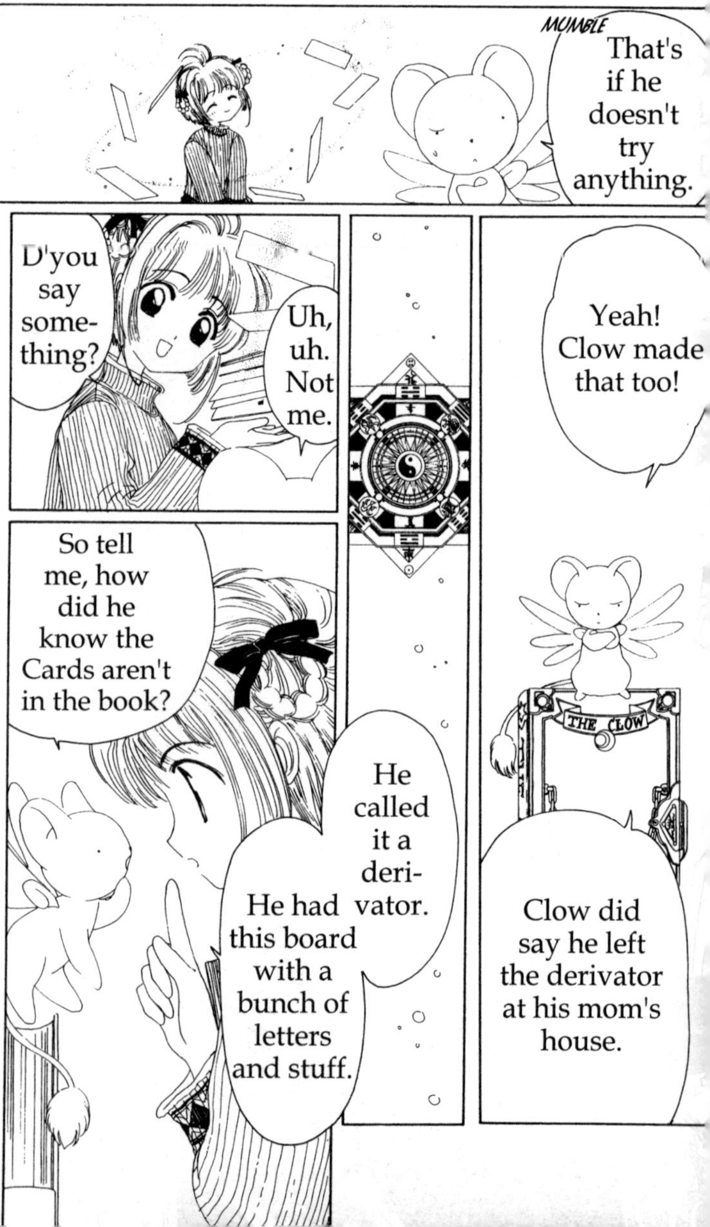
MUMBLE
That's if he doesn't try anything.
D'you say some-thing?
Uh, uh. Not me.
So tell me, how did he know the Cards aren't in the book?
He called it a deri-vator.
He had this board with a bunch of letters and stuff.
Yeah! Clow made that too!
THE CLOW
Clow did say he left the derivator at his mom's house.

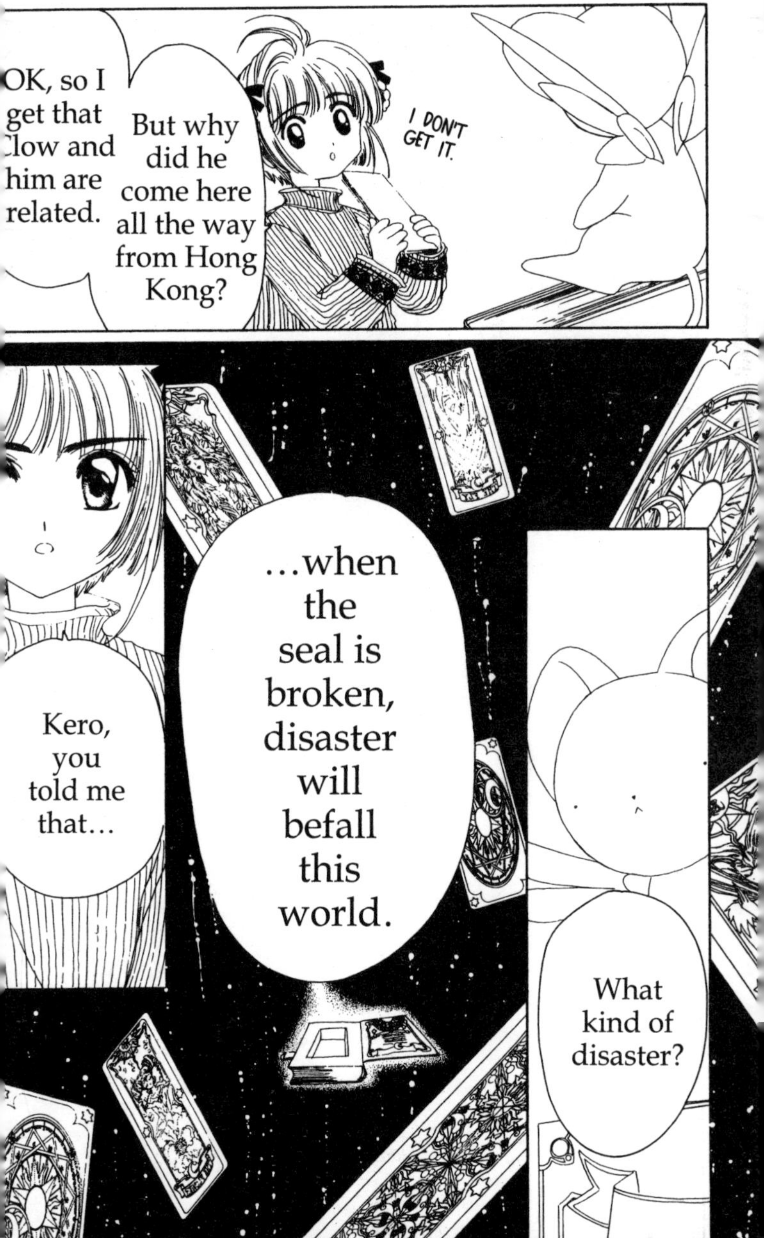
OK, so I get that Clow and him are related.
But why did he come here all the way from Hong Kong?
I DON'T GET IT.
Kero, you told me that…
…when the seal is broken, disaster will befall this world.
What kind of disaster?

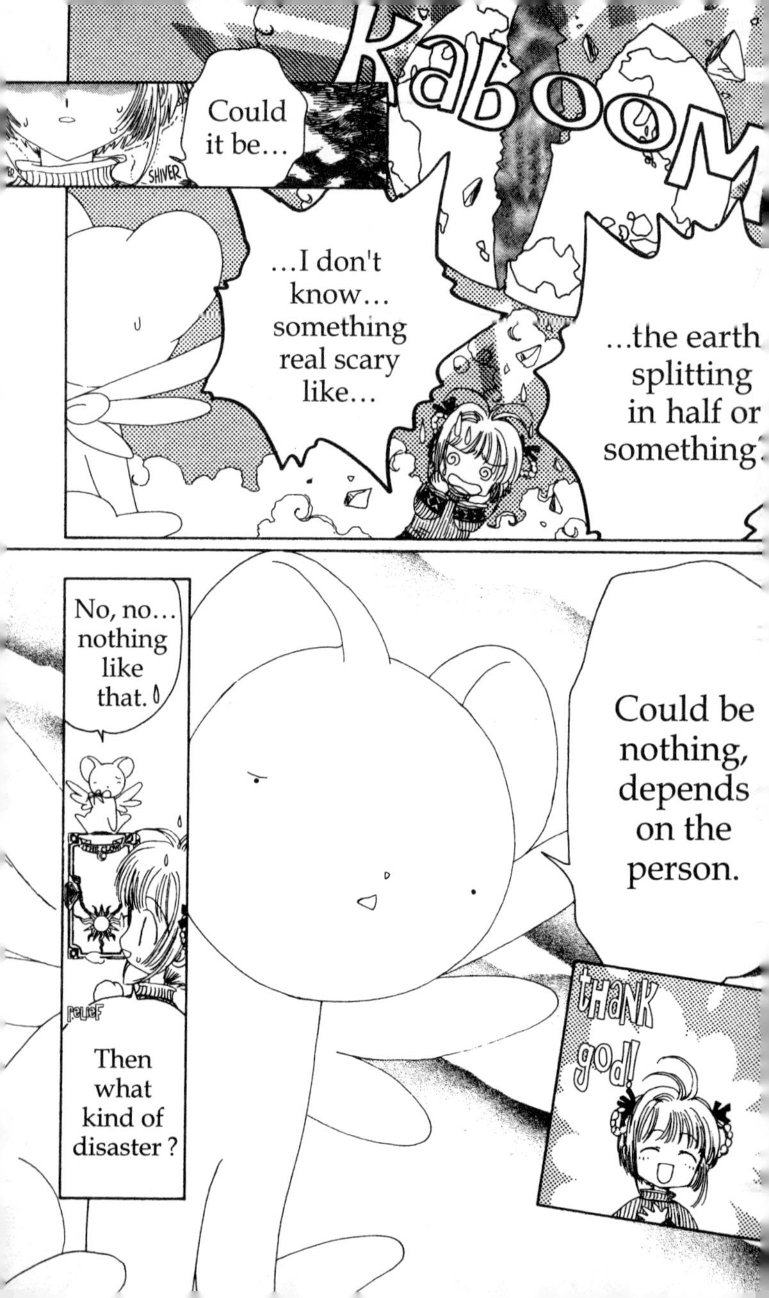
Could it be…
SHIVER
KaBOOOM
…I don't know… something real scary like…
…the earth splitting in half or something?
No, no… nothing like that.
RELIEF
Then what kind of disaster ?
Could be nothing, depends on the person.
THANK god!

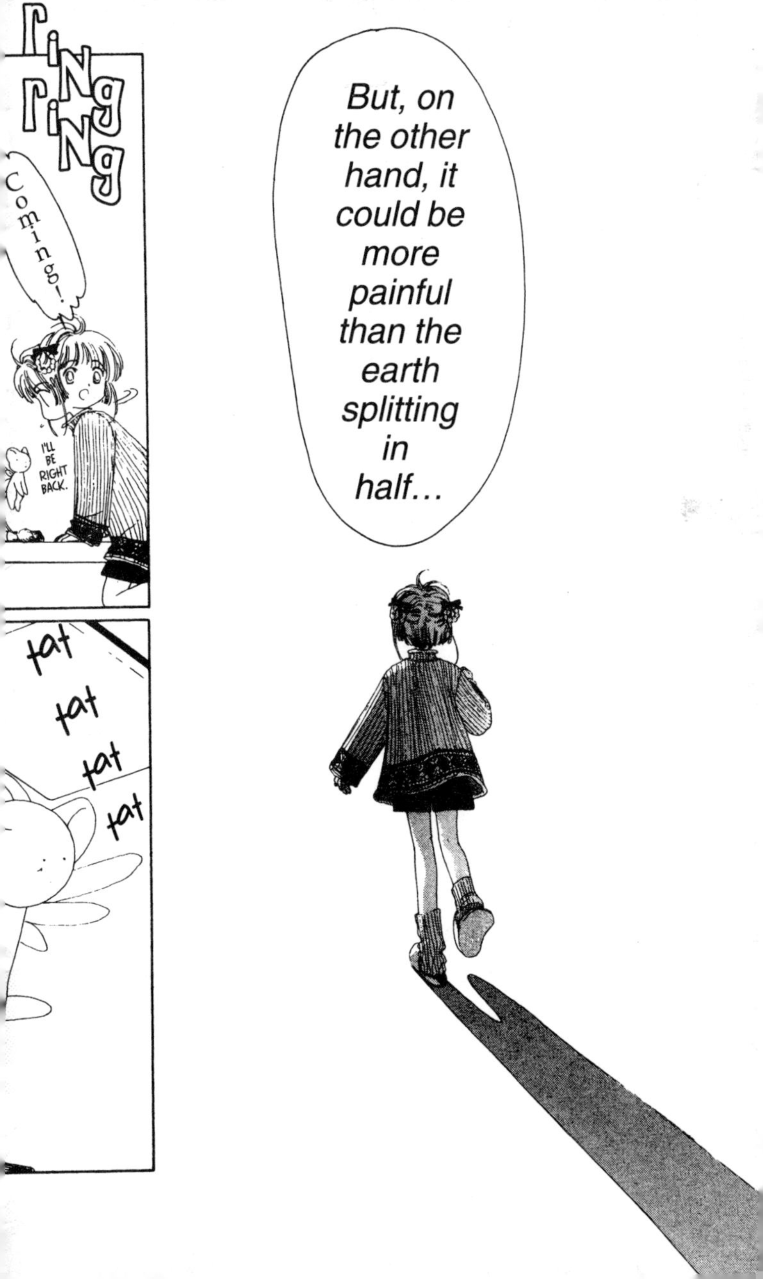
ring ring
Coming!
I'LL BE RIGHT BACK.
tat tat tat tat
But, on the other hand, it could be more painful than the earth splitting in half...

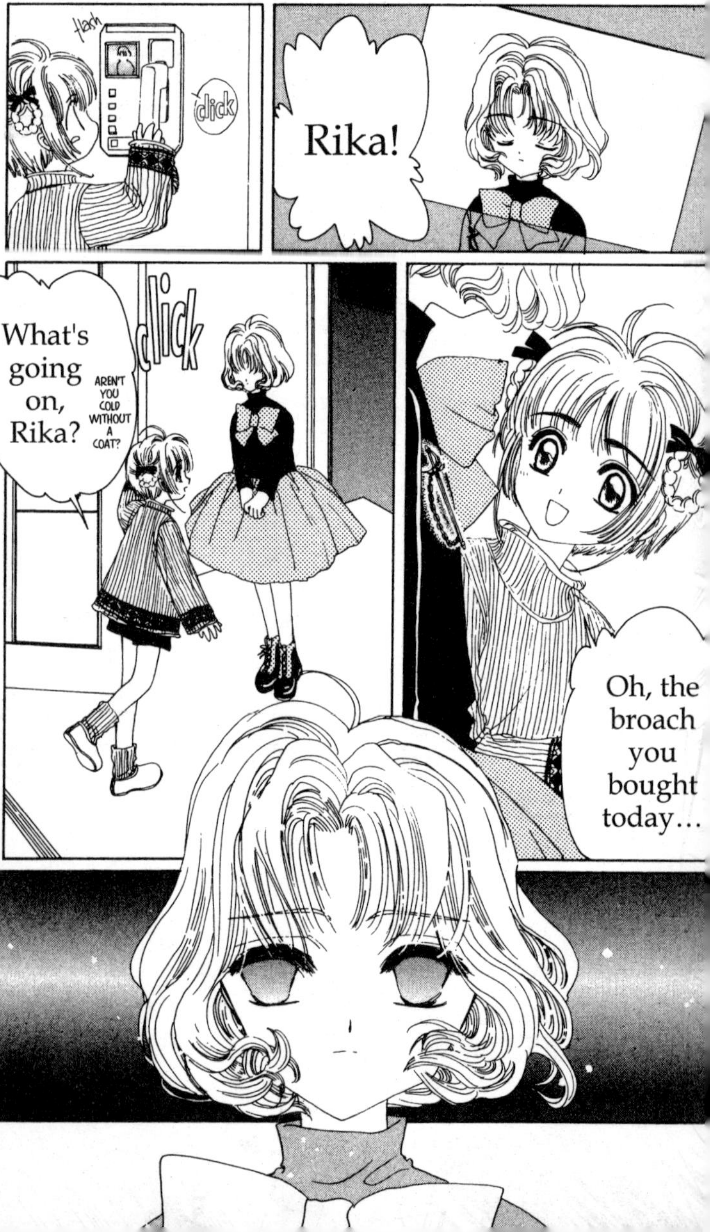
flash
click
Rika!
click
What's going on, Rika?
AREN'T YOU COLD WITHOUT A COAT?
Oh, the broach you bought today…

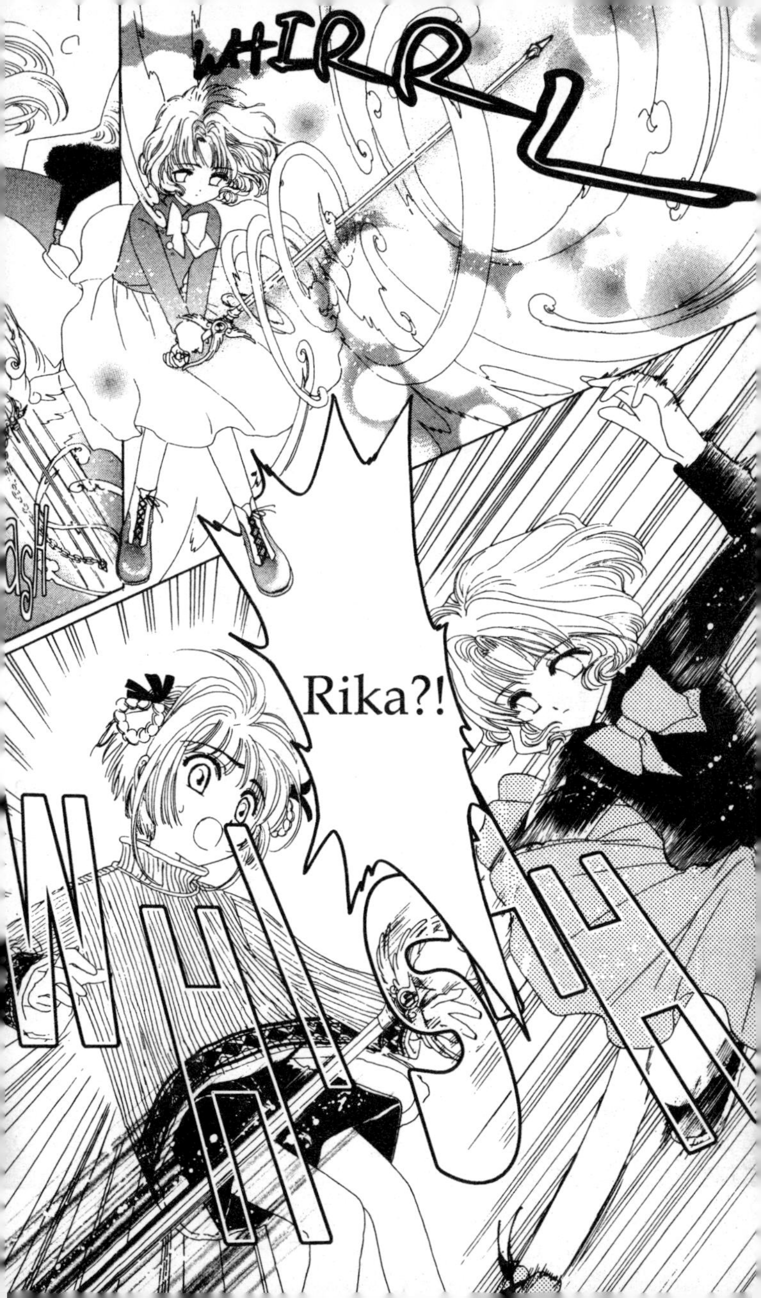
WHIRRL
Rika?!
WHISH

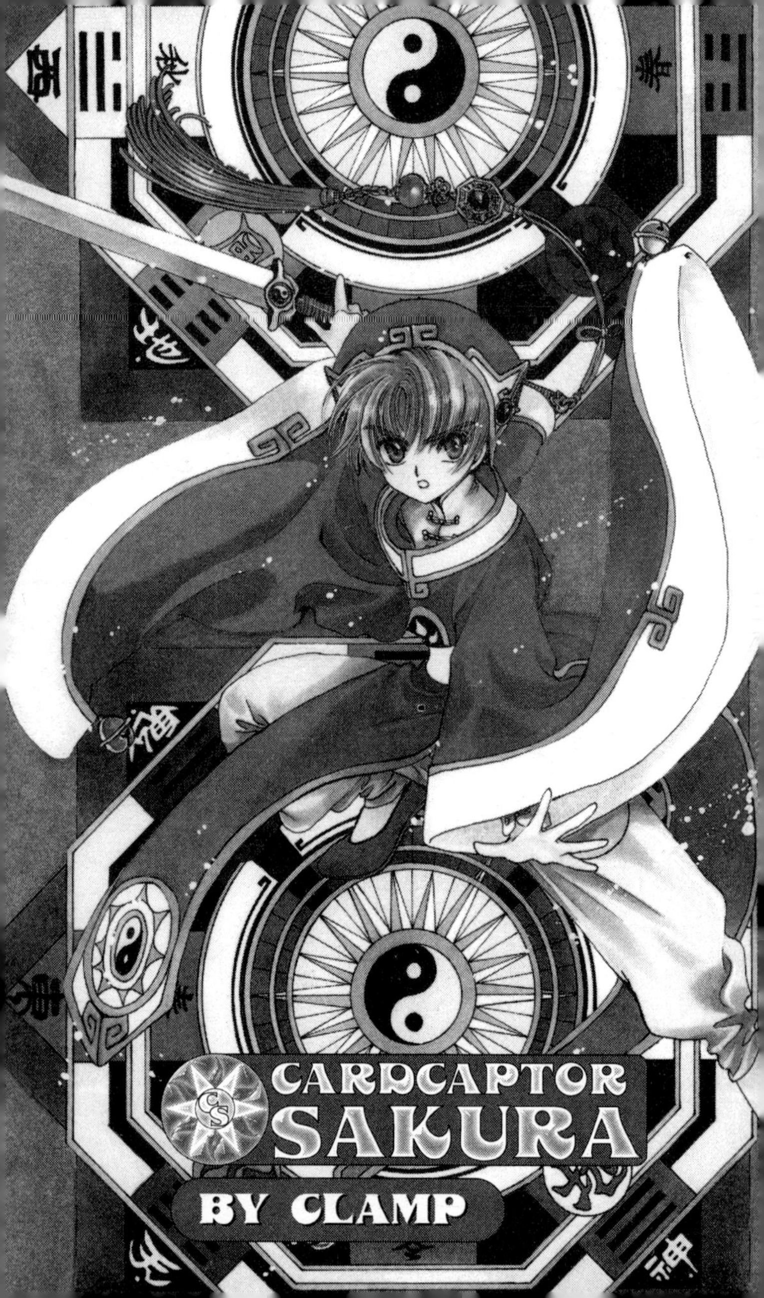
CARDCAPTOR SAKURA
BY CLAMP

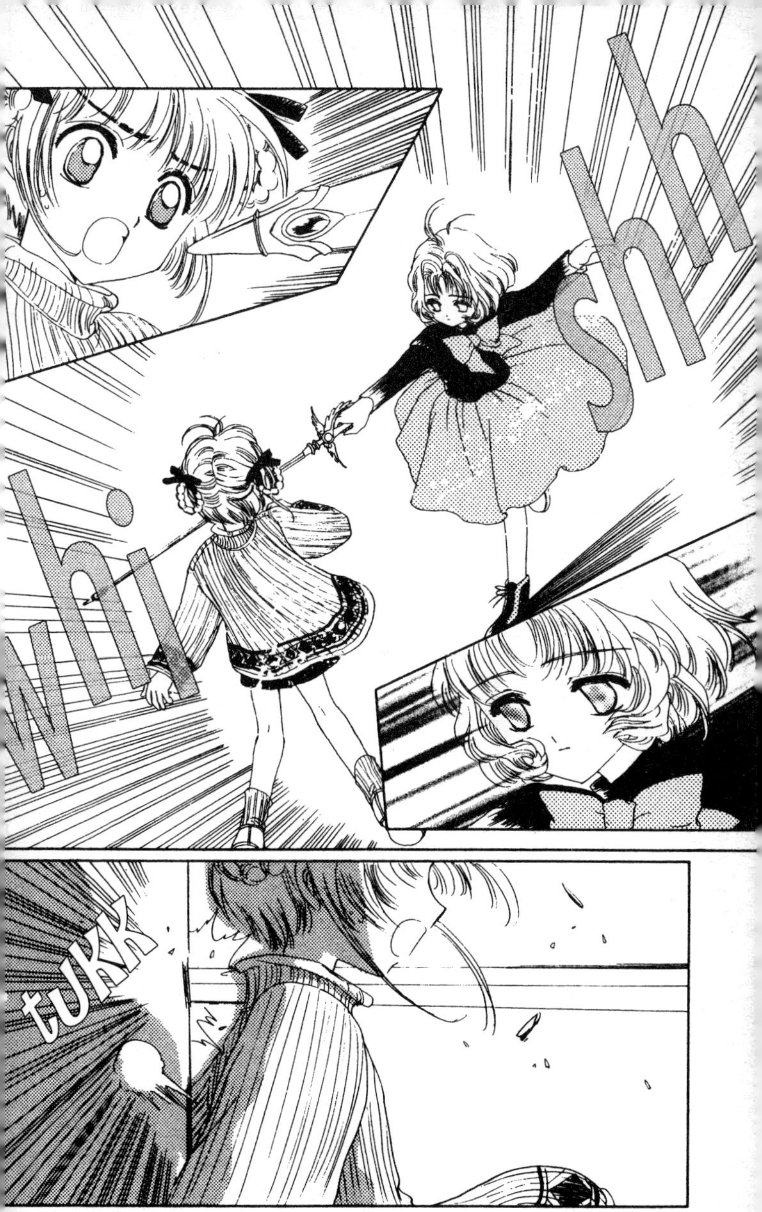
whi
shh
tukk

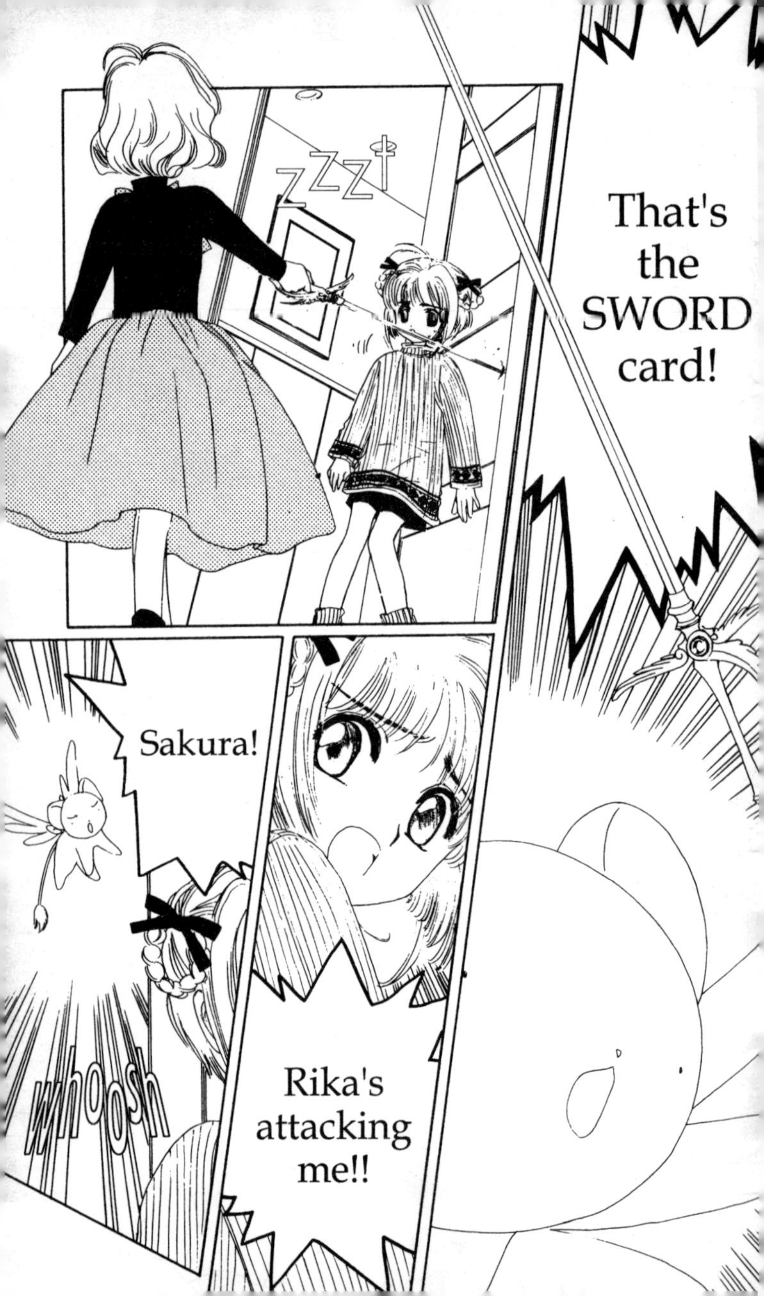
zzzt
Sakura!
whoosh
Rika's attacking me!!
That's the SWORD card!

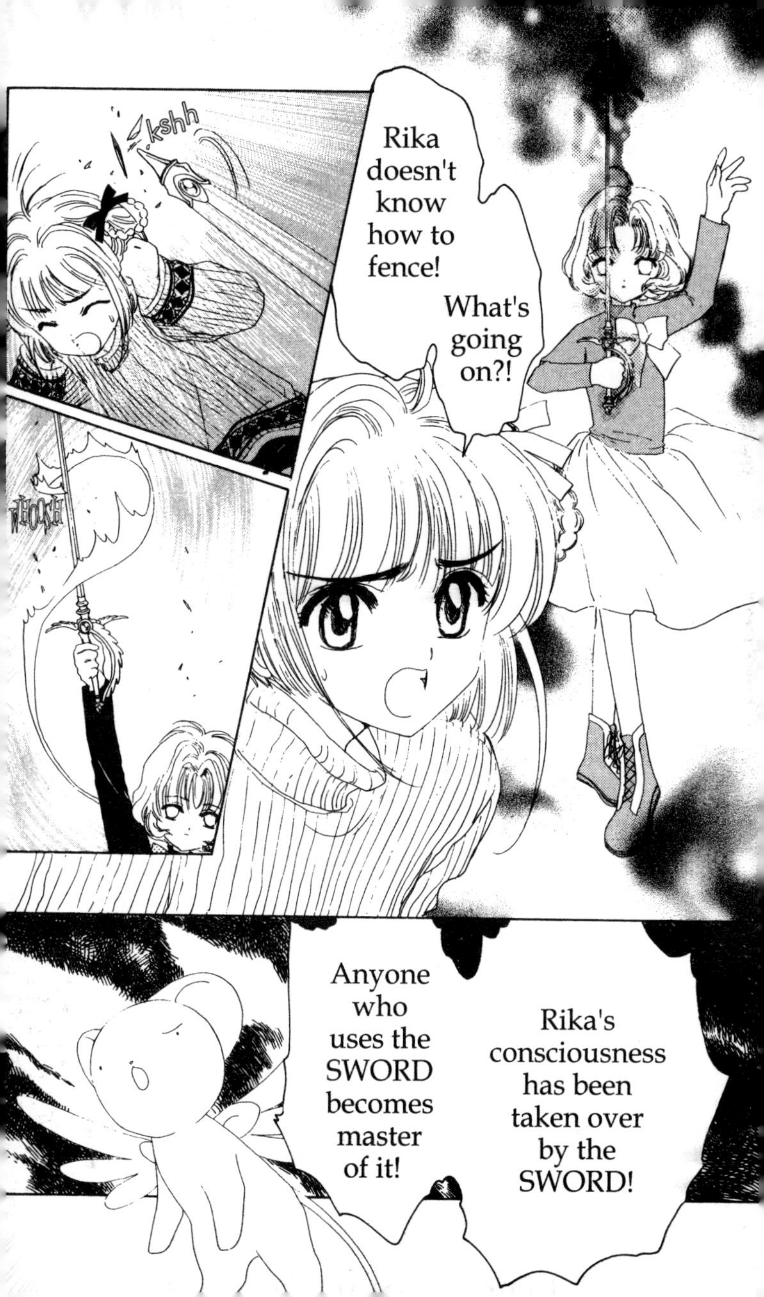
kshh
WHOOSH
Rika doesn't know how to fence!
What's going on?!
Anyone who uses the SWORD becomes master of it!
Rika's consciousness has been taken over by the SWORD!

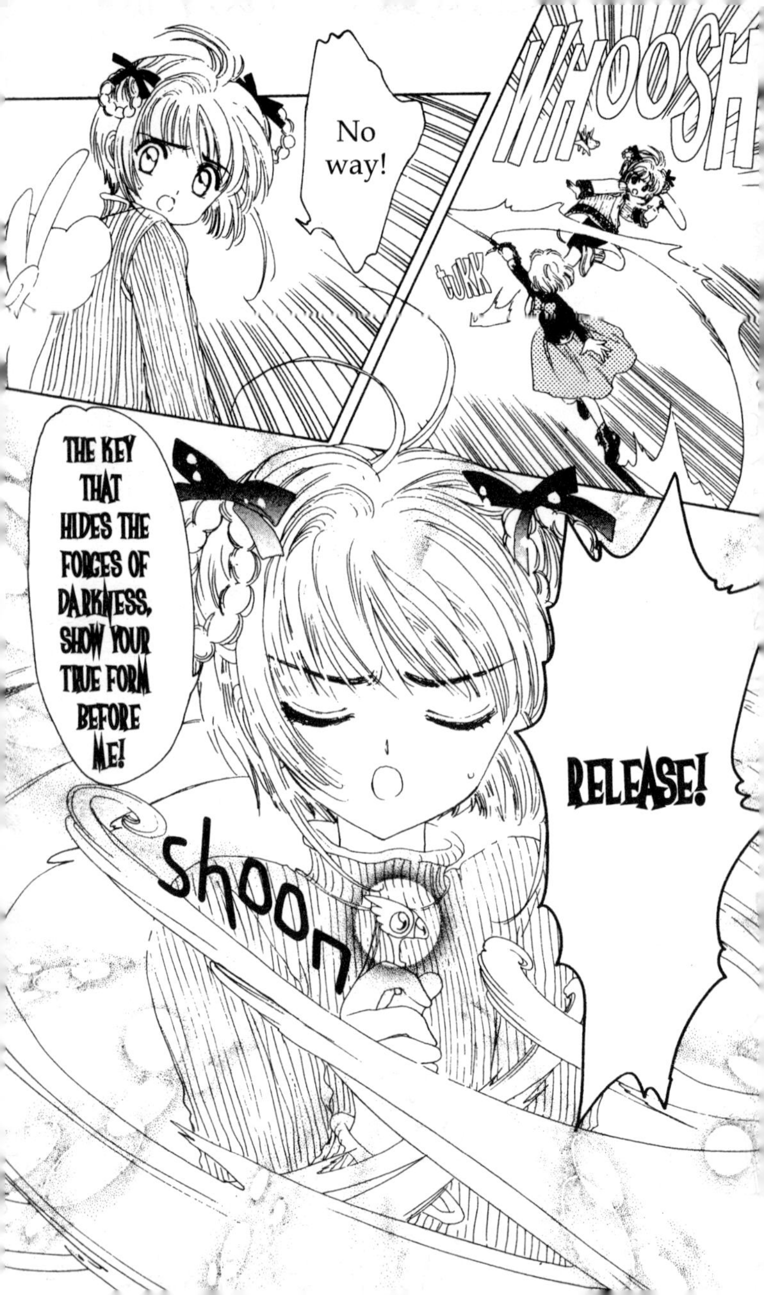
No way!
WHOOSH
tuKK
THE KEY THAT HIDES THE FORCES OF DARKNESS, SHOW YOUR TRUE FORM BEFORE ME!
RELEASE!
shoon

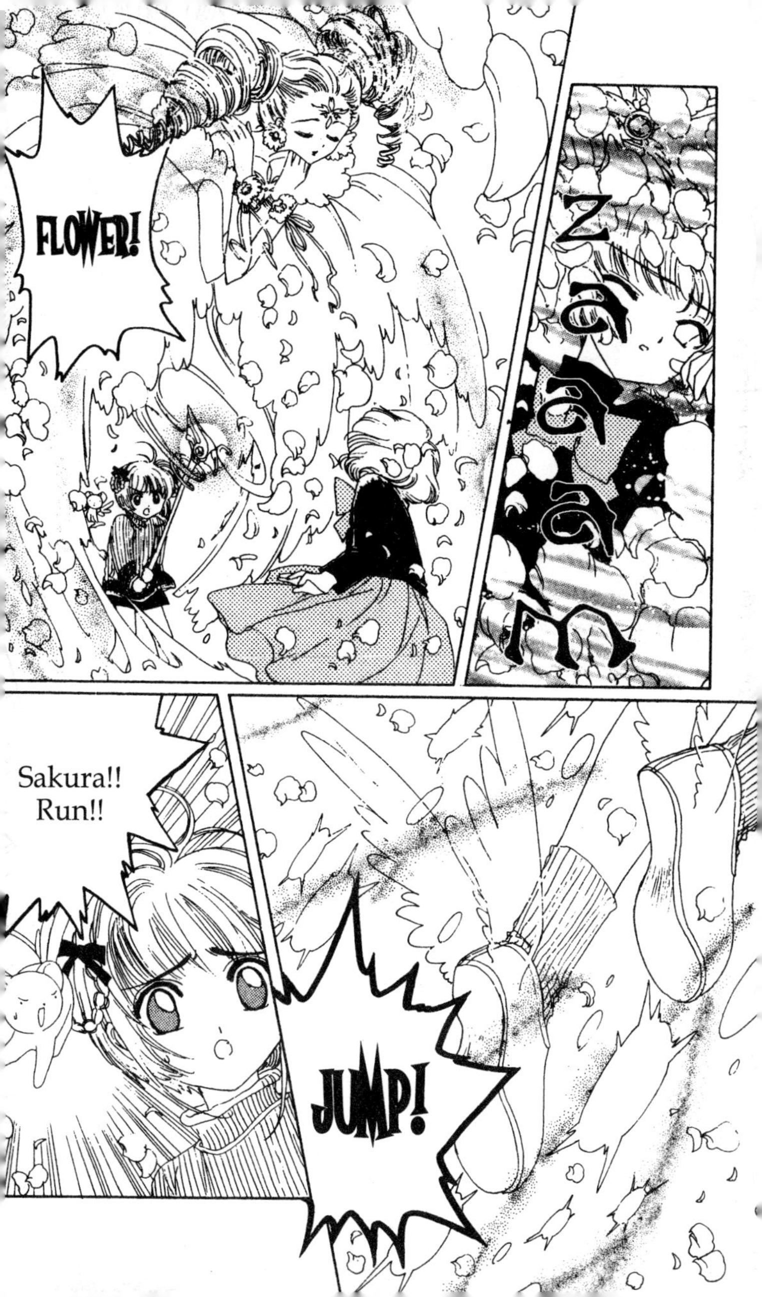
FLOWER!
Zaaaam
Sakura!! Run!!
JUMP!

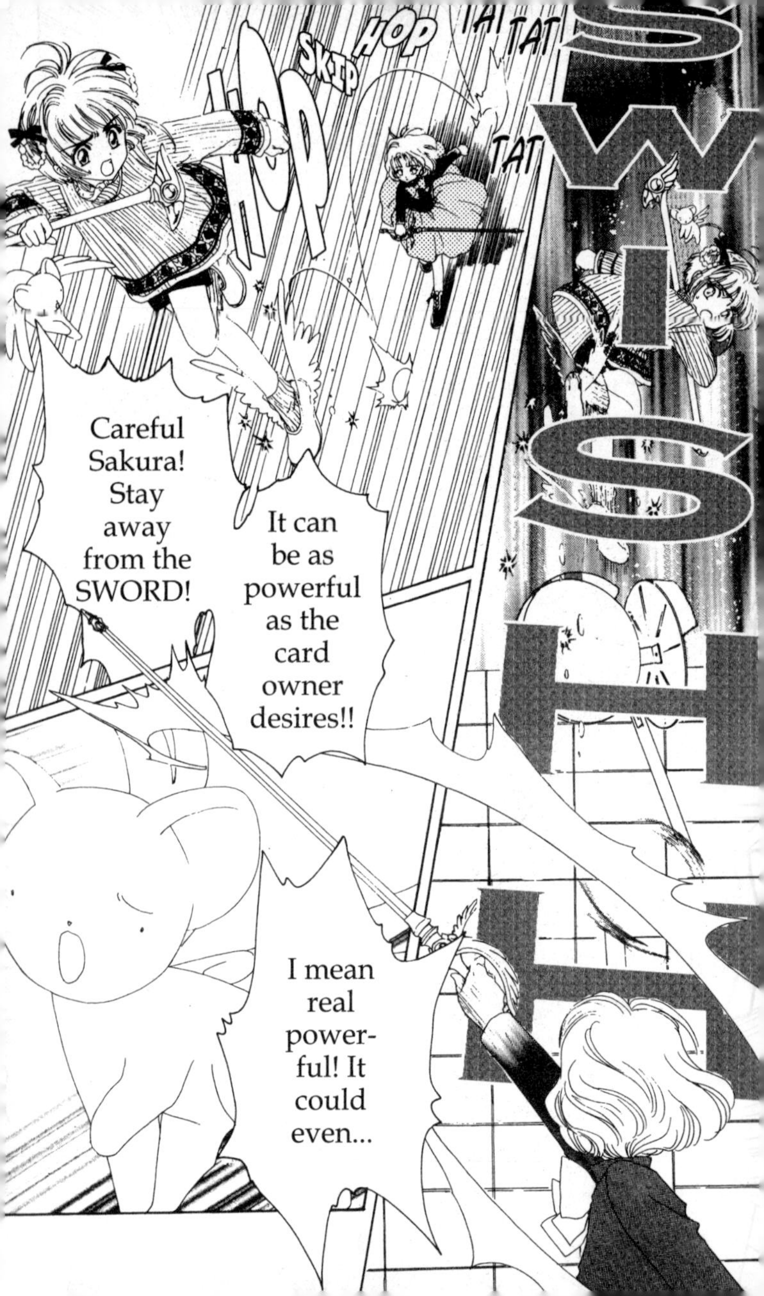
HOP
SKIP
HOP
TAT
TAT
SWISH
Careful Sakura! Stay away from the SWORD!
It can be as powerful as the card owner desires!!
I mean real power-ful! It could even...

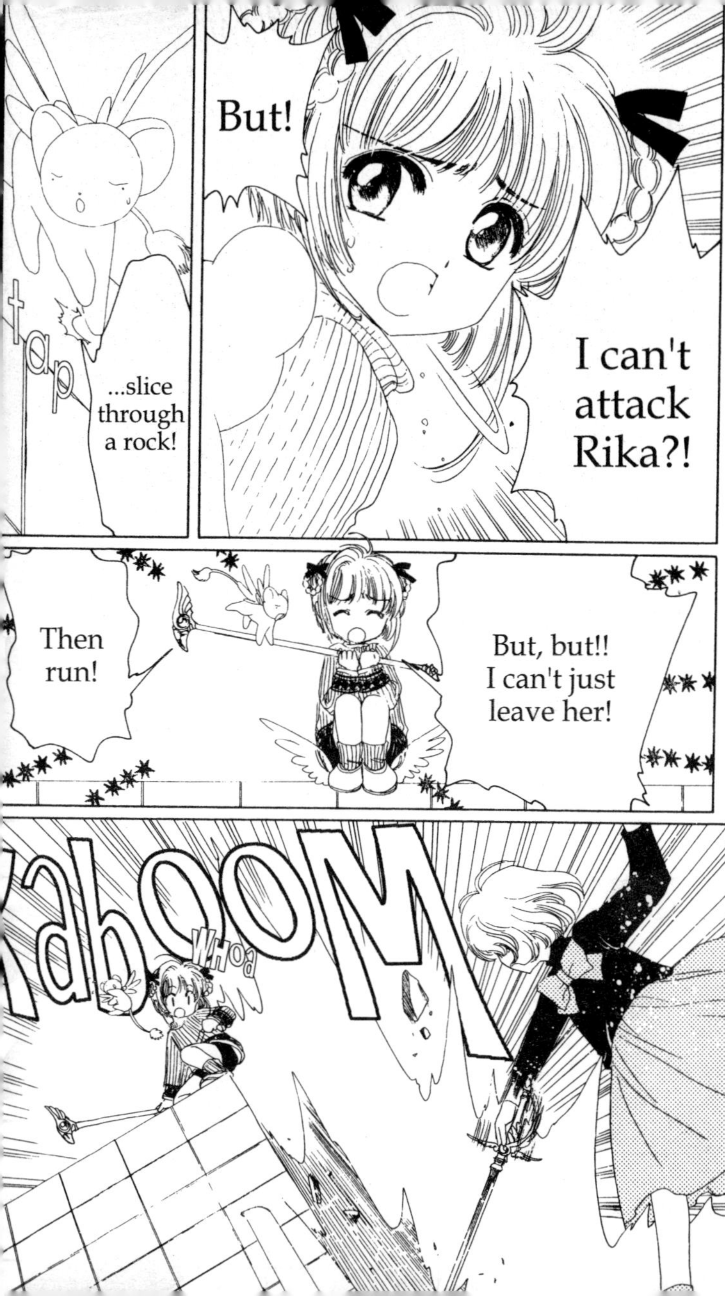
tap
...slice through a rock!
But!
I can't attack Rika?!
Then run!
But, but!! I can't just leave her!
kaboom
WHOA

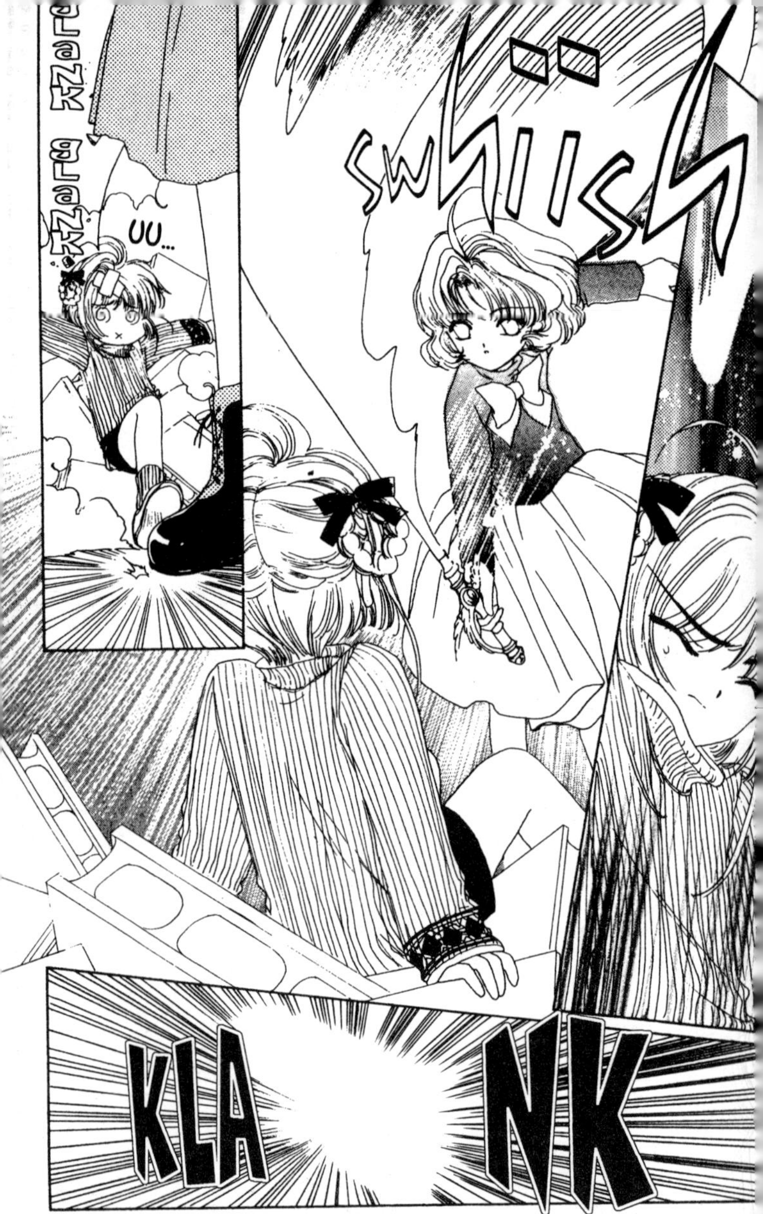
KZALG KZALG
UU...
SWHIISH
KLANK

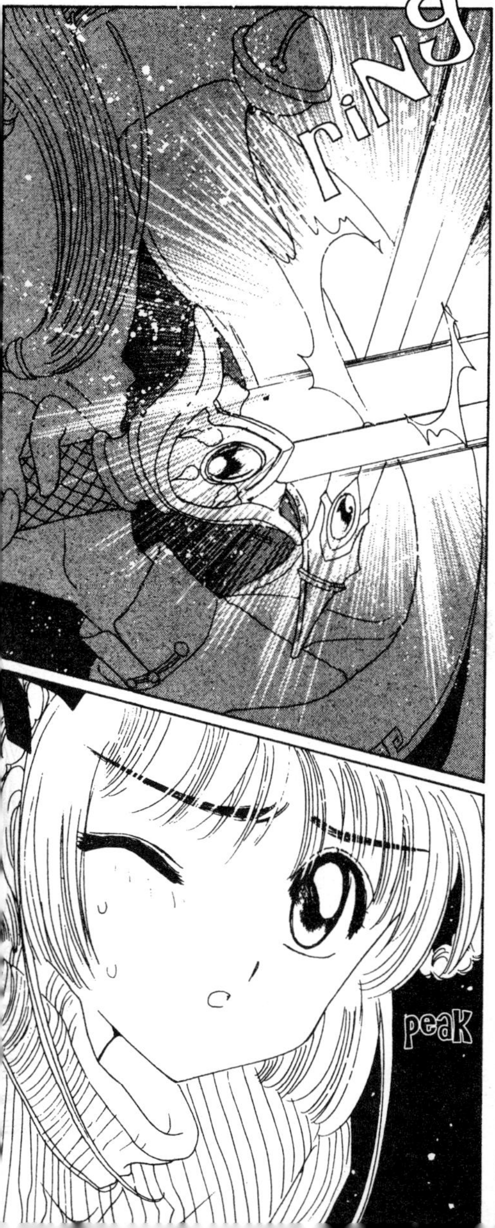
ring
peak

8

Nadeshiko Kinomoto

Birthday
May 20th
Occupation
Model
Favorite Foods
Sweets, Tea
Least Favorite Foods
None
Favorite Thing
The warm rays of the sun
Favorite Color
White
Favorite Recipe
Can't cook
Things I'm not good at
Remembering people's faces and names
Hobby
Sleeping
Special skills
Can fall asleep anywhere

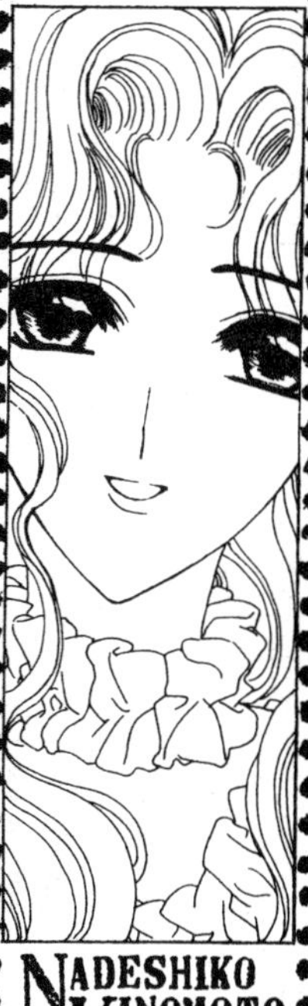

NADESHIKO KINOMOTO

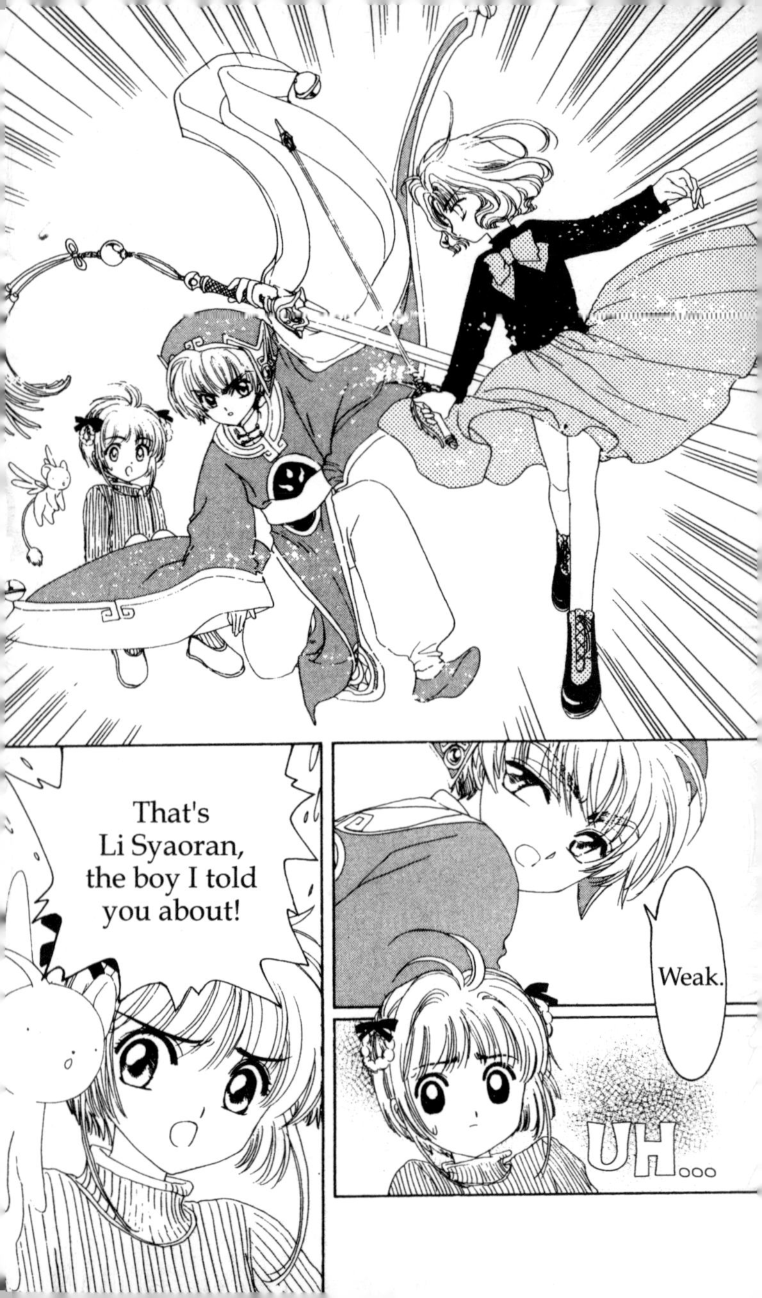
That's Li Syaoran, the boy I told you about!
Weak.
UH...

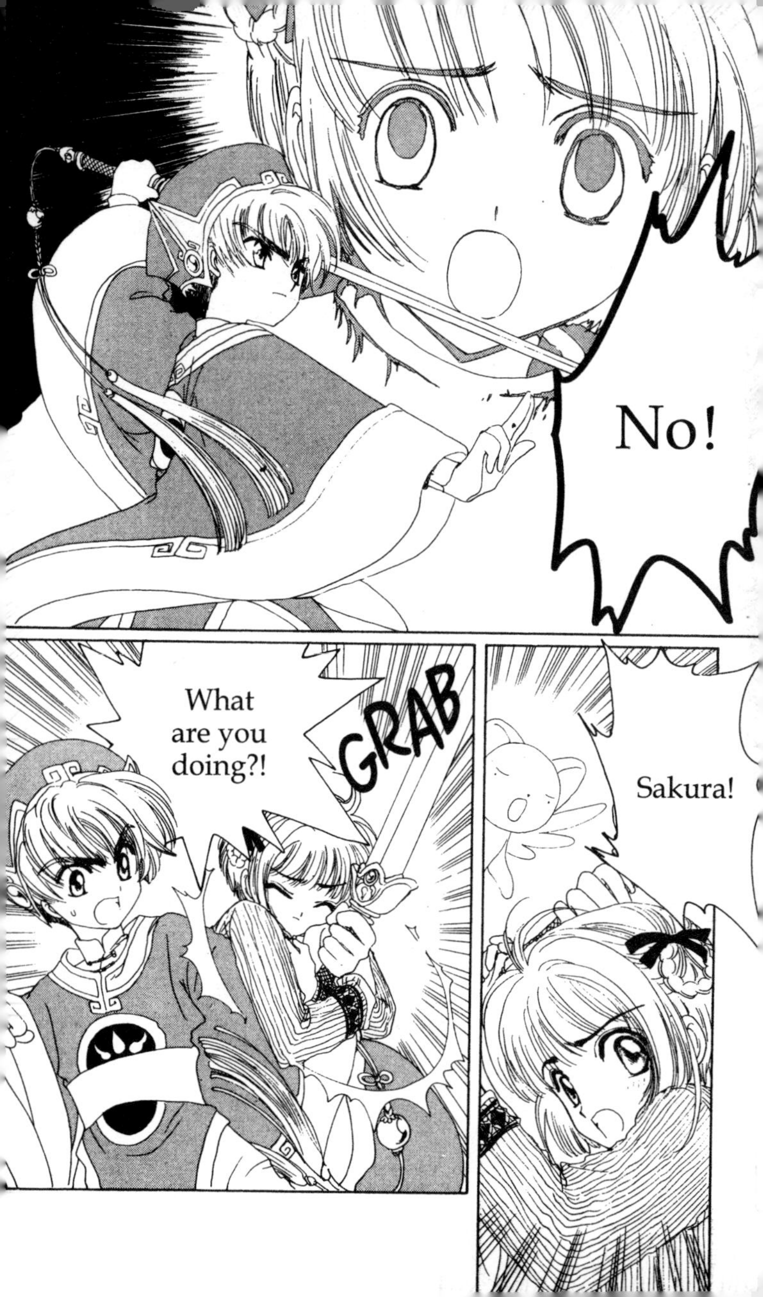
No!
What are you doing?!
GRAB
Sakura!

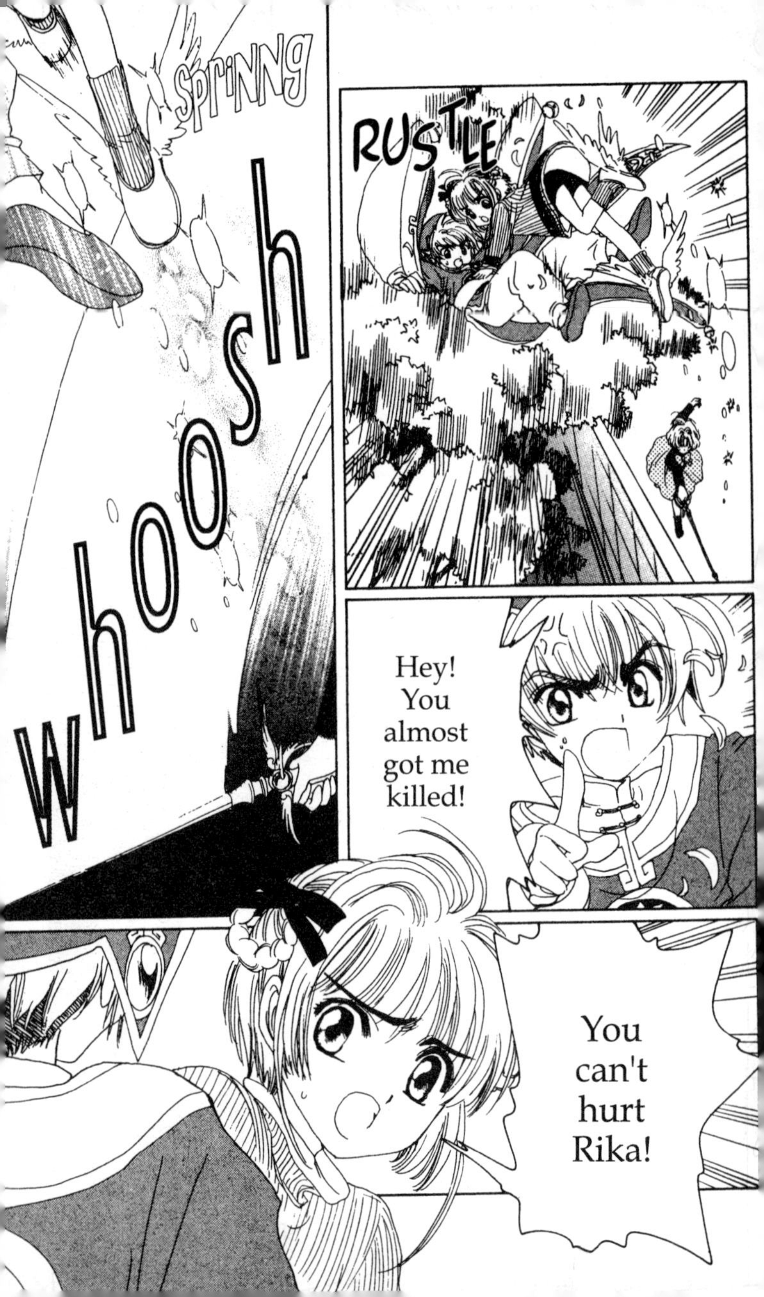
SpriNNg
whoosh
RUSTLE
Hey! You almost got me killed!
You can't hurt Rika!

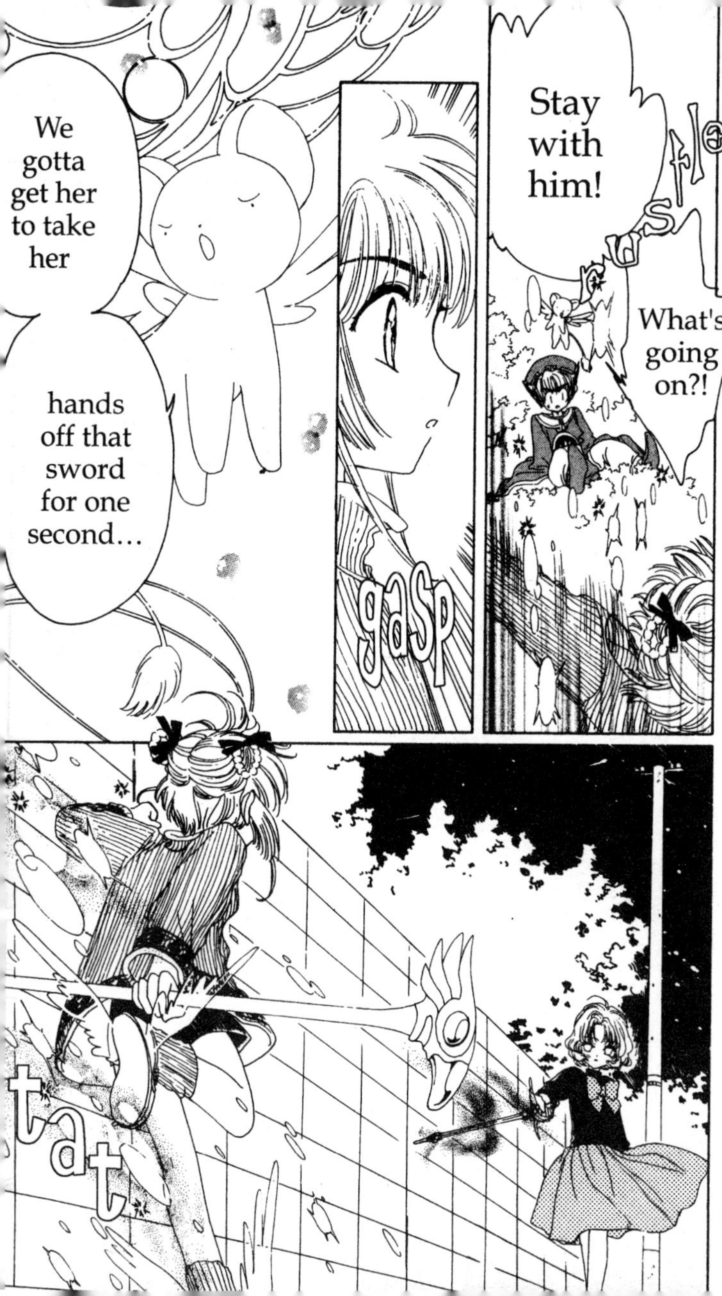
We gotta get her to take her
hands off that sword for one second...
gasp
Stay with him!
rustle
What's going on?!
tat

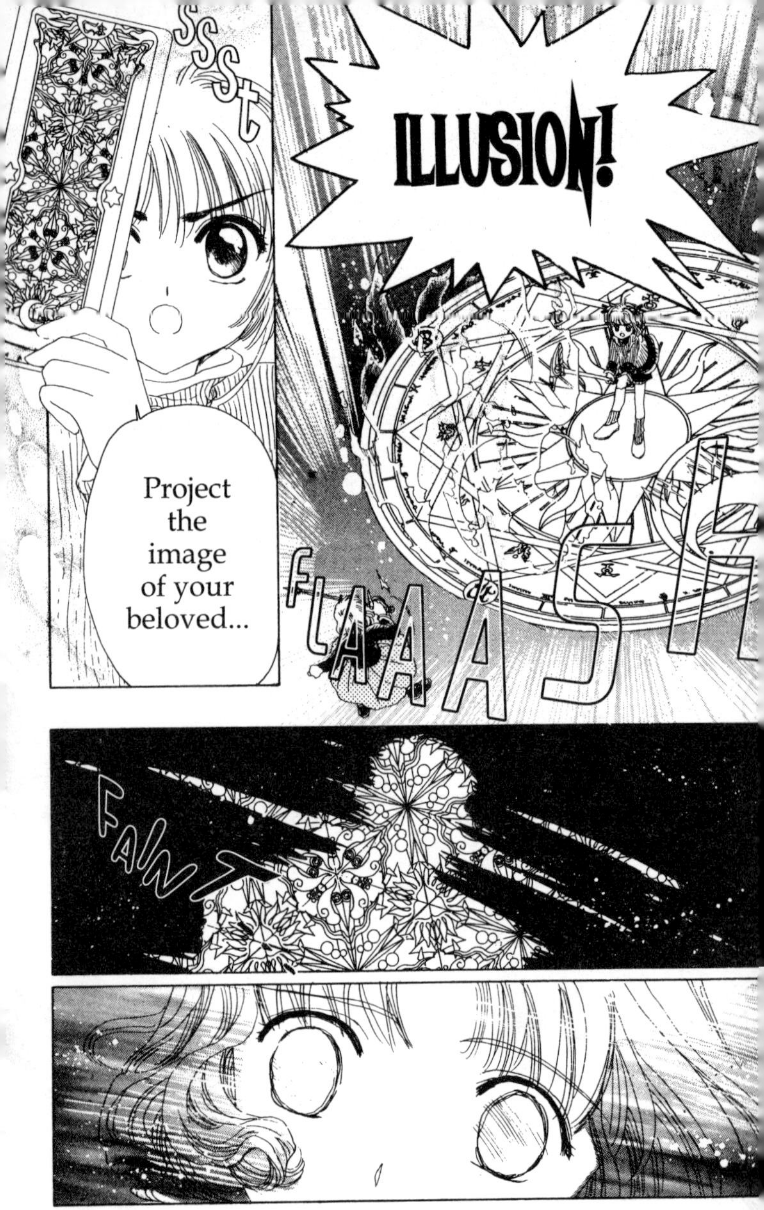
SSSt
ILLUSION!
Project the image of your beloved...
FLAAASH
FAINT

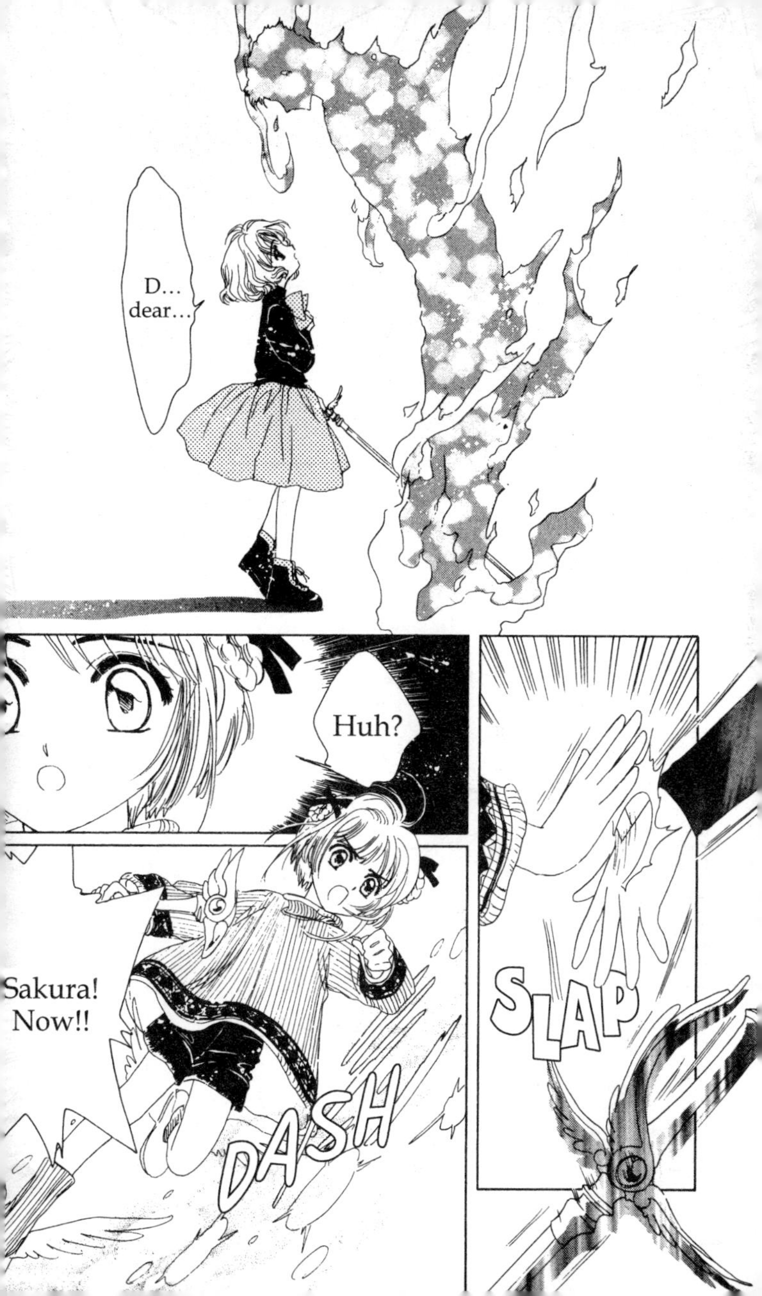
D... dear...
Huh?
Sakura! Now!!
DASH
SLAP

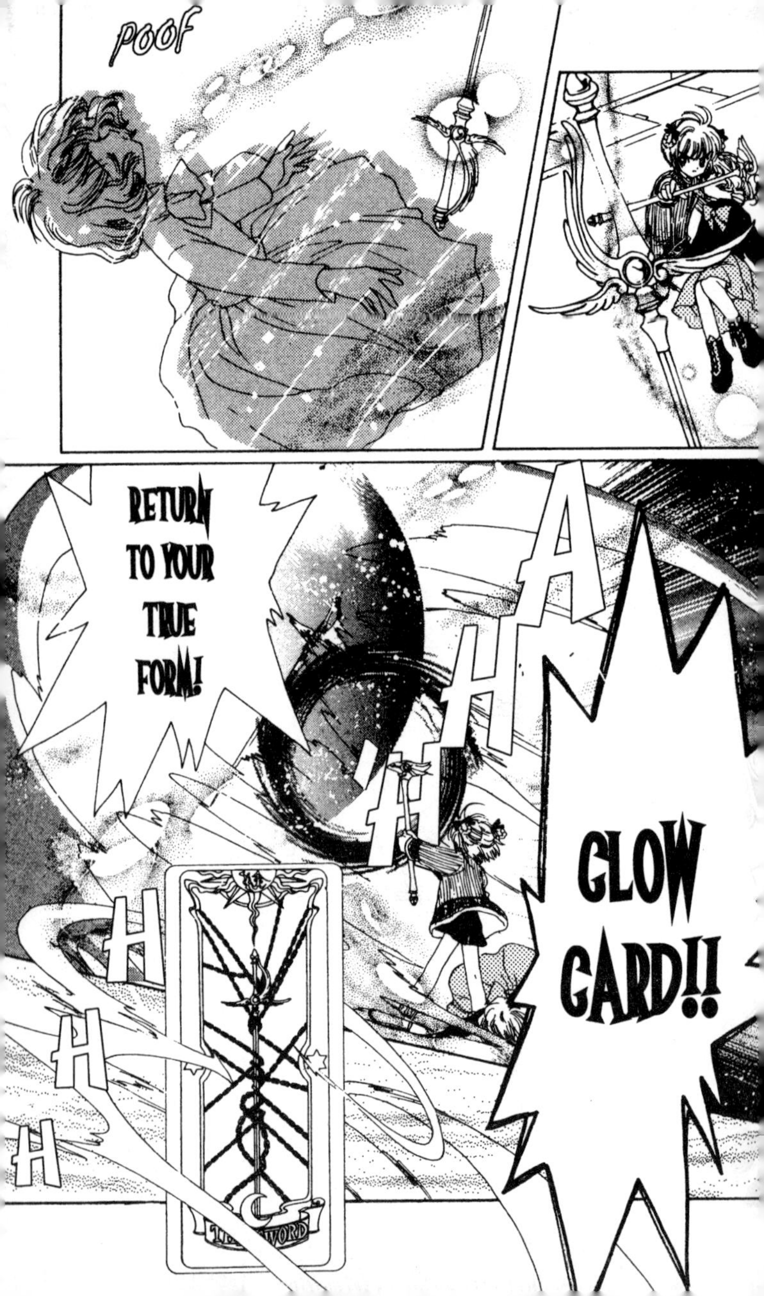
POOF
RETURN TO YOUR TRUE FORM!
AHHHHH
GLOW CARD!!

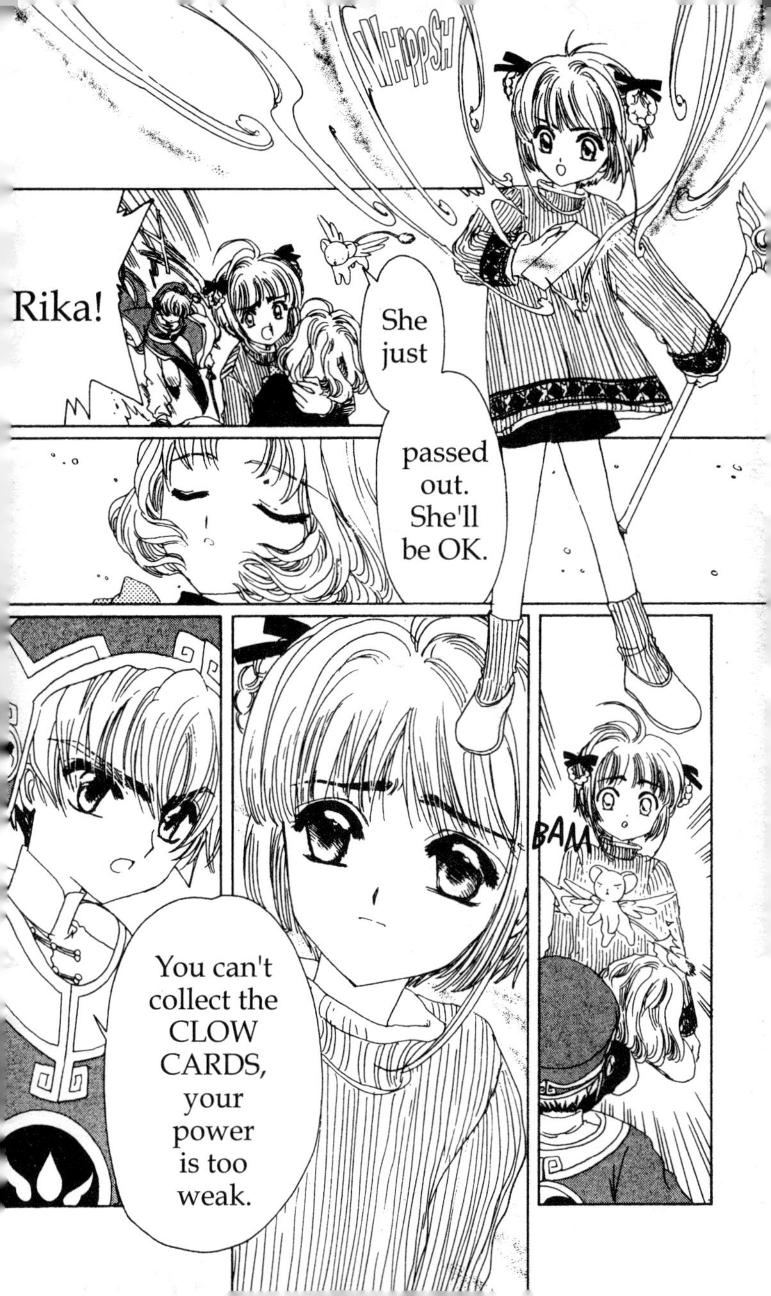
WHIPPSH
Rika!
She just passed out. She'll be OK.
You can't collect the CLOW CARDS, your power is too weak.
BAM

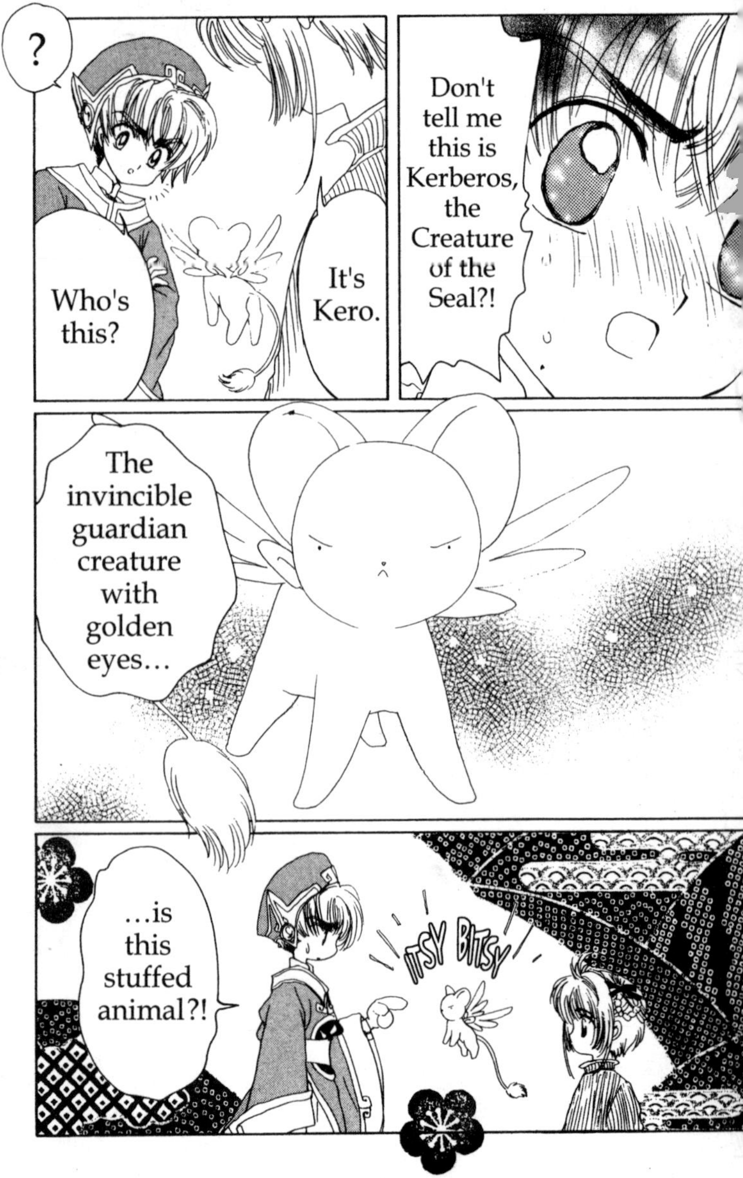
?
Who's this?
It's Kero.
Don't tell me this is Kerberos, the Creature of the Seal?!
The invincible guardian creature with golden eyes…
…is this stuffed animal?!
ITSY BITSY

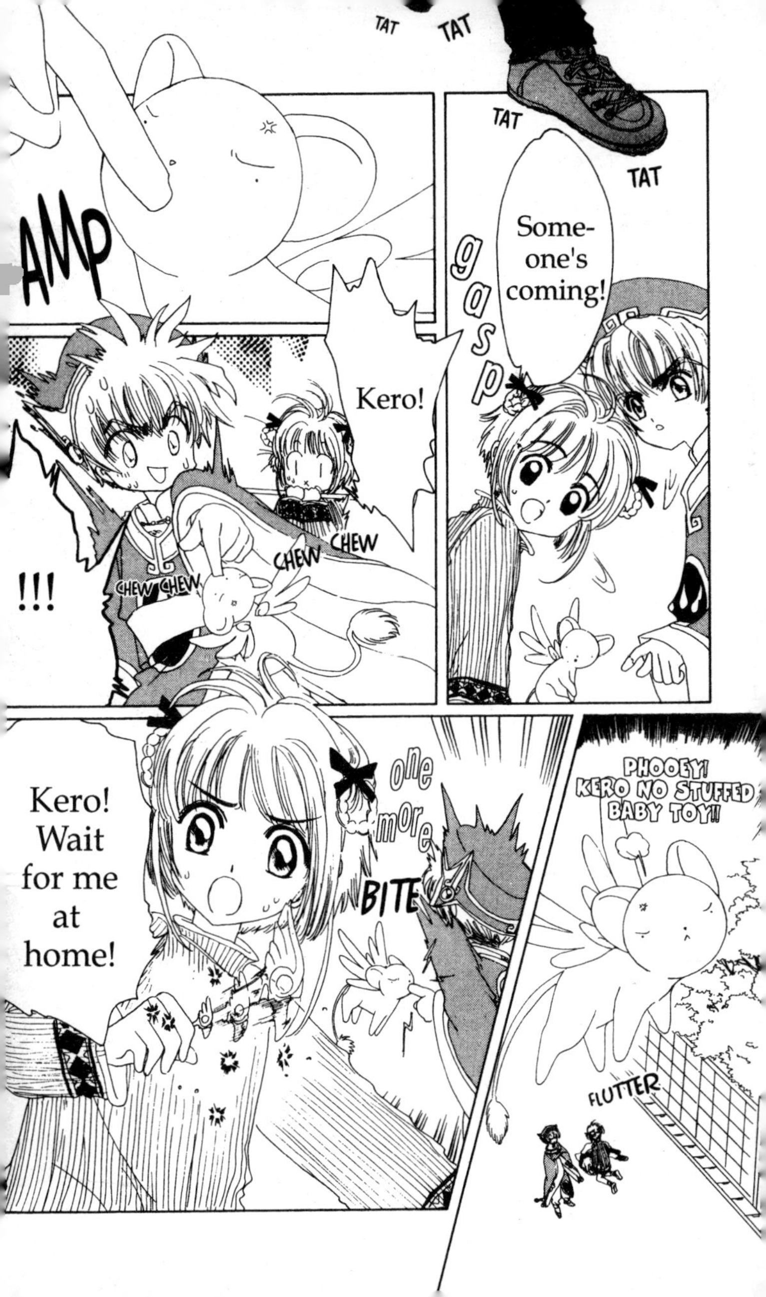

AMP
Kero!
CHEW CHEW
CHEW CHEW
!!!
TAT TAT
TAT
TAT
Some-one's coming!
gasp
Kero! Wait for me at home!
one more
BITE
PHOOEY! KERO NO STUFFED BABY TOY!!
FLUTTER

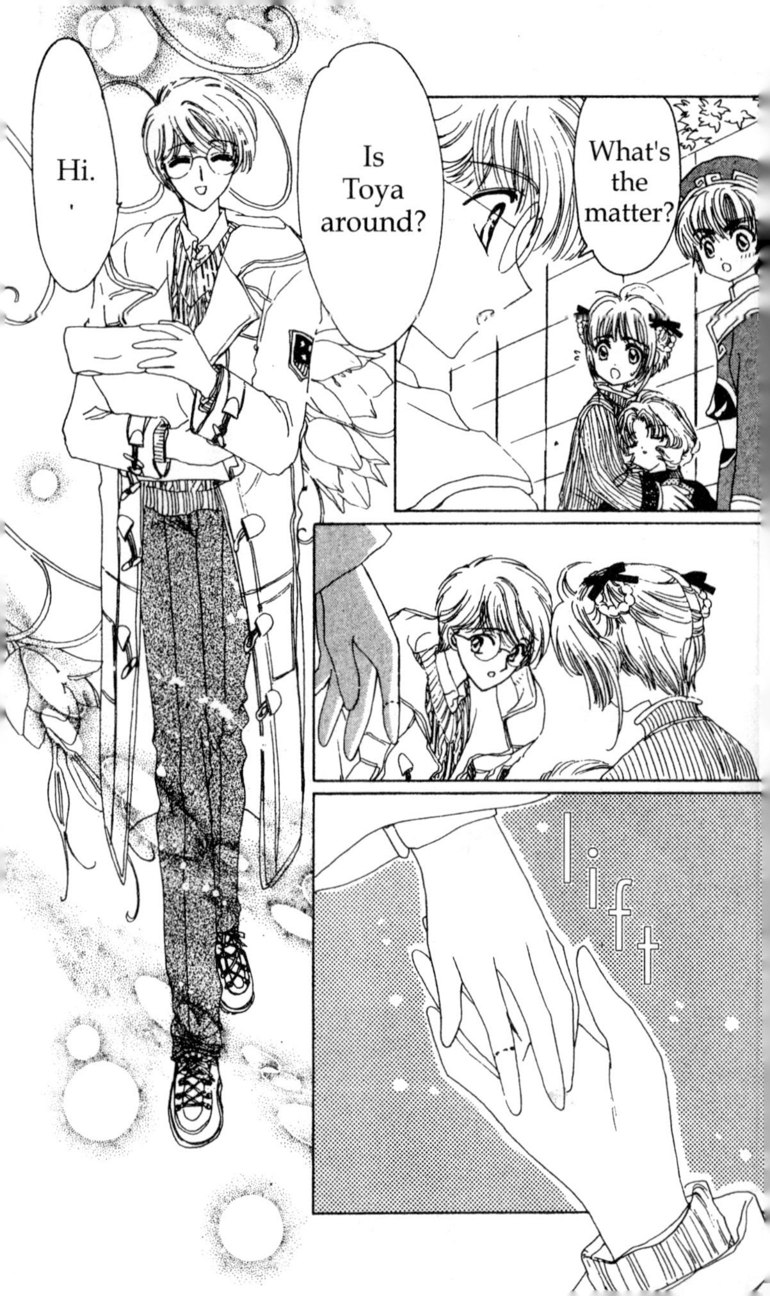
Hi.
Is Toya around?
What's the matter?
lift

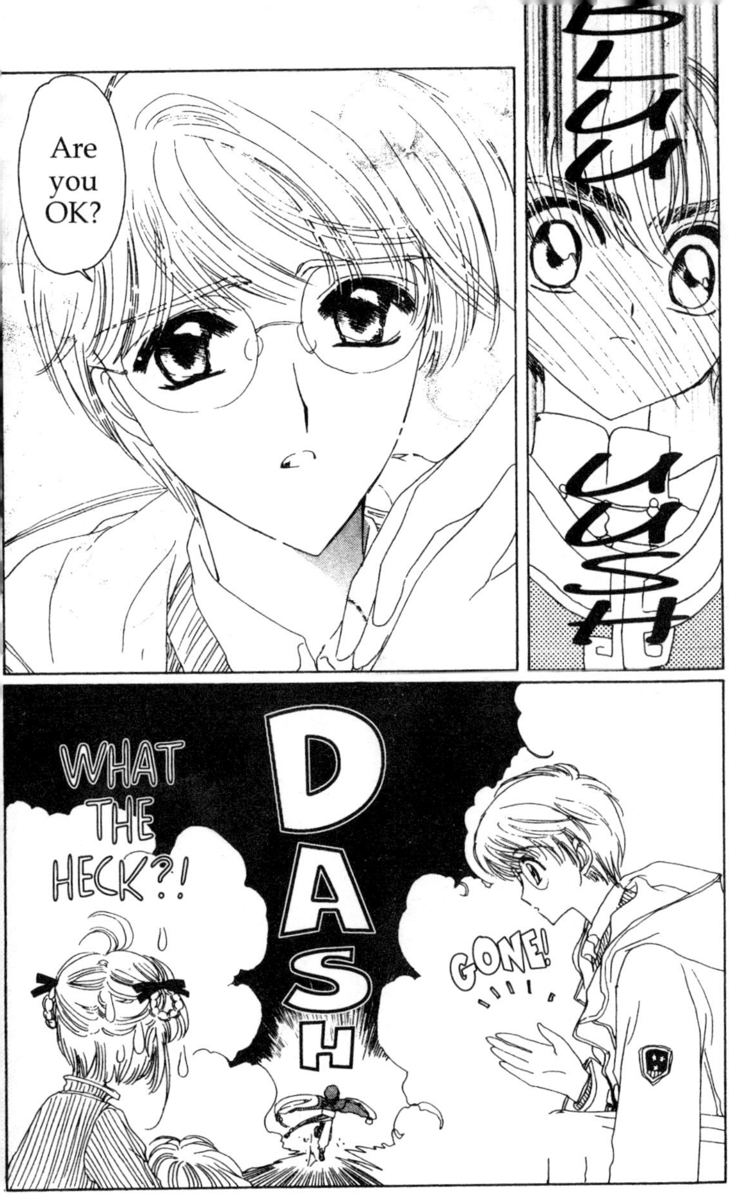
Are you OK?
BLUUUUSH
WHAT THE HECK?!
DASH
GONE!

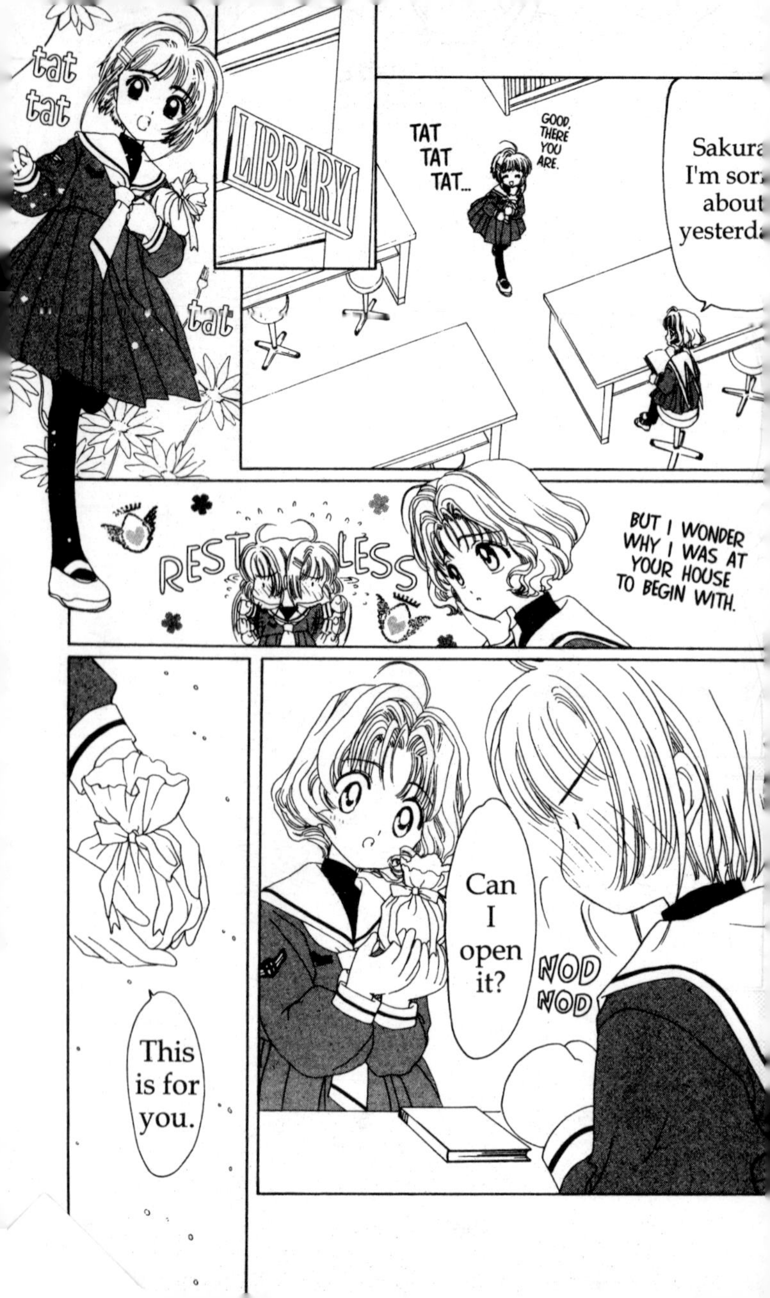
tat tat
tat
LIBRARY
TAT TAT TAT...
GOOD, THERE YOU ARE.
Sakura I'm sor about yesterda
RESTLESS
BUT I WONDER WHY I WAS AT YOUR HOUSE TO BEGIN WITH.
This is for you.
Can I open it?
NOD NOD

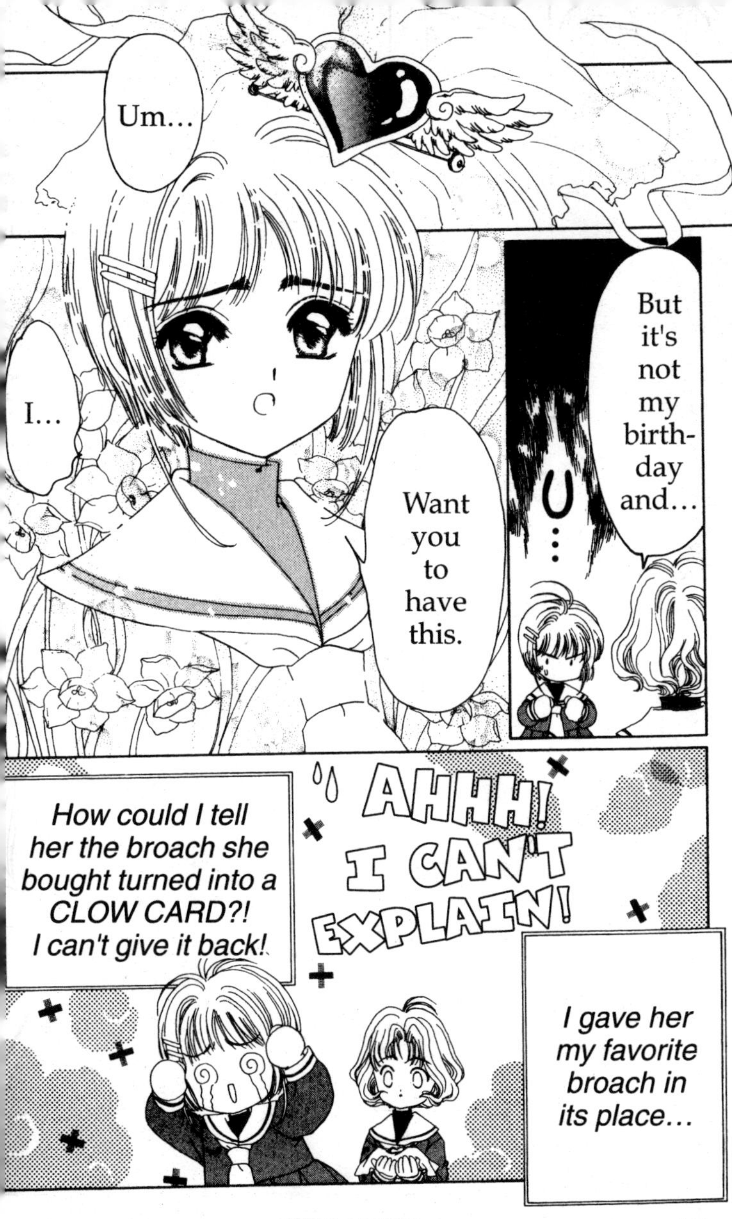
Um…
I…
Want you to have this.
But it's not my birthday and…
…
How could I tell her the broach she bought turned into a CLOW CARD?! I can't give it back!
AHHH! I CAN'T EXPLAIN!
I gave her my favorite broach in its place…

She didn't probe because she knew I was stuck for an answer..

Thank you! I'll cherish it!

Rika's nice, pretty and mature. She's great.

impressed

smile *smile*

Could it be an older boy friend's influence?

Well. I'll see you later.

RATTLE

GOOD MORNING.

GOOD MORNING, MR. TERADA!

BOW

tat tat tat tat tat

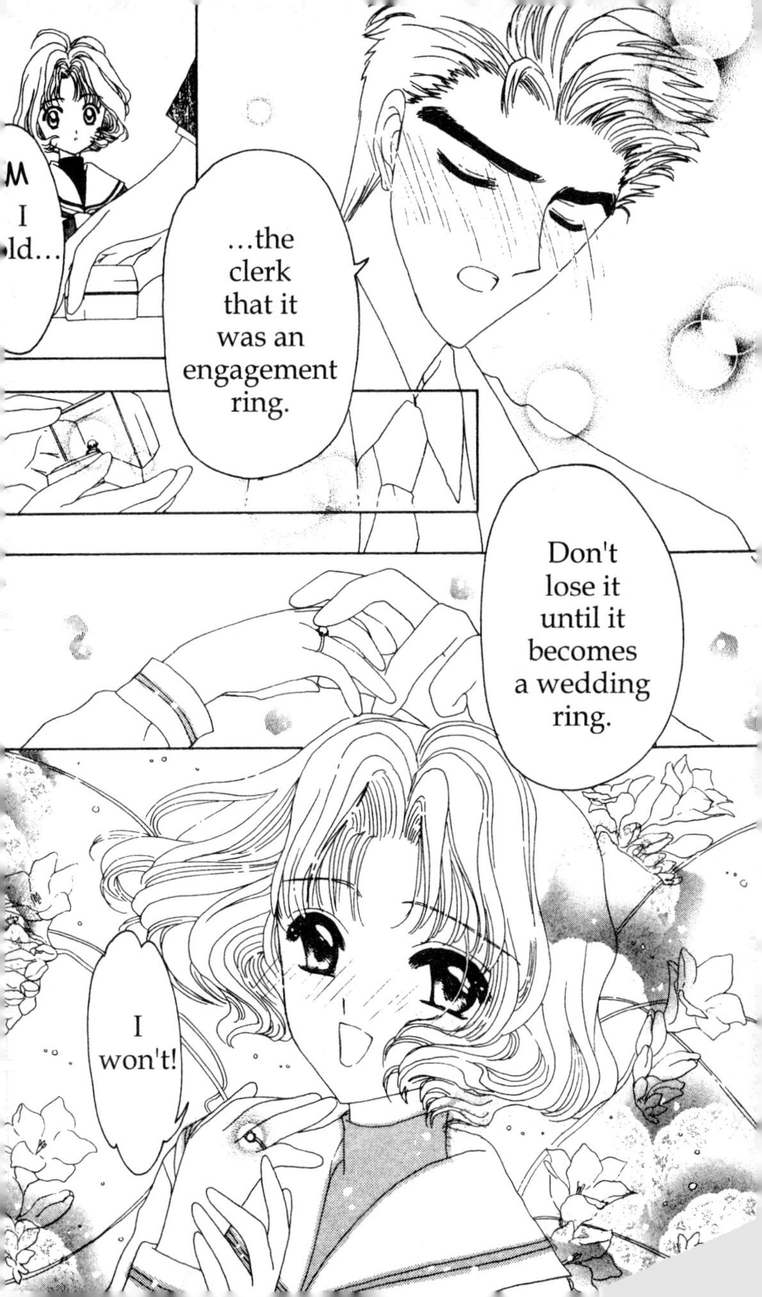
M
I
ld...
...the clerk that it was an engagement ring.
Don't lose it until it becomes a wedding ring.
I won't!

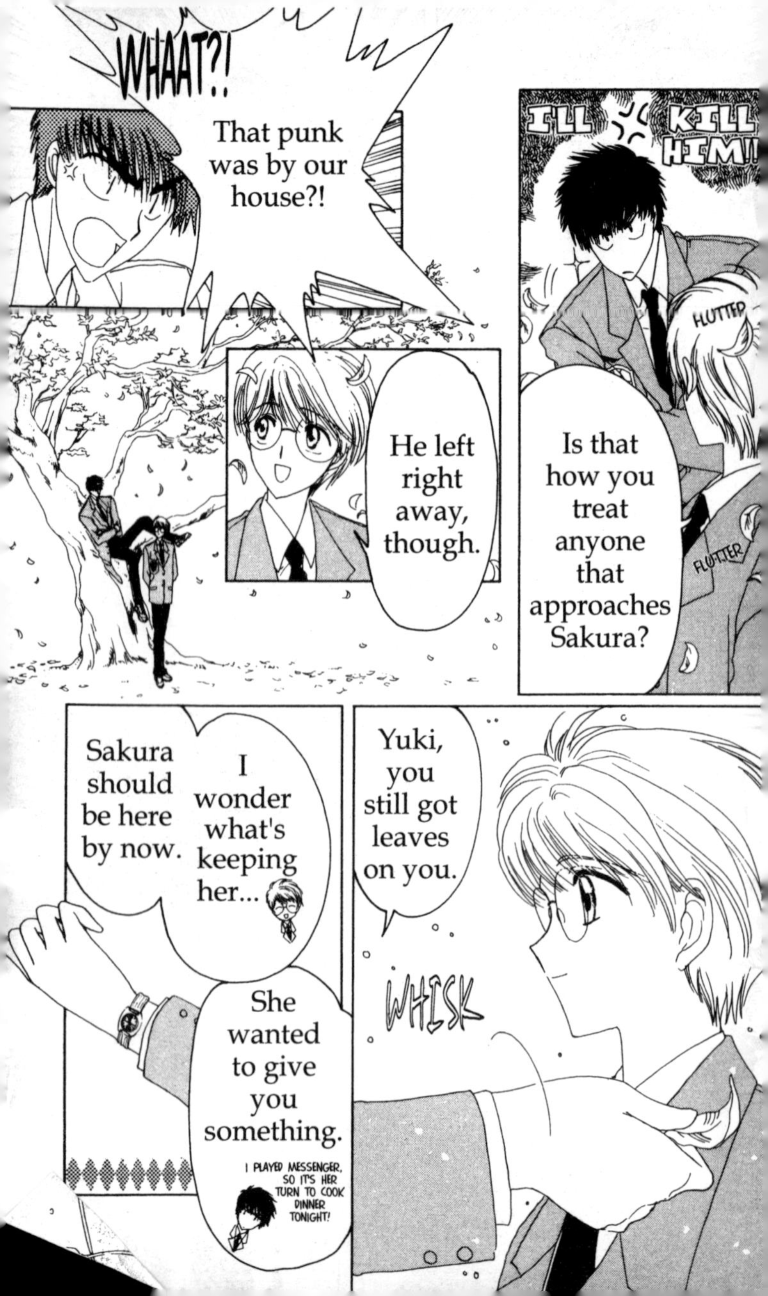
WHAAT?!
That punk was by our house?!
He left right away, though.
I'LL KILL HIM!
FLUTTER
FLUTTER
Is that how you treat anyone that approaches Sakura?
Sakura should be here by now.
I wonder what's keeping her...
She wanted to give you something.
I PLAYED MESSENGER, SO IT'S HER TURN TO COOK DINNER TONIGHT!
Yuki, you still got leaves on you.
WHISK

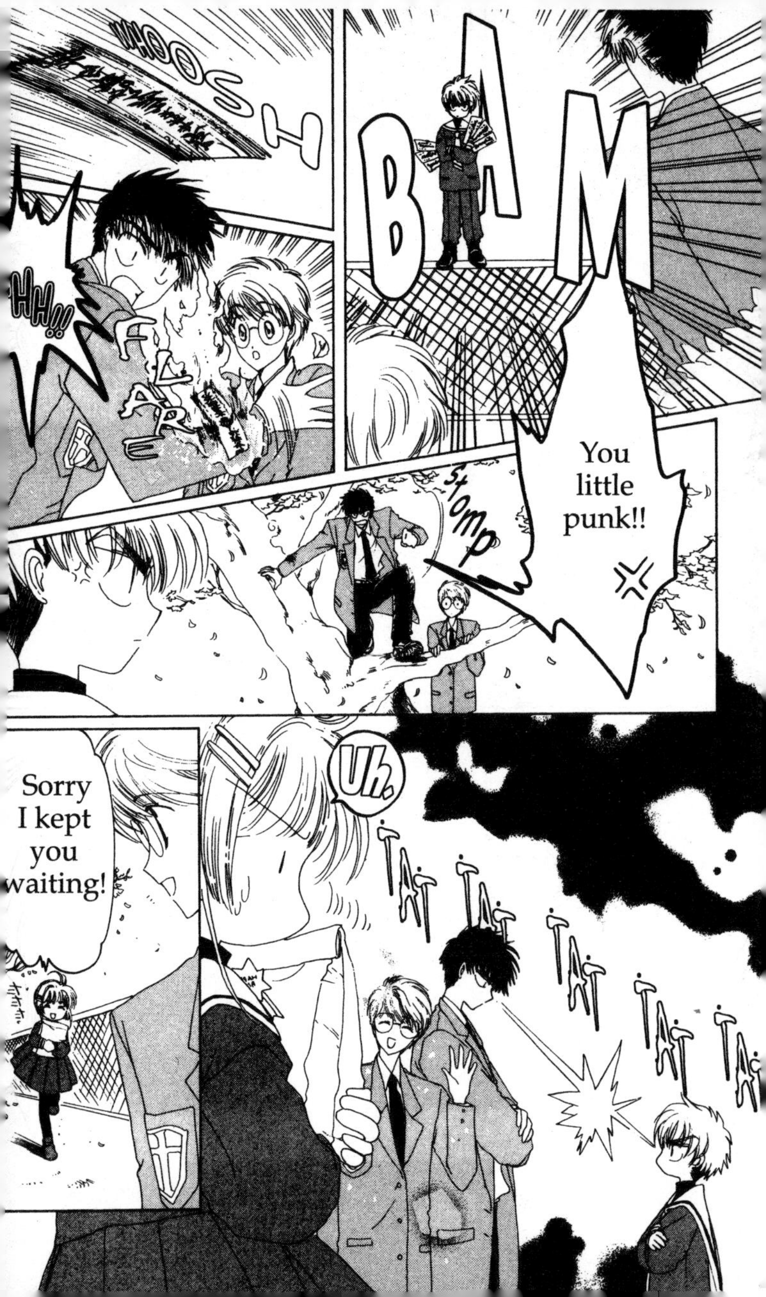
WHOOSH
HHH!!
FLARE
BAM
stomp
You little punk!!
Sorry I kept you waiting!
Uh.
TAT TAT TAT TAT TAT

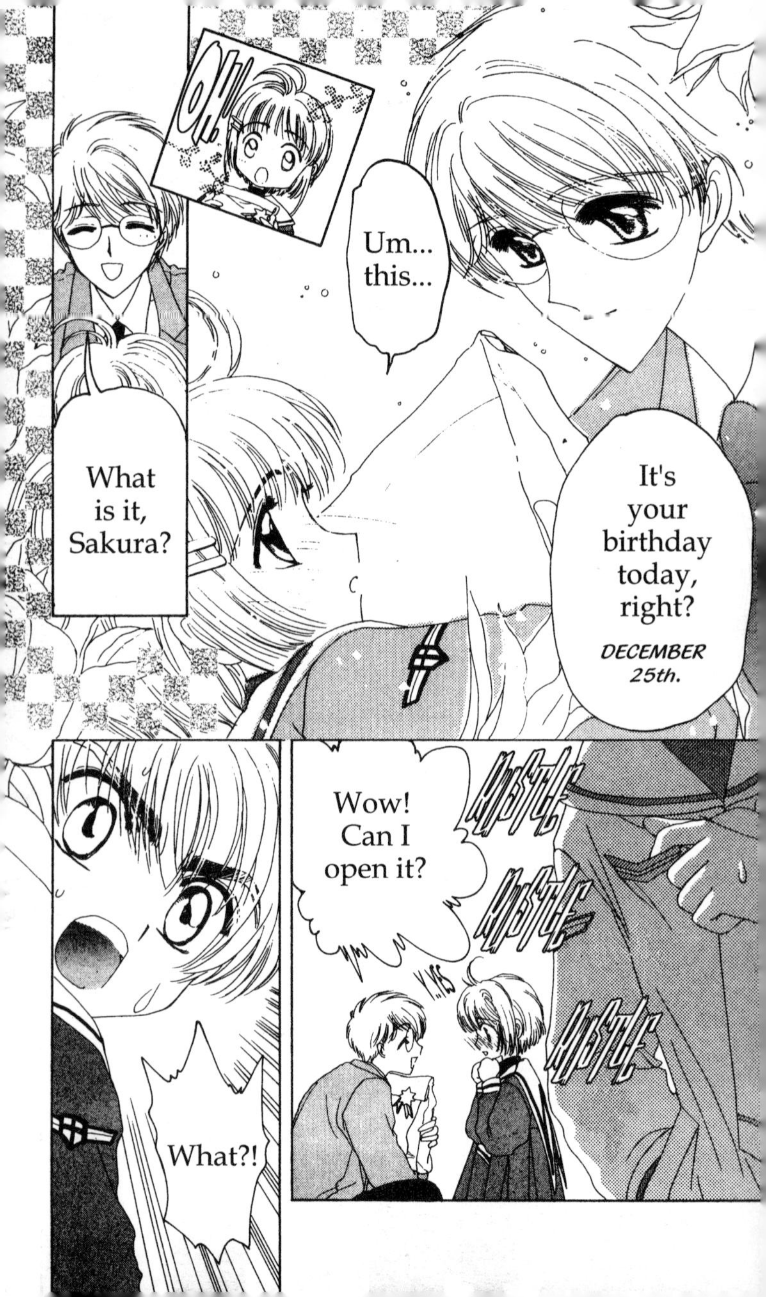
What is it, Sakura?
Um... this...
It's your birthday today, right?
DECEMBER 25th.
What?!
Wow! Can I open it?

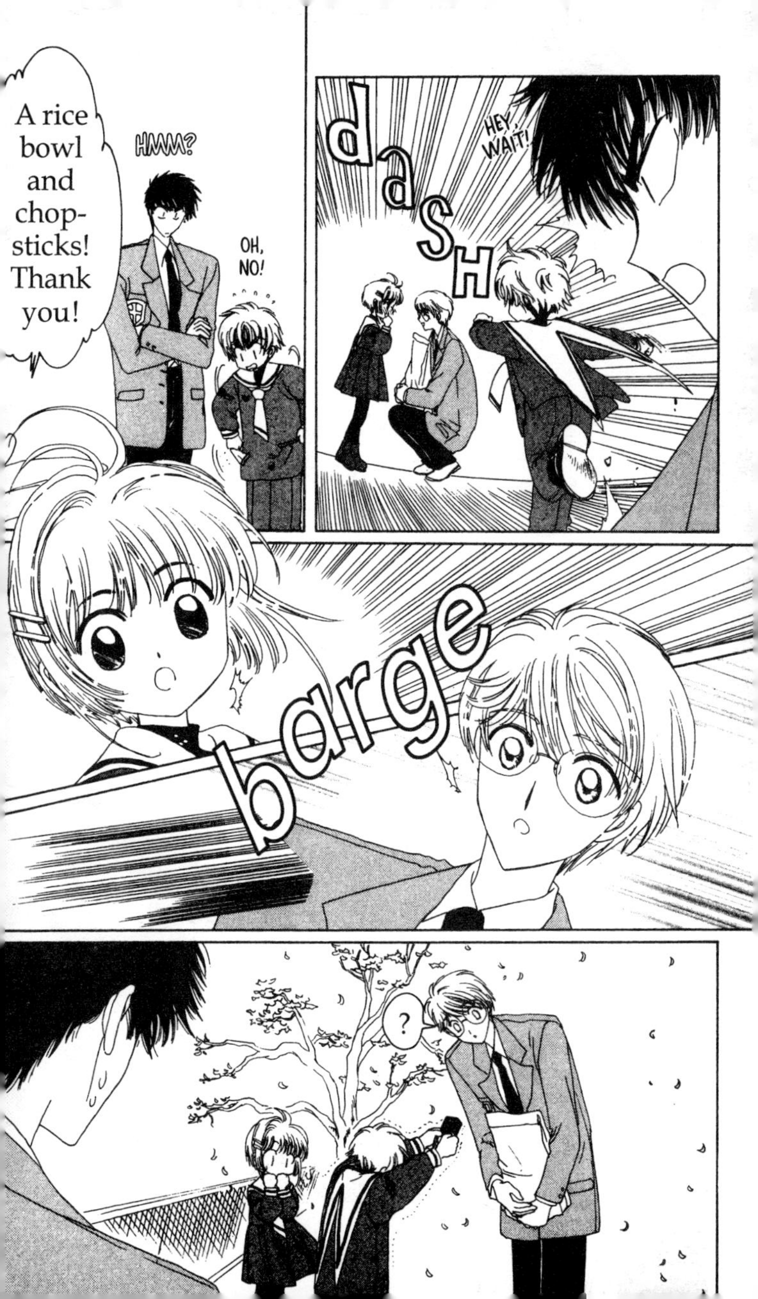
A rice bowl and chop-sticks! Thank you!
HMM?
OH, NO!
dash
HEY, WAIT!
barge
?

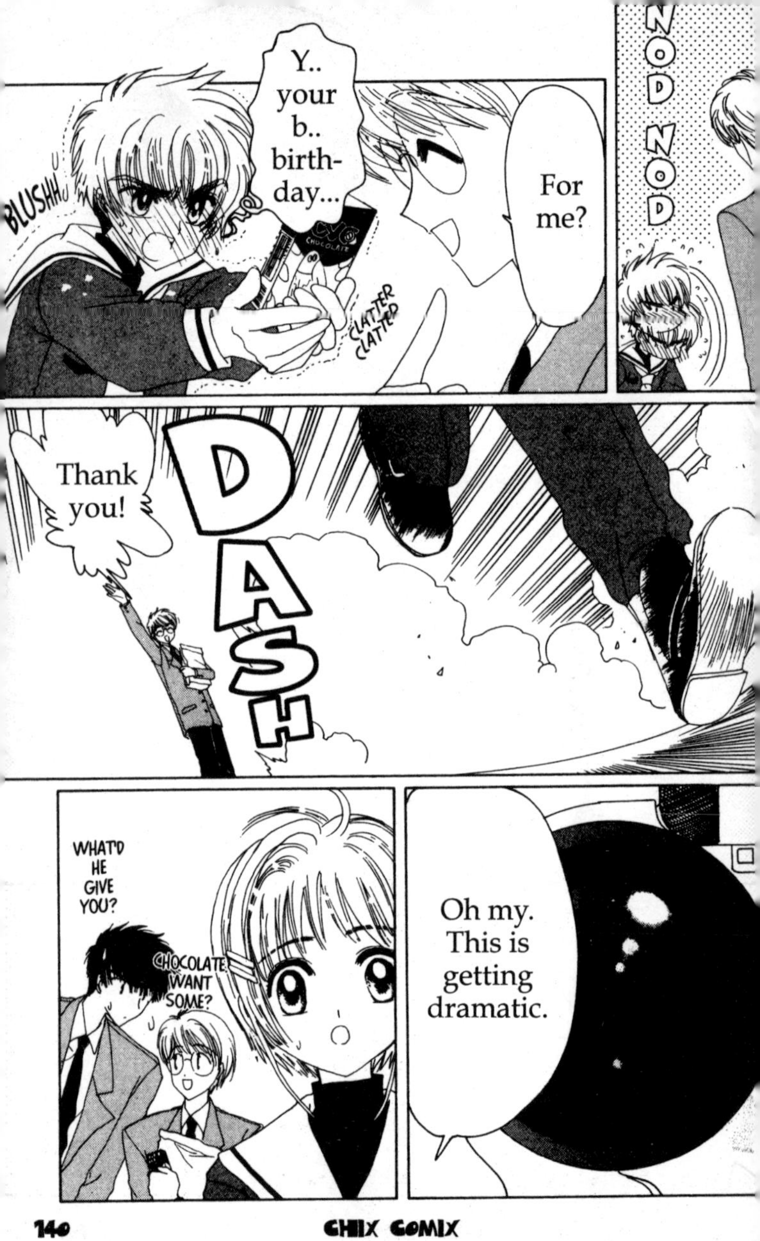

BLUSHH
Y.. your b.. birthday...
CHOCOLATE
CLATTER CLATTER
For me?
NOD NOD NOD
Thank you!
DASH
WHAT'D HE GIVE YOU?
CHOCOLATE. WANT SOME?
Oh my. This is getting dramatic.

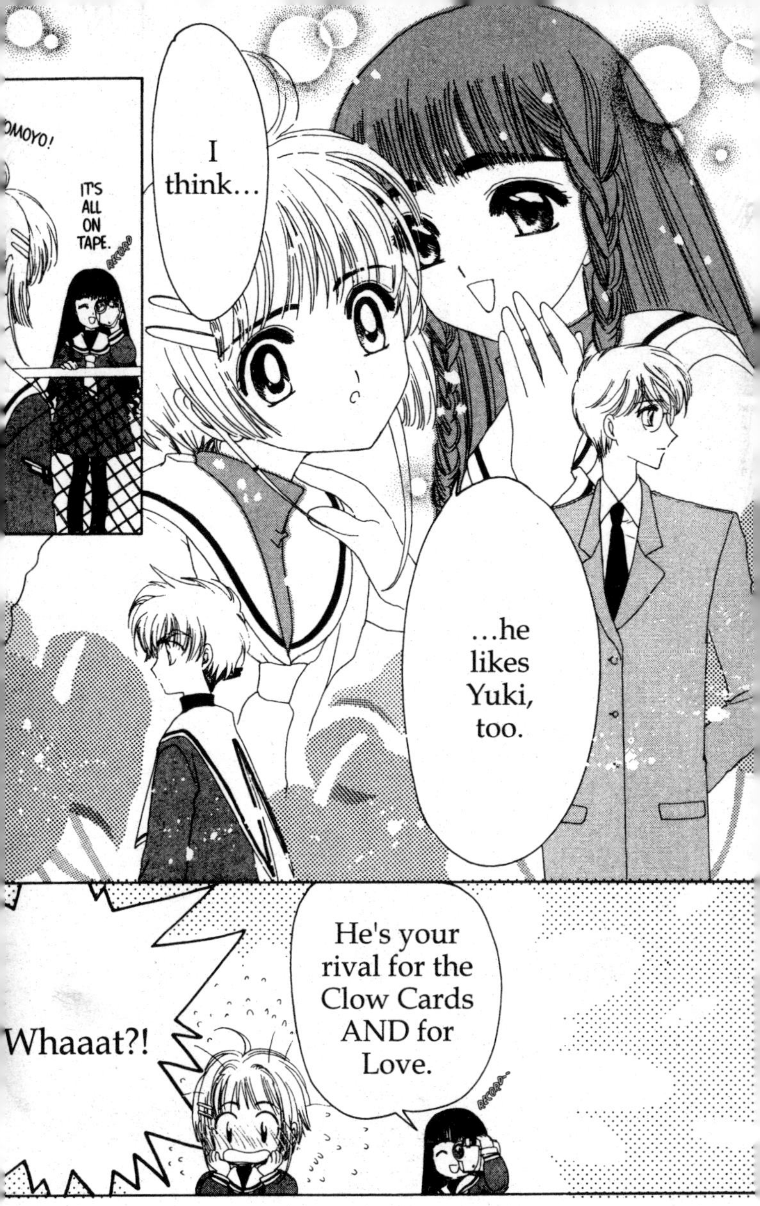

OMOYO!
IT'S ALL ON TAPE.
RECORD
I think…
…he likes Yuki, too.
Whaaat?!
He's your rival for the Clow Cards AND for Love.
RECORD~

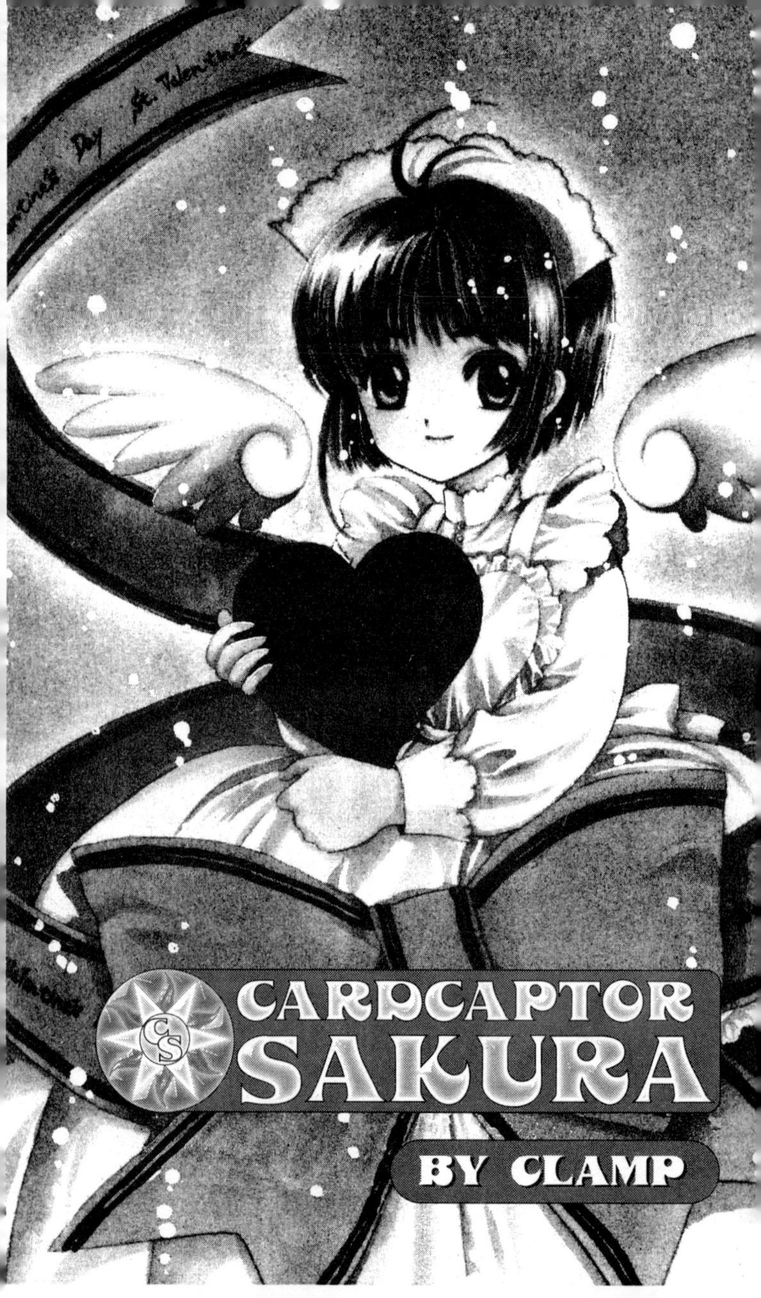
Day St. Valentine's
CARDCAPTOR SAKURA
BY CLAMP

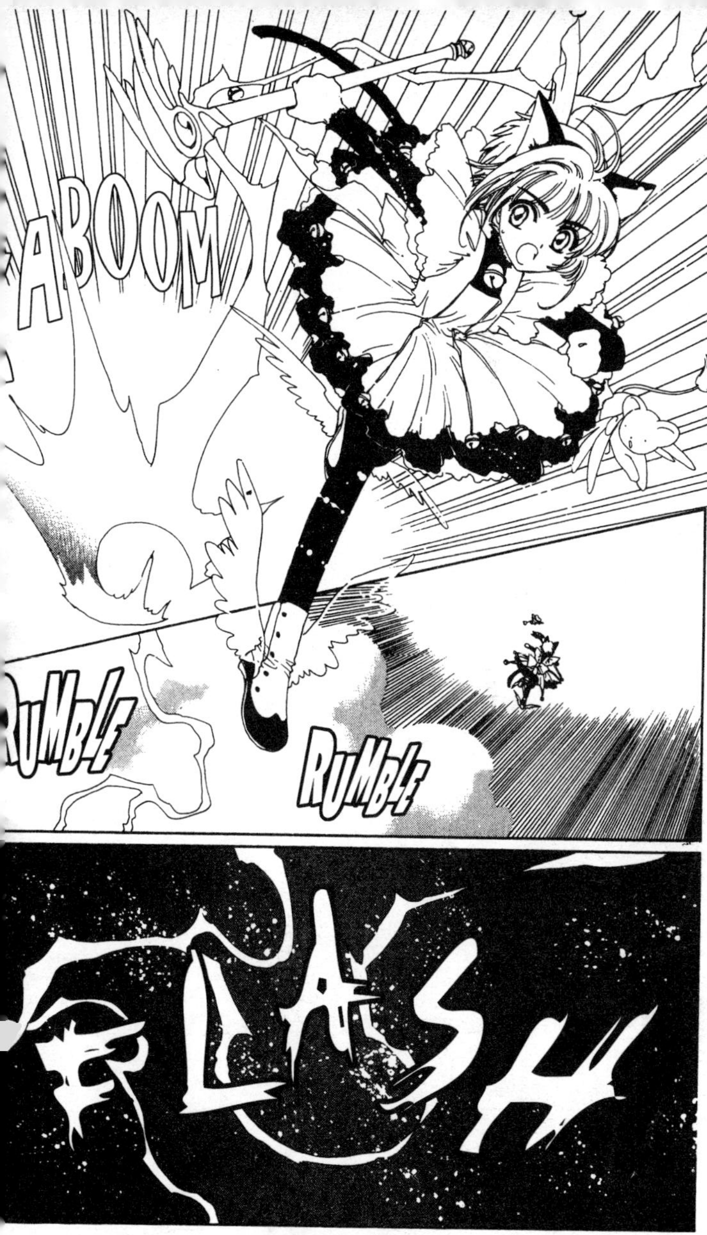
KABOOM
RUMBLE
RUMBLE
FLASH

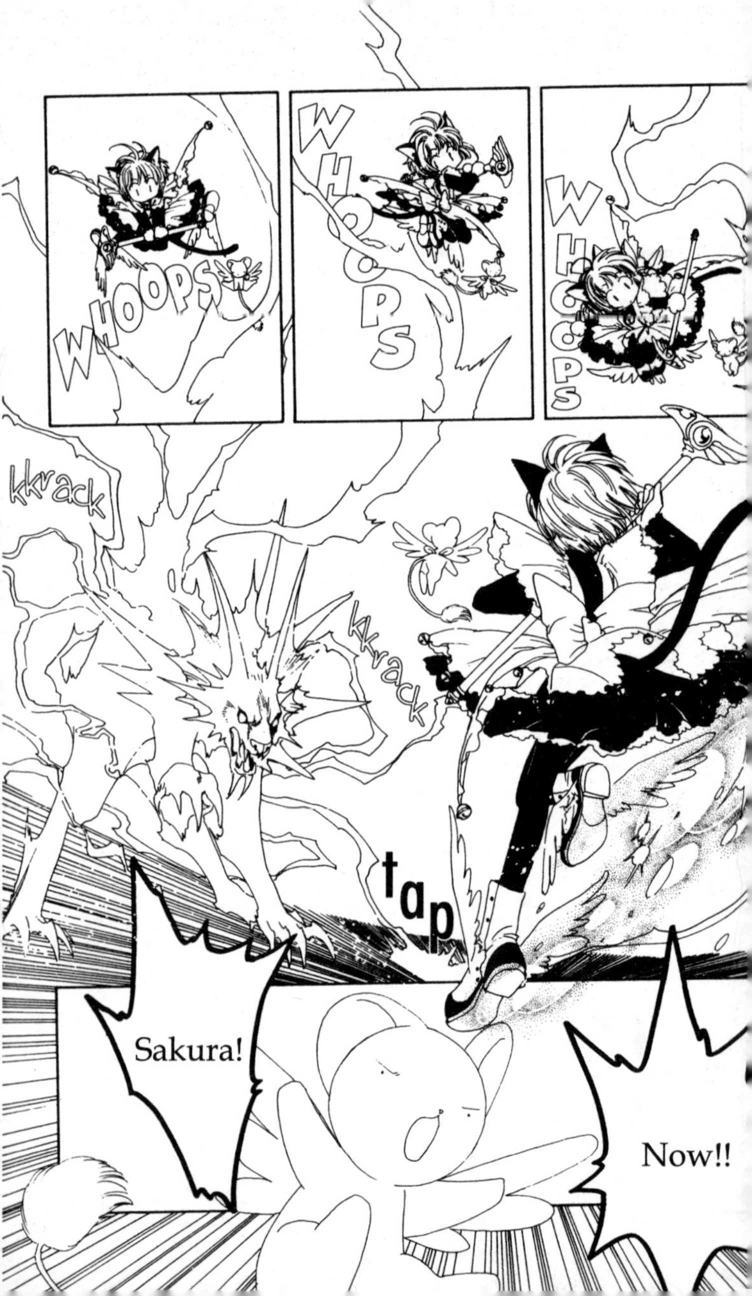
WHOOPS
WHOOPS
WHOOPS
kkrack
kkrack
tap
Sakura!
Now!!

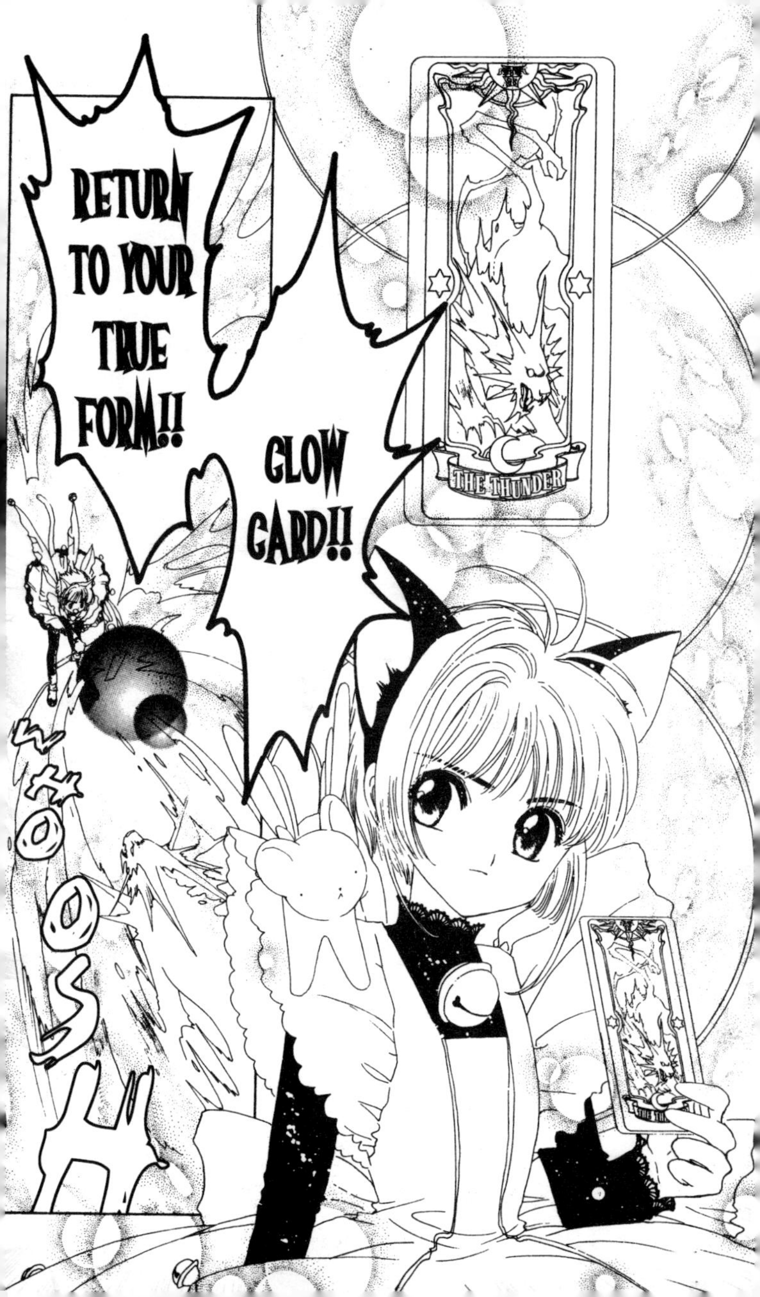
RETURN TO YOUR TRUE FORM!!
GLOW CARD!!
THE THUNDER

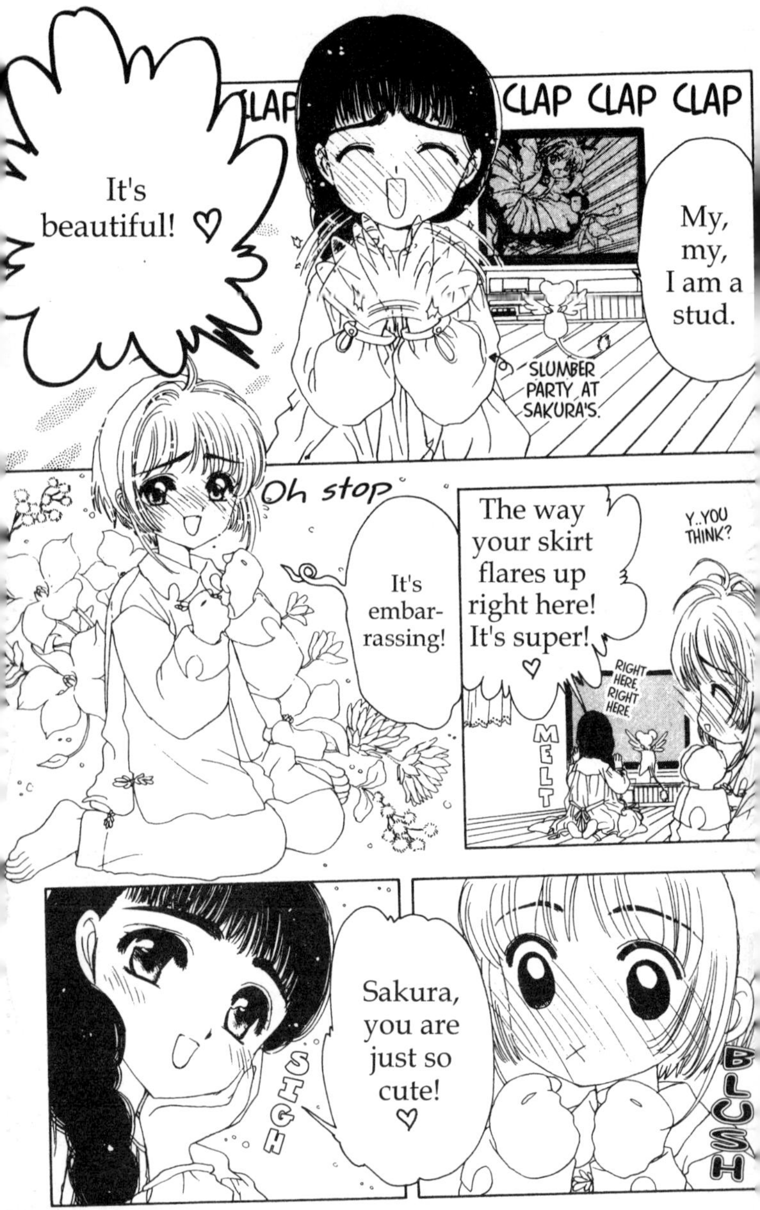
LAP
It's beautiful! ♡
CLAP CLAP CLAP
My, my, I am a stud.
SLUMBER PARTY AT SAKURA'S.
Oh stop
It's embar-rassing!
The way your skirt flares up right here! It's super! ♡
Y..YOU THINK?
RIGHT HERE, RIGHT HERE
MELT
Sakura, you are just so cute! ♡
SIGH
BLUSH

We still need a lot more cards.

You're still letting that little pookie boy bug you?

That Li Syaoran kid.

Teenie... weenie... pookie...

HE'S A TEENIE WEENIE POOKIE POOH IF YOU ASK ME!

Kero's mad because Li called him a stuffed animal!

Oh...

HMPH!

Cheer up, Sakura!

Your magical powers are stronger now!

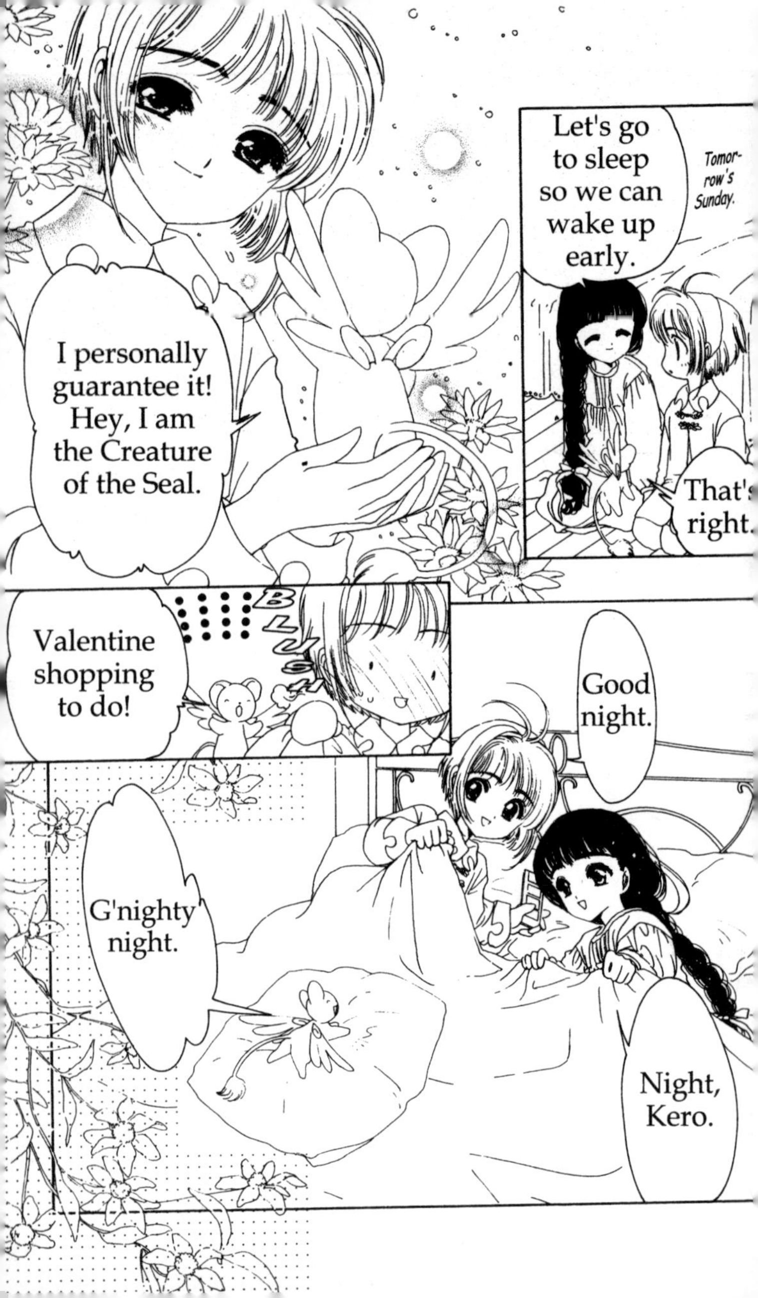
Let's go to sleep so we can wake up early.
Tomorrow's Sunday.
That's right.
I personally guarantee it! Hey, I am the Creature of the Seal.
BLUSH
Valentine shopping to do!
Good night.
G'nighty night.
Night, Kero.

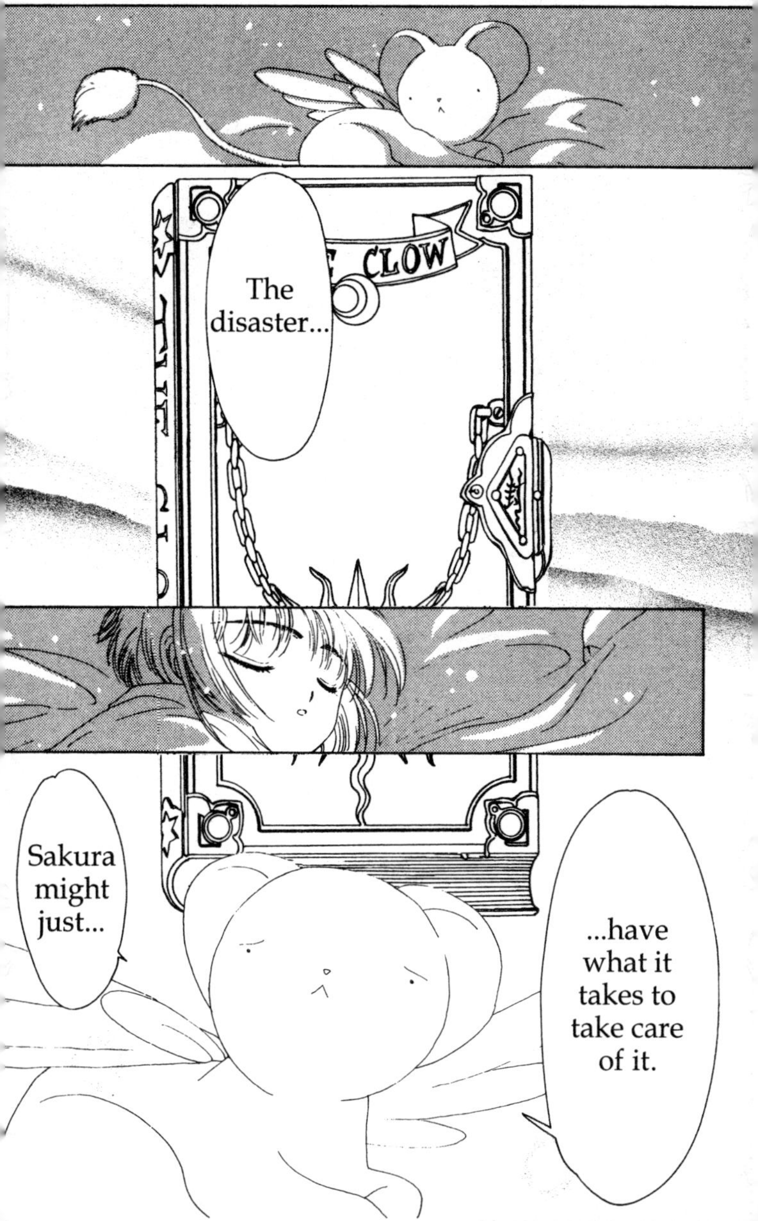
CLOW
The disaster...
Sakura might just...
...have what it takes to take care of it.

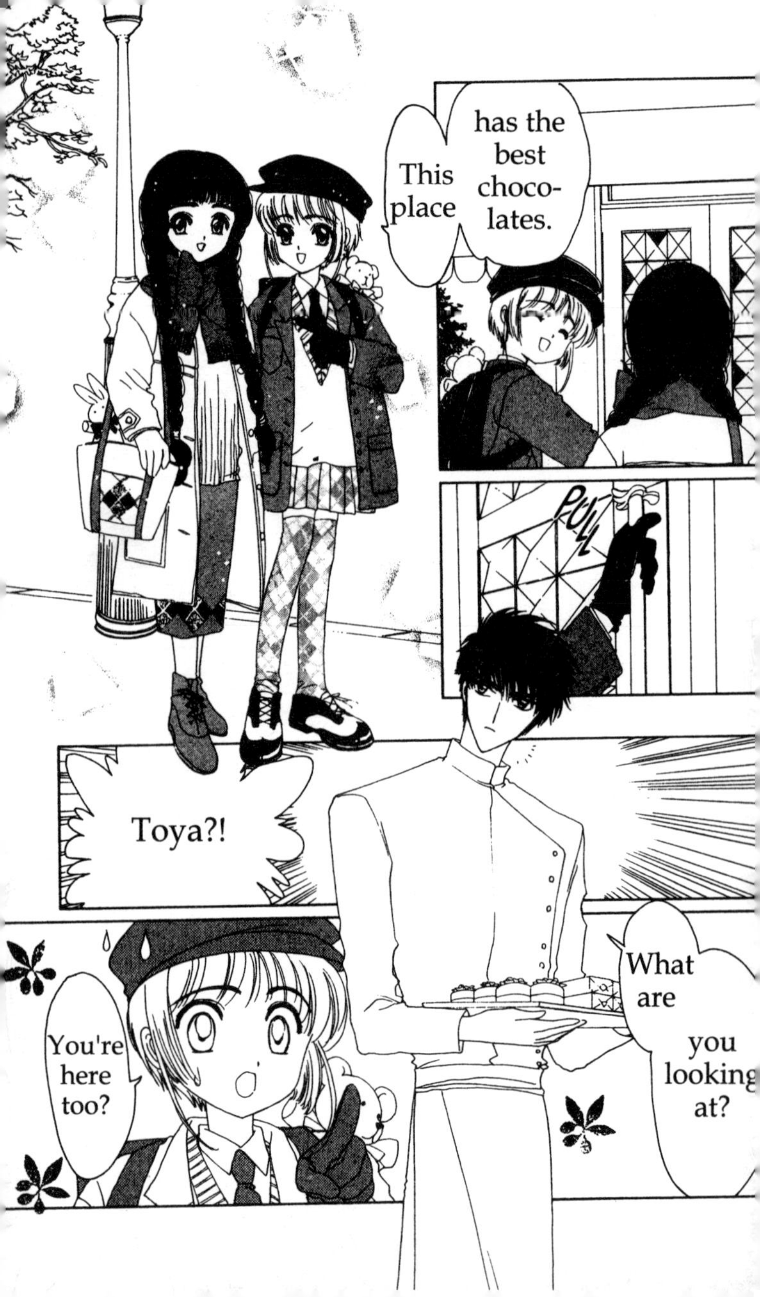
This place has the best choco-lates.
PULL
Toya?!
You're here too?
What are you looking at?

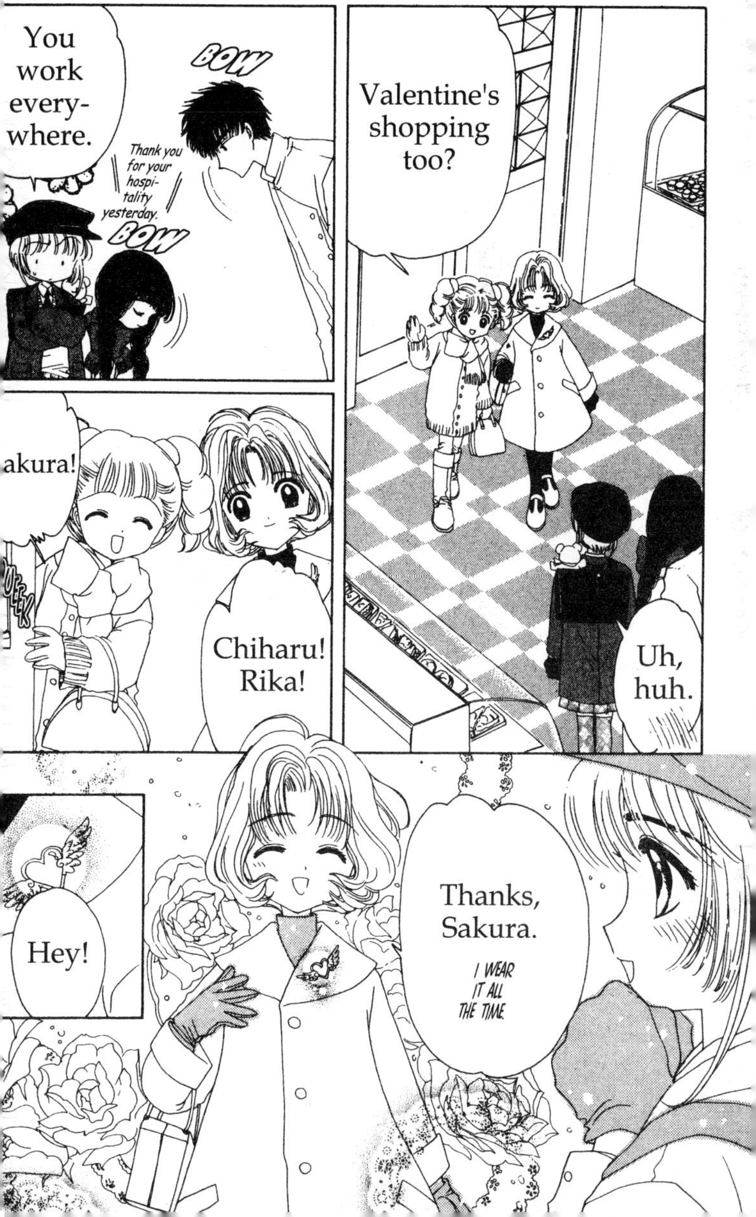
You work every-where.
BOW
Thank you for your hospi-tality yesterday.
BOW
akura!
Chiharu! Rika!
Valentine's shopping too?
Uh, huh.
Hey!
Thanks, Sakura.
I WEAR IT ALL THE TIME.

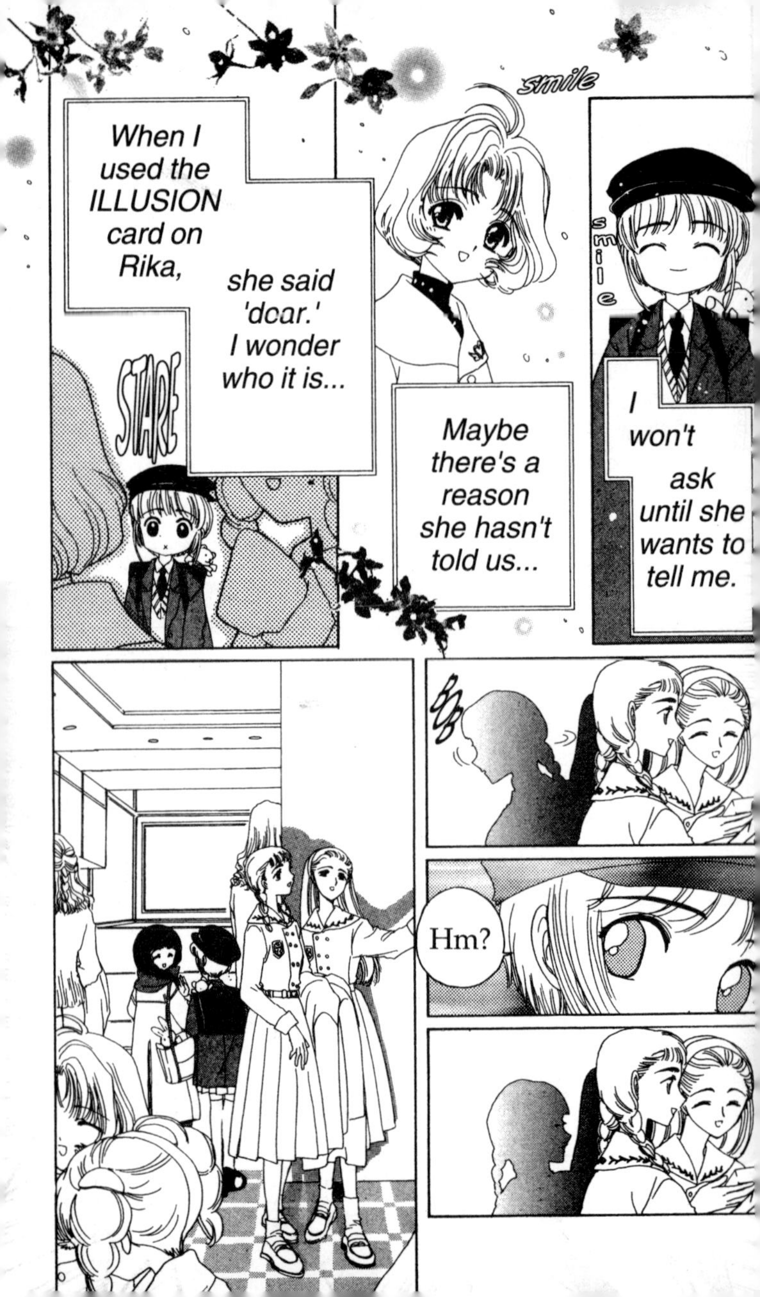
STARE
When I used the ILLUSION card on Rika,
she said 'dear.' I wonder who it is...
smile
Maybe there's a reason she hasn't told us...
smile
I won't ask until she wants to tell me.
Hm?

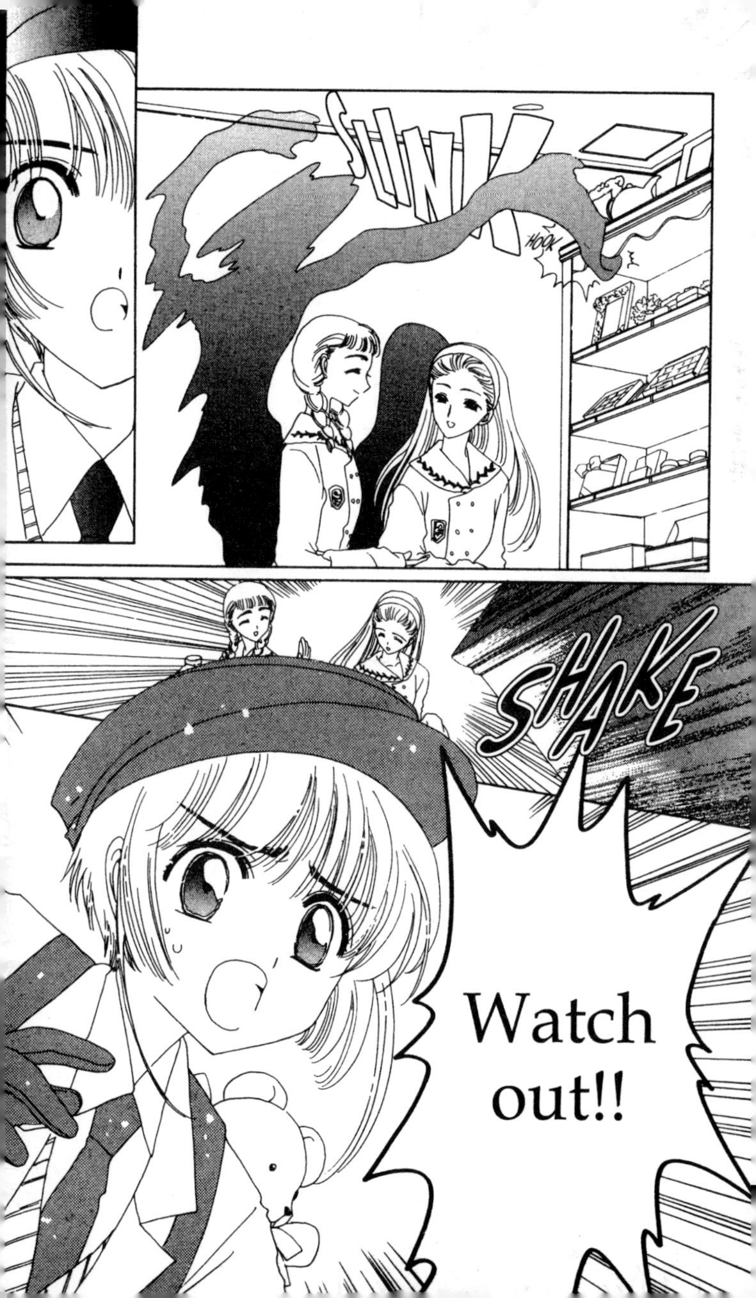
SHINK
HOOK
SHAKE
Watch out!!

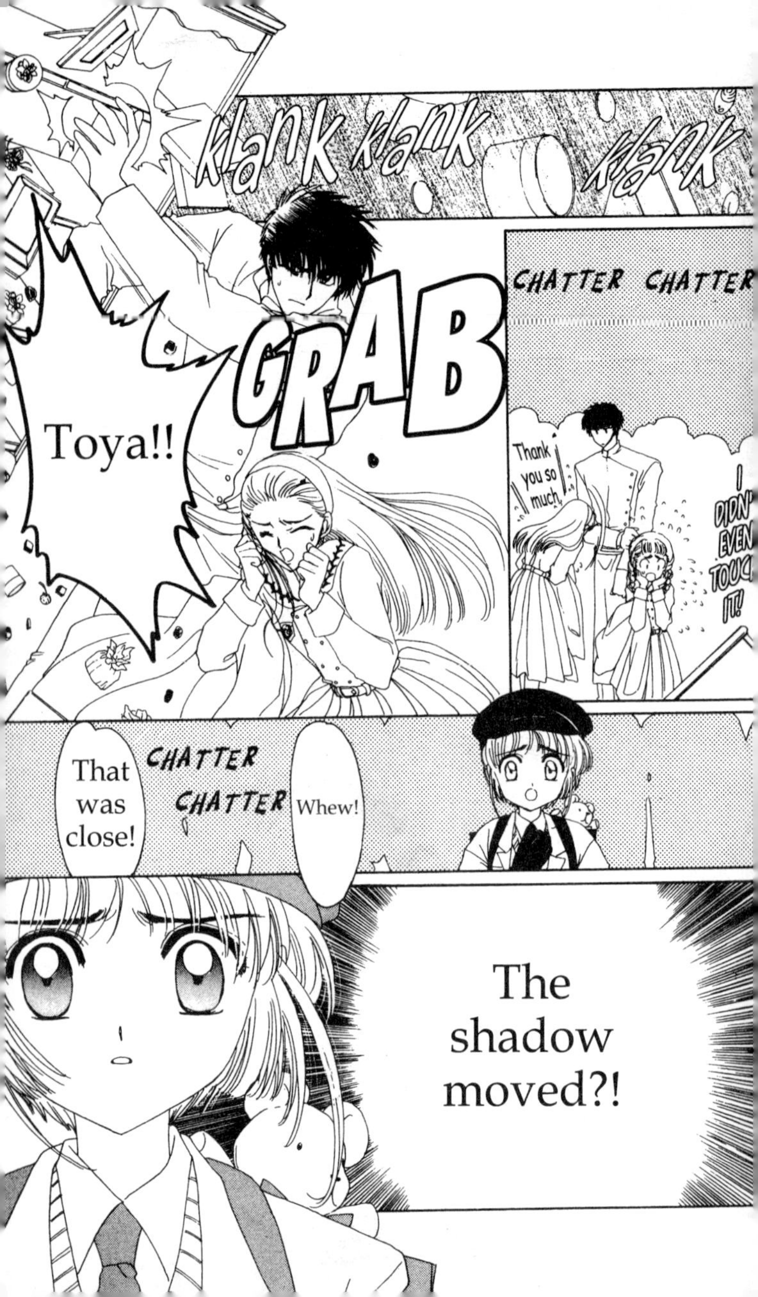
klank klank klank
Toya!!
GRAB
CHATTER CHATTER
Thank you so much
I DIDN' EVEN TOUC IT!
That was close!
CHATTER CHATTER
Whew!
The shadow moved?!

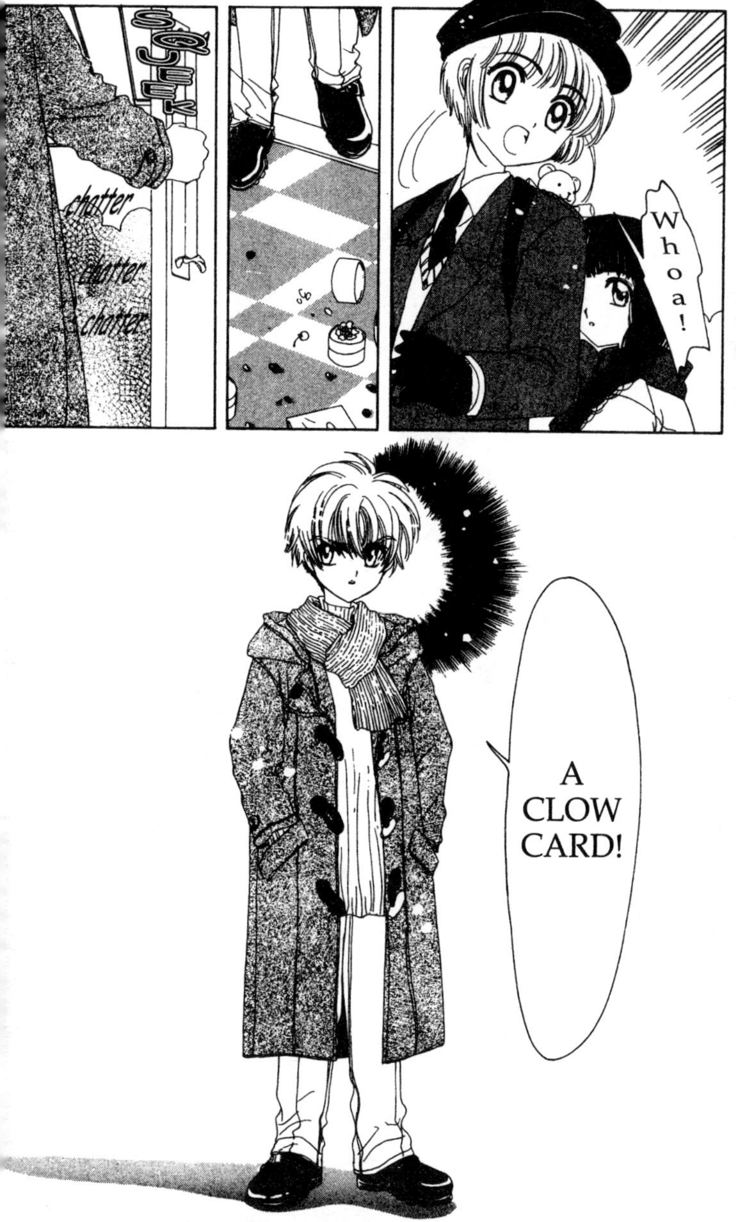
SQUEEK
chatter
chatter
chatter
Whoa!
A CLOW CARD!

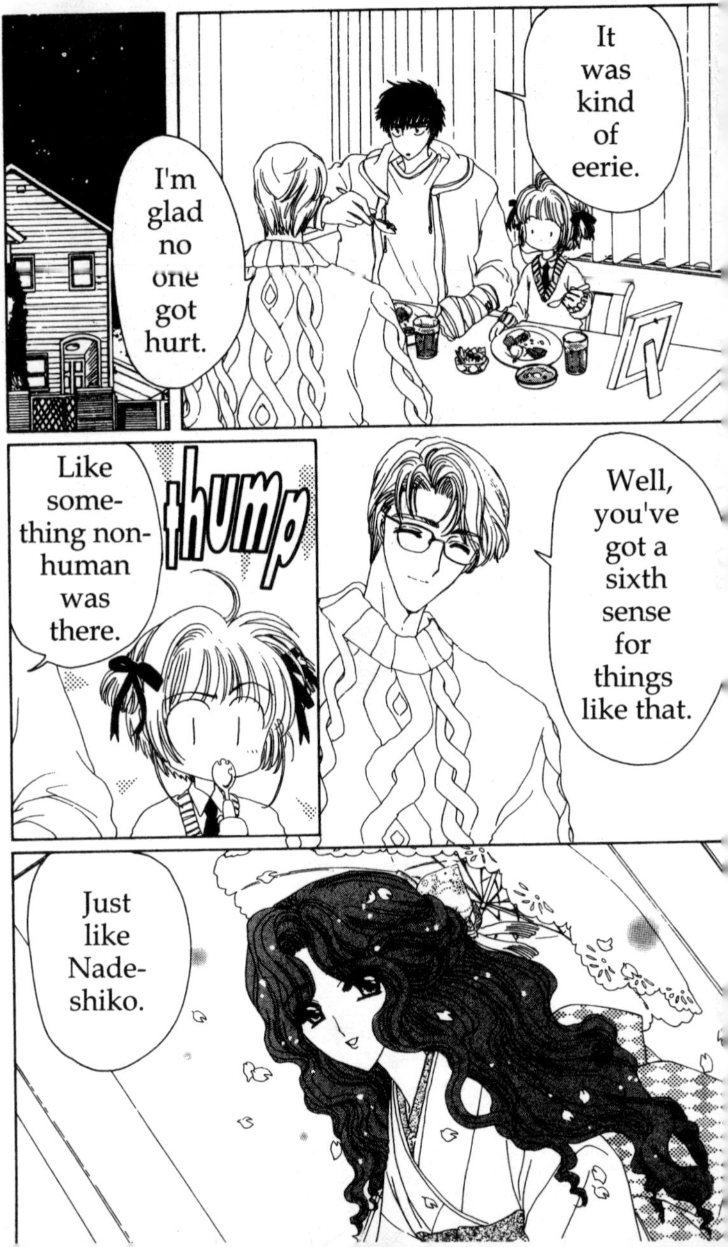
It was kind of eerie.
I'm glad no one got hurt.
Like something non-human was there.
thump
Well, you've got a sixth sense for things like that.
Just like Nadeshiko.

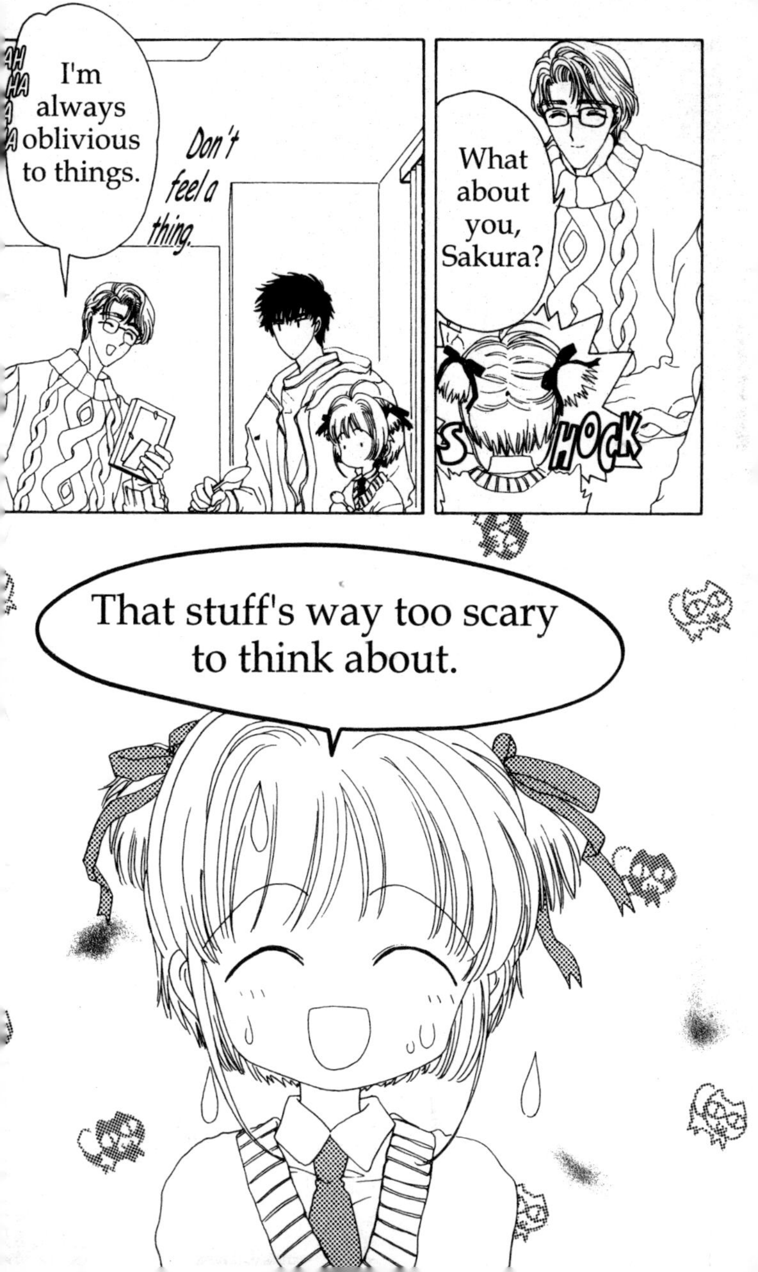
AH HA A A
I'm always oblivious to things.
Don't feel a thing.
What about you, Sakura?
SHOCK
That stuff's way too scary to think about.

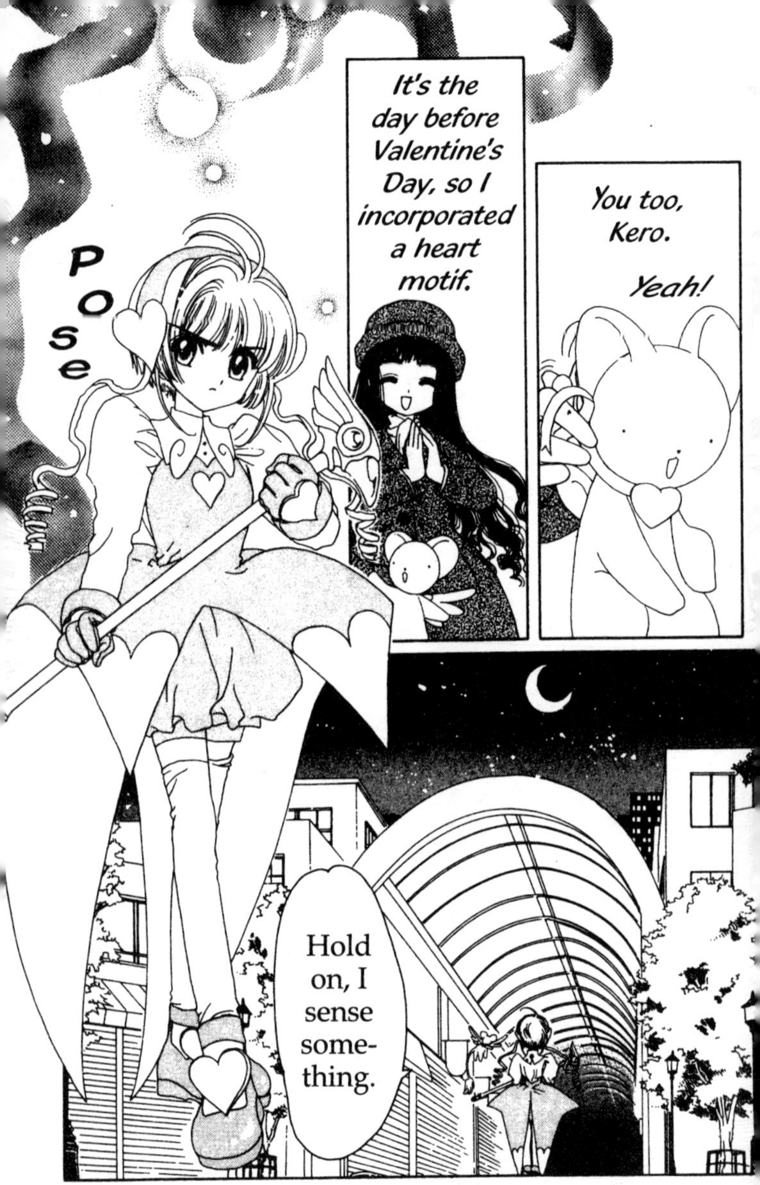
Pose
It's the day before Valentine's Day, so I incorporated a heart motif.
You too, Kero.
Yeah!
Hold on, I sense some-thing.

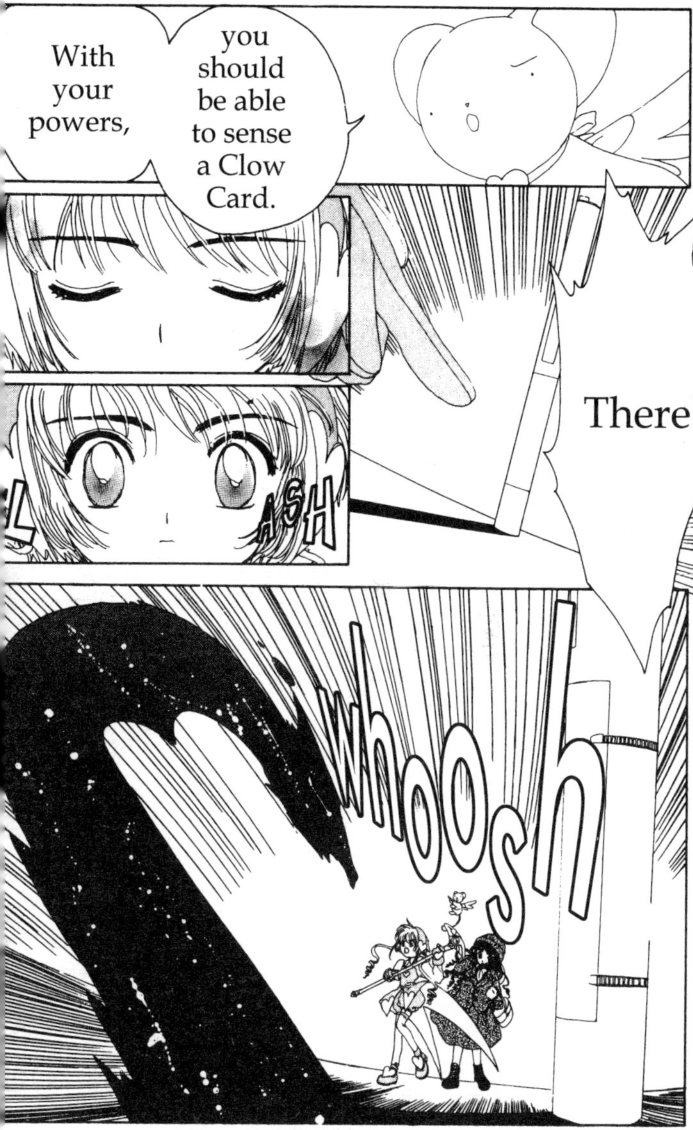

With your powers,
you should be able to sense a Clow Card.
LASH
There!
whoOsh

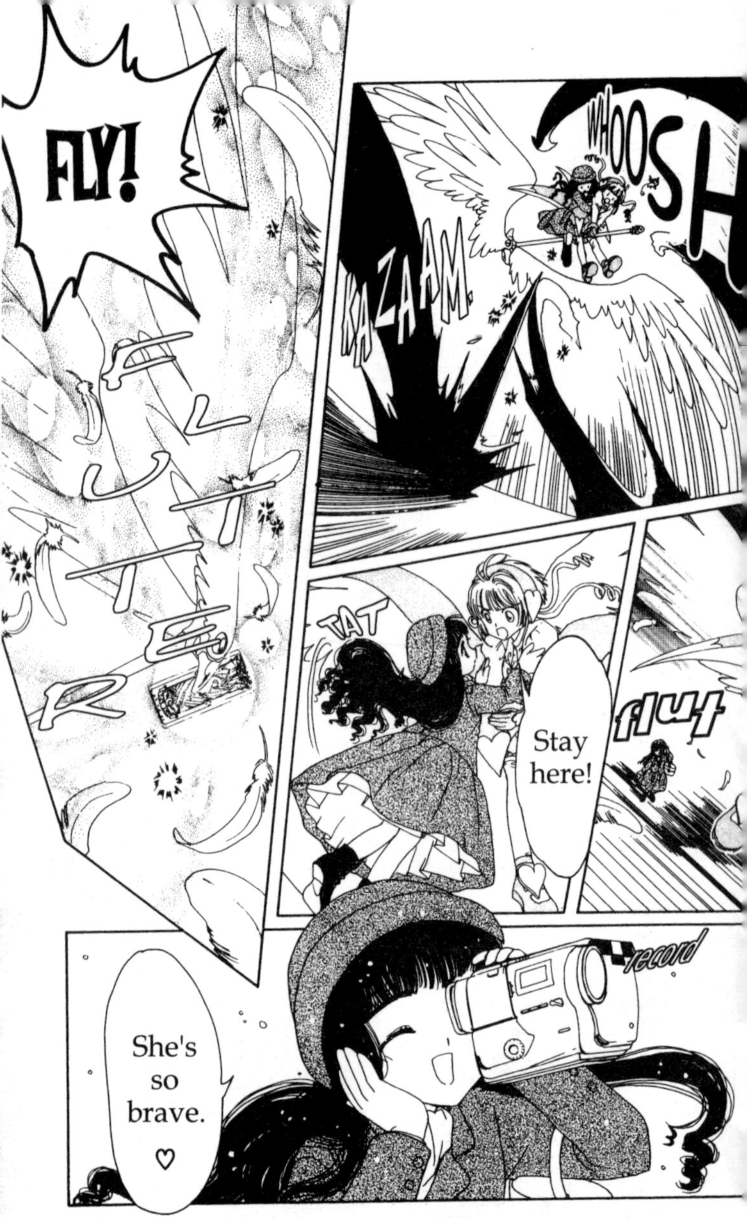
FLY!
FLUTTER
KAZAAM
WHOOSH
TAT
Stay here!
fluf
She's so brave. ♡
record

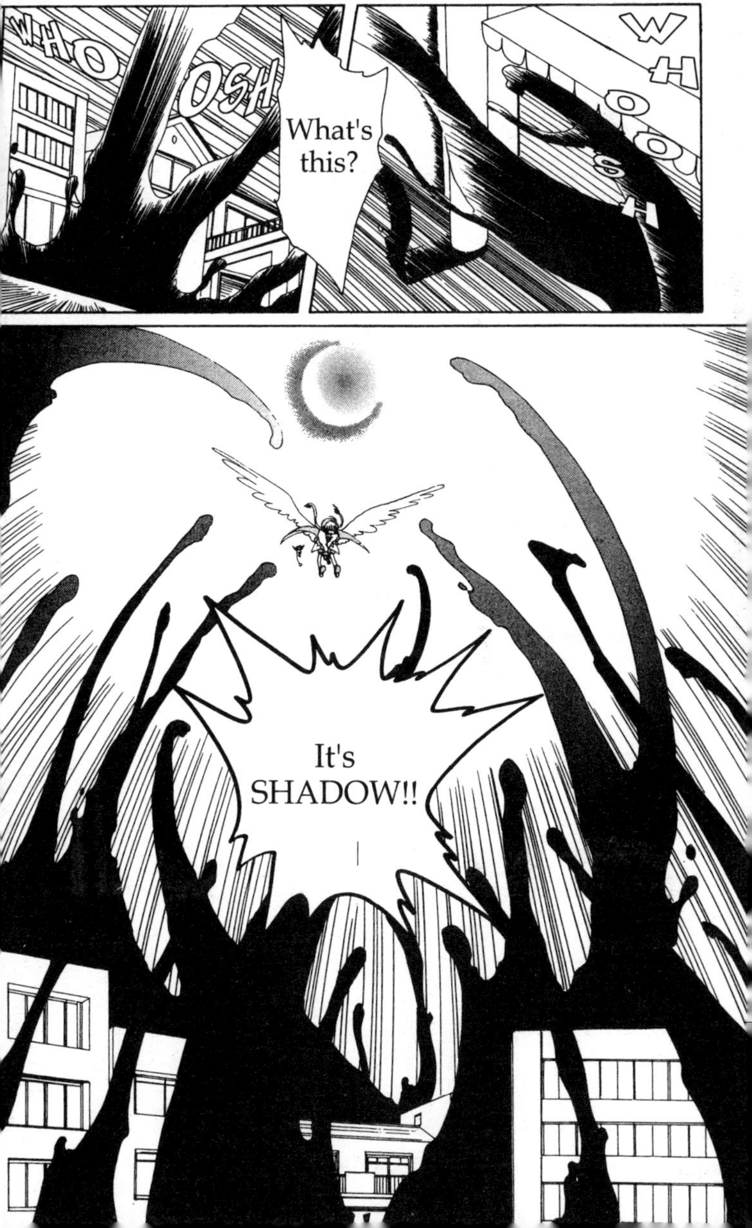
WHOOSH
What's this?
WHOOSH
It's SHADOW!!

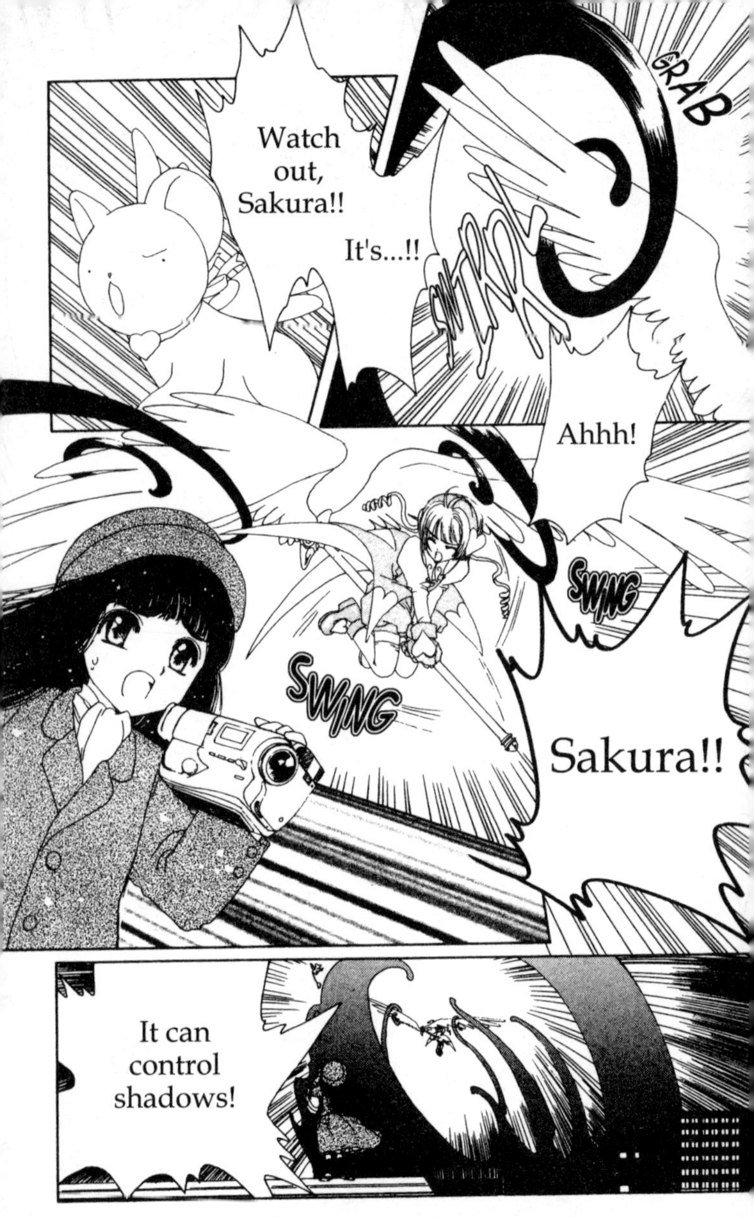
Watch out, Sakura!!
It's...!!
GRAB
Ahhh!
SWING
SWING
Sakura!!
It can control shadows!

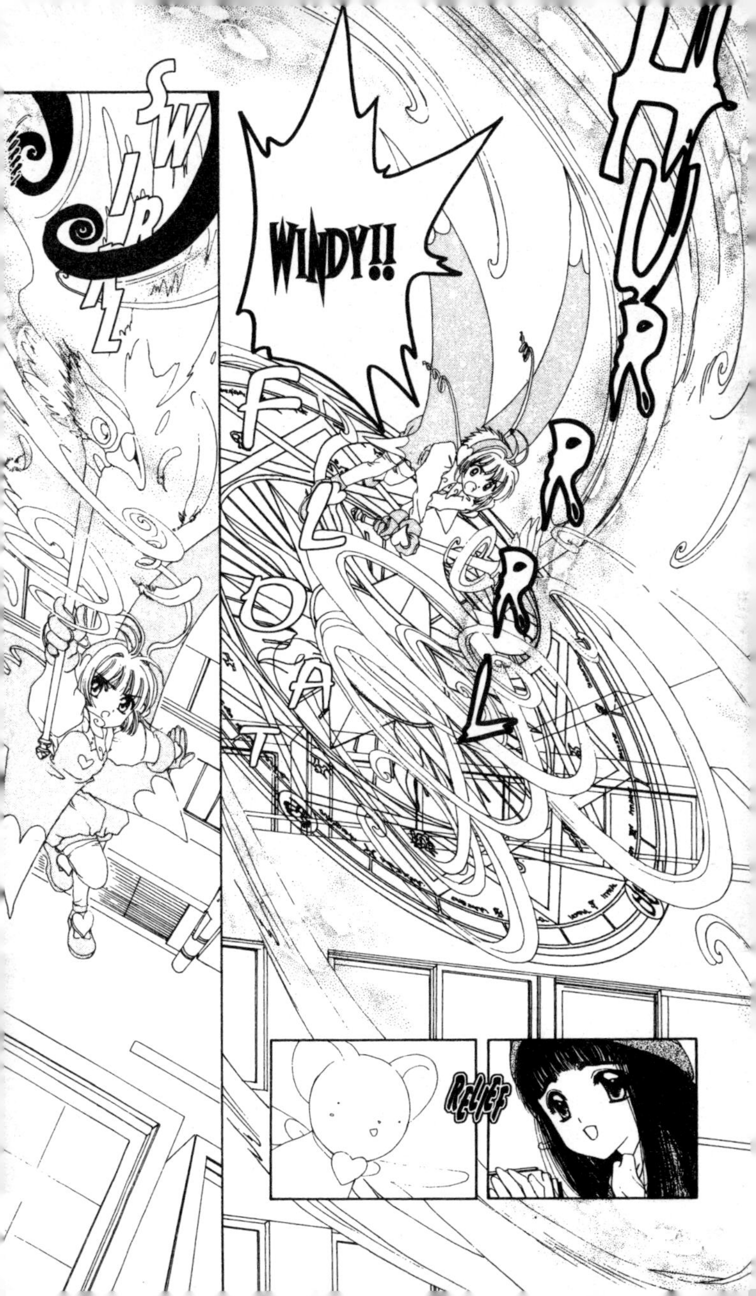
SWIRL
WINDY!!
FLOAT
RELIEF

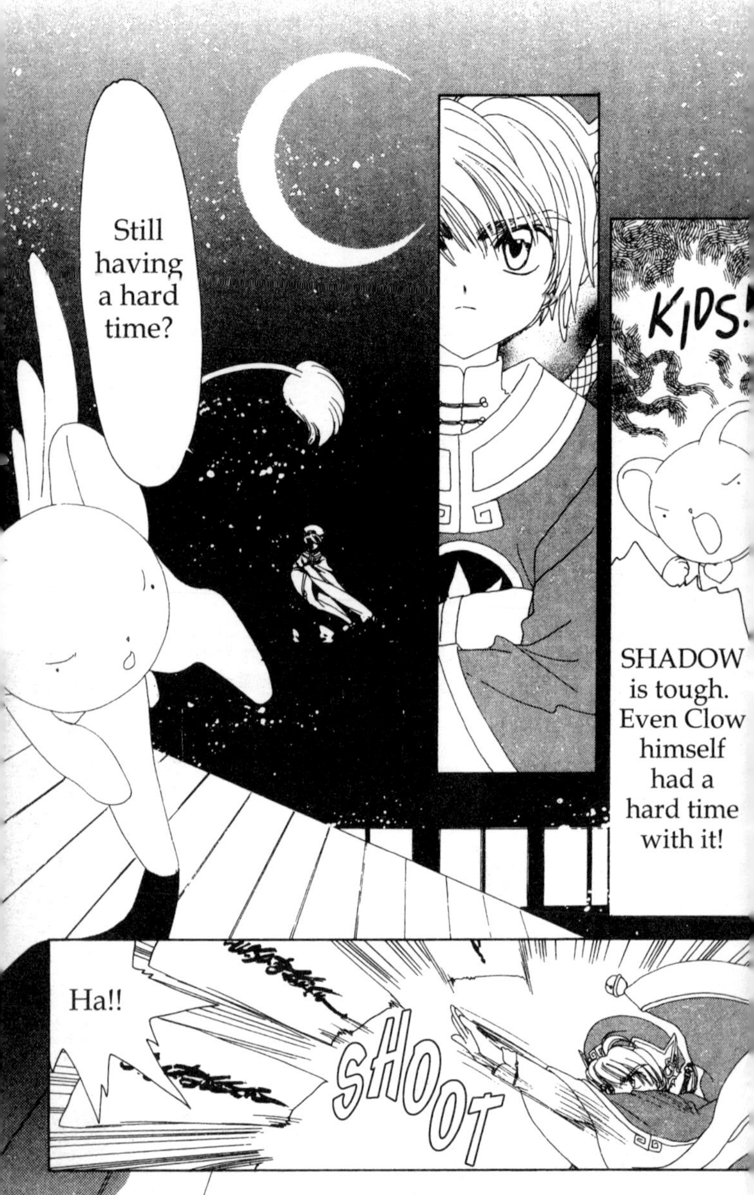
Still having a hard time?
KIDS!
SHADOW is tough. Even Clow himself had a hard time with it!
Ha!!
SHOOT

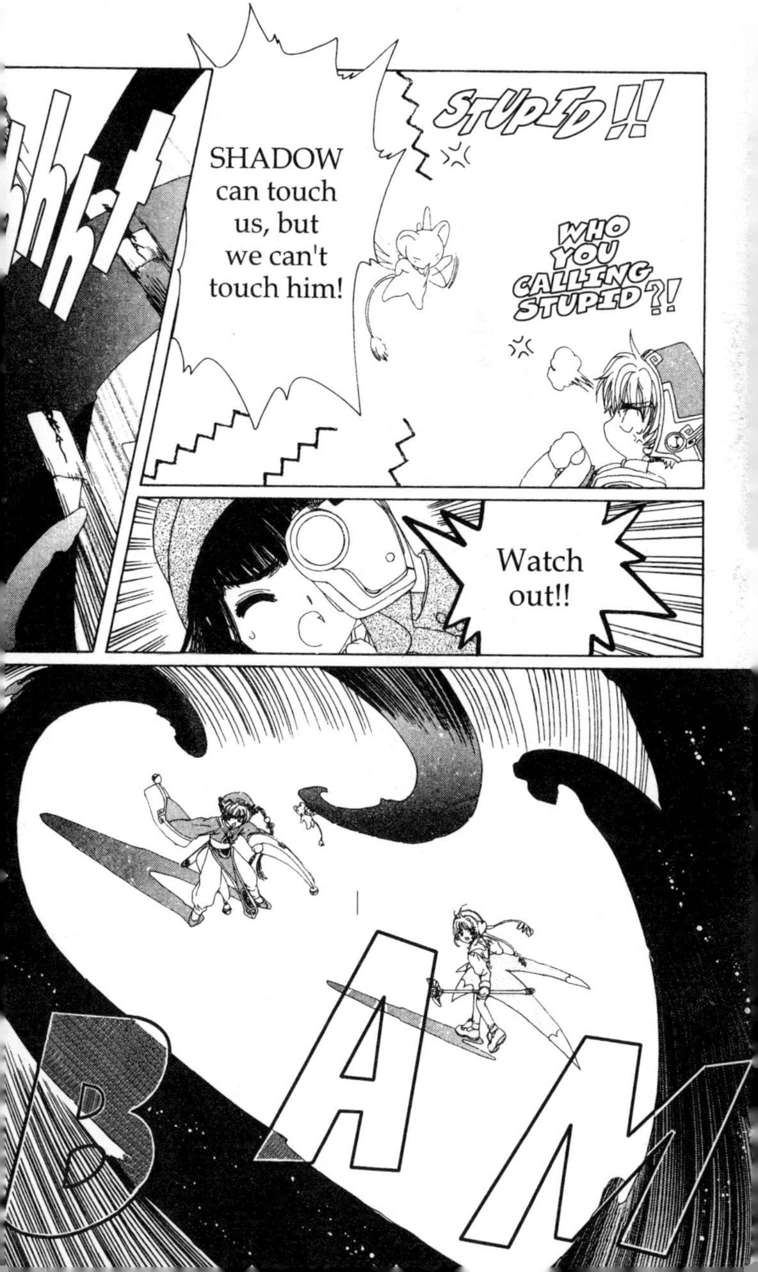
SHADOW can touch us, but we can't touch him!
STUPID!!
WHO YOU CALLING STUPID?!
Watch out!!
BAM

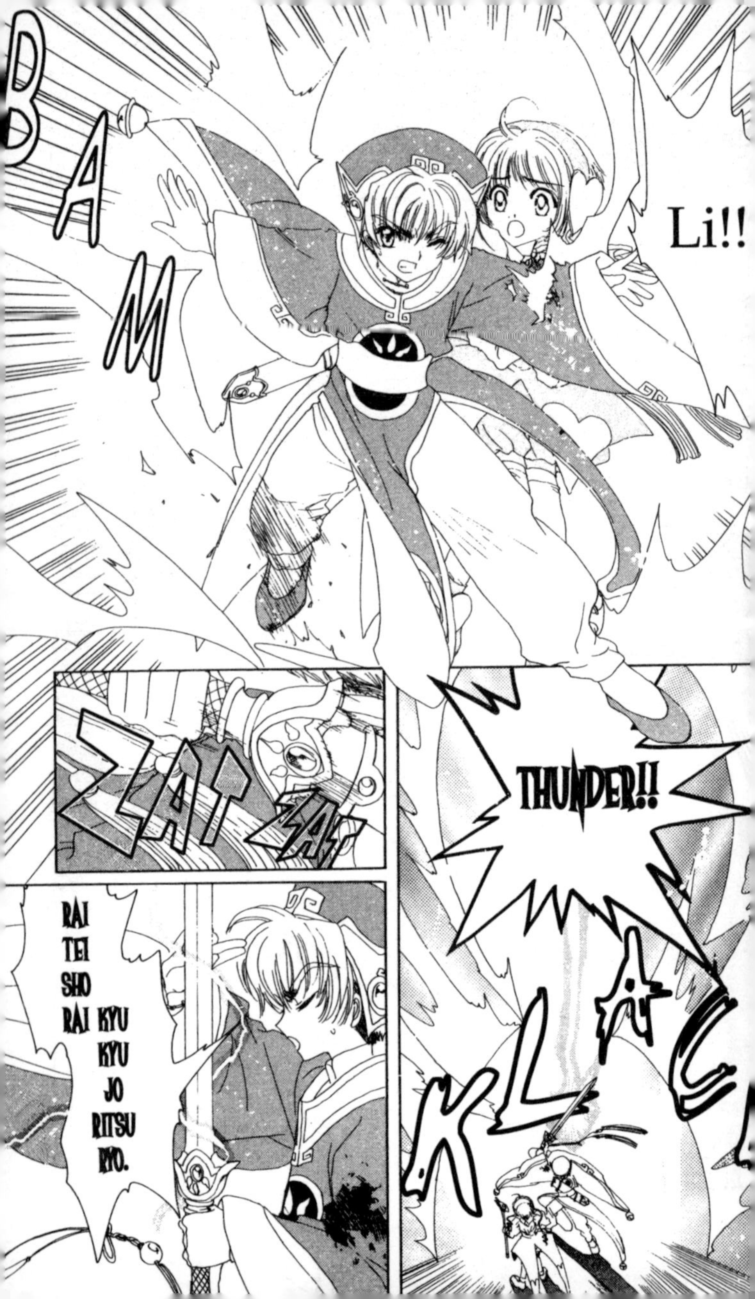
BAM
Li!!
ZAT ZAT
RAI TEI SHO RAI KYU KYU JO RITSU RYO.
THUNDER!!
KLAC

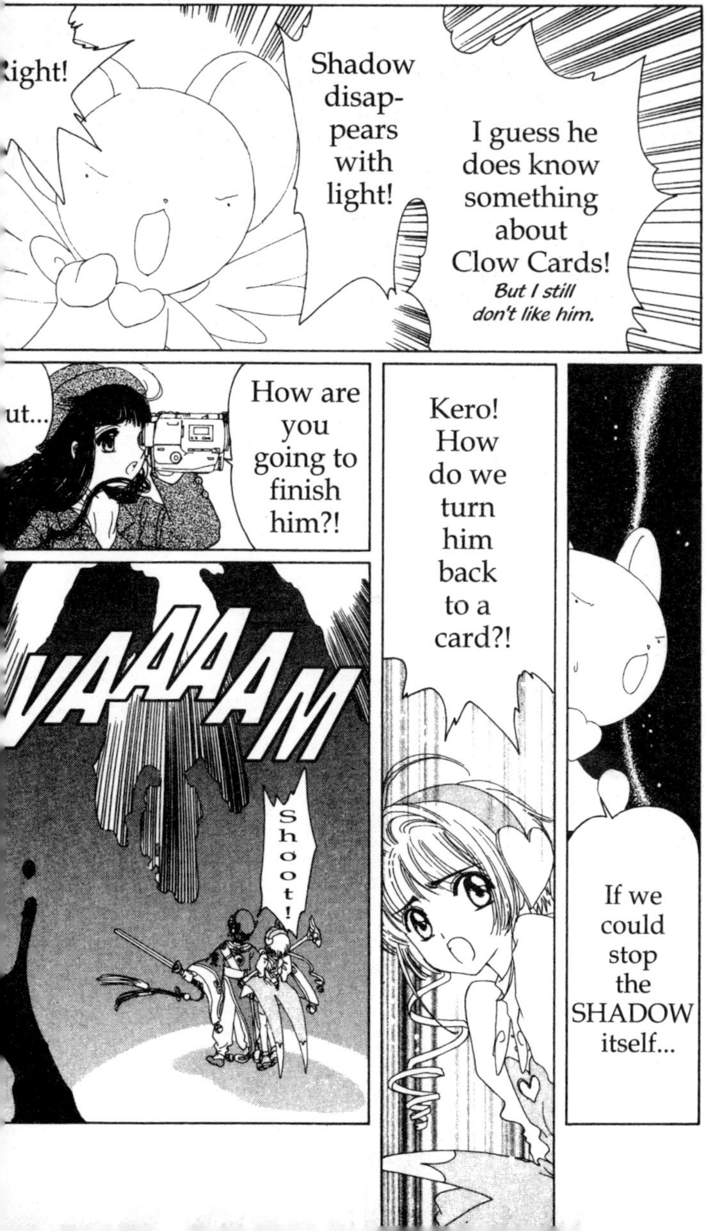
ight!
Shadow disap- pears with light!
I guess he does know something about Clow Cards!
But I still don't like him.
ut...
How are you going to finish him?!
AAAAM
Shoooot!
Kero! How do we turn him back to a card?!
If we could stop the SHADOW itself...

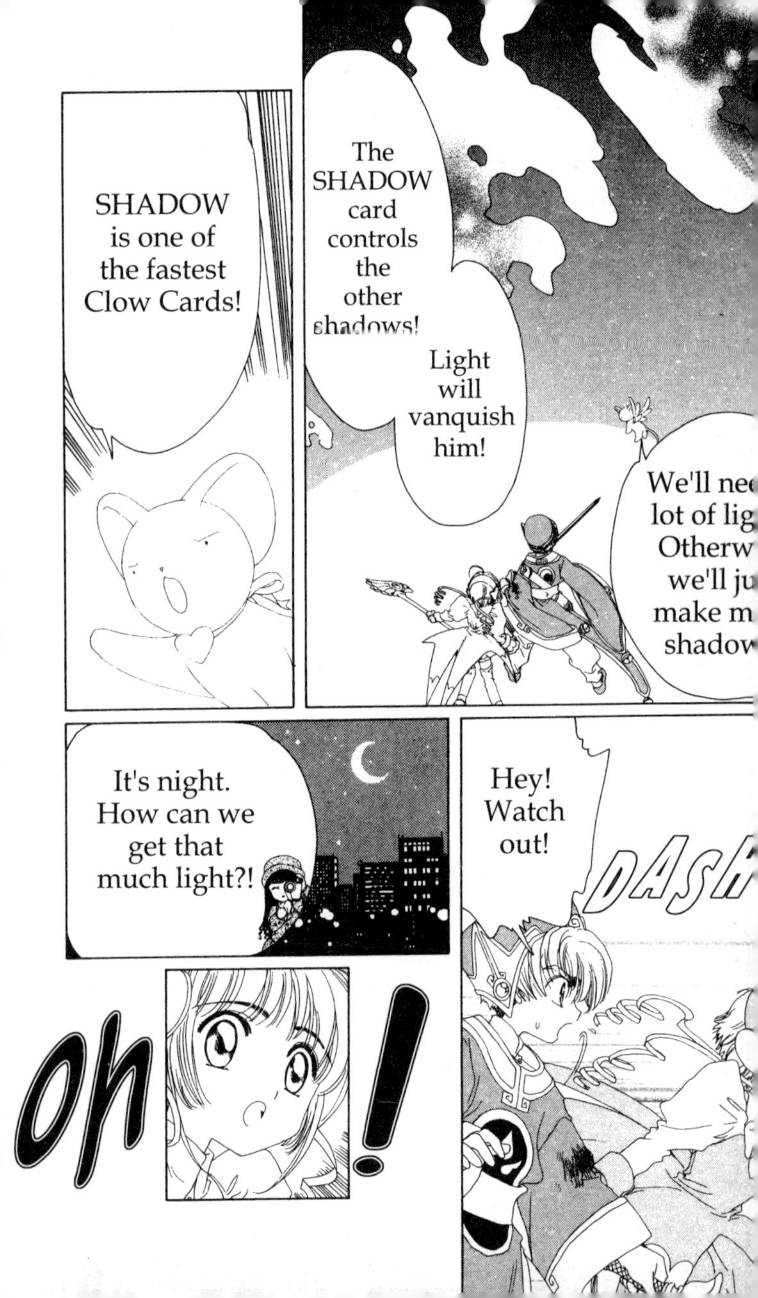
SHADOW is one of the fastest Clow Cards!
The SHADOW card controls the other shadows!
Light will vanquish him!
We'll nee lot of lig Otherw we'll ju make m shadow
It's night. How can we get that much light?!
Oh!
Hey! Watch out!
DASH

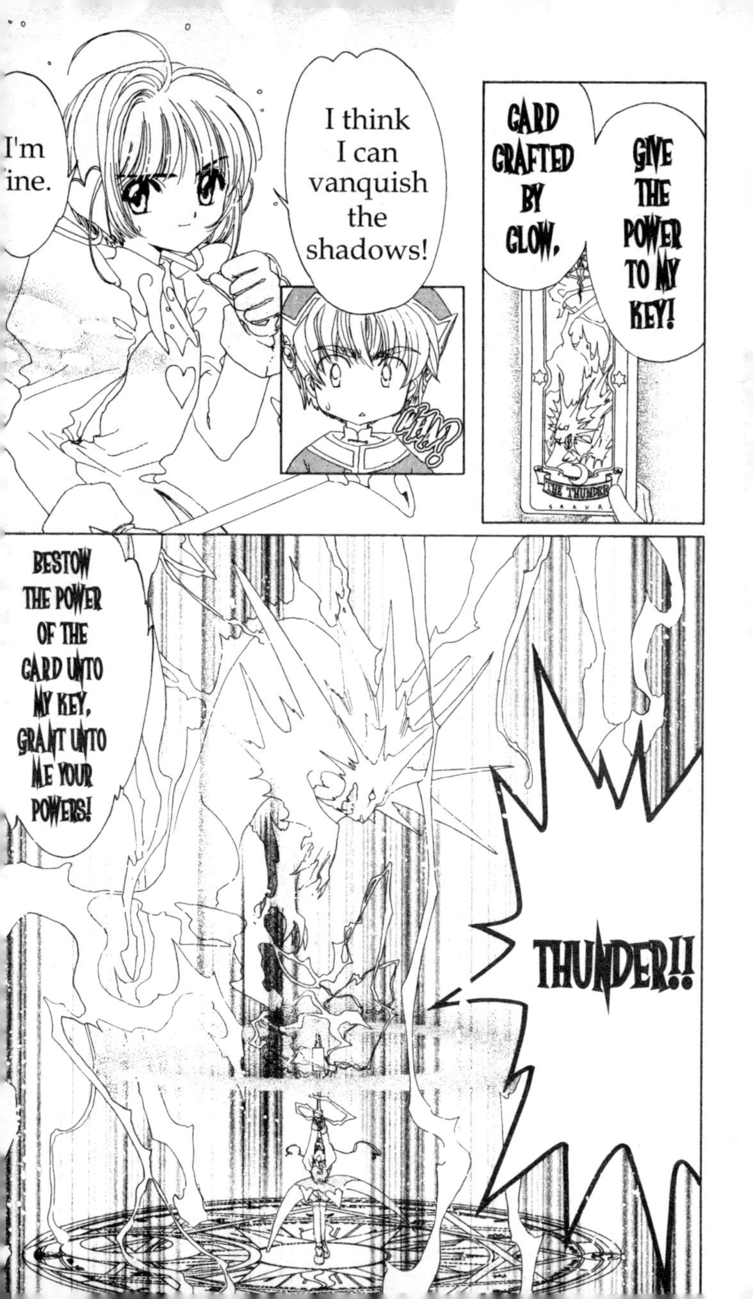
I'm ine.
I think I can vanquish the shadows!
CARD CRAFTED BY GLOW,
GIVE THE POWER TO MY KEY!
THE THUNDER
SAKURA
BESTOW THE POWER OF THE CARD UNTO MY KEY, GRANT UNTO ME YOUR POWERS!
THUNDER!!

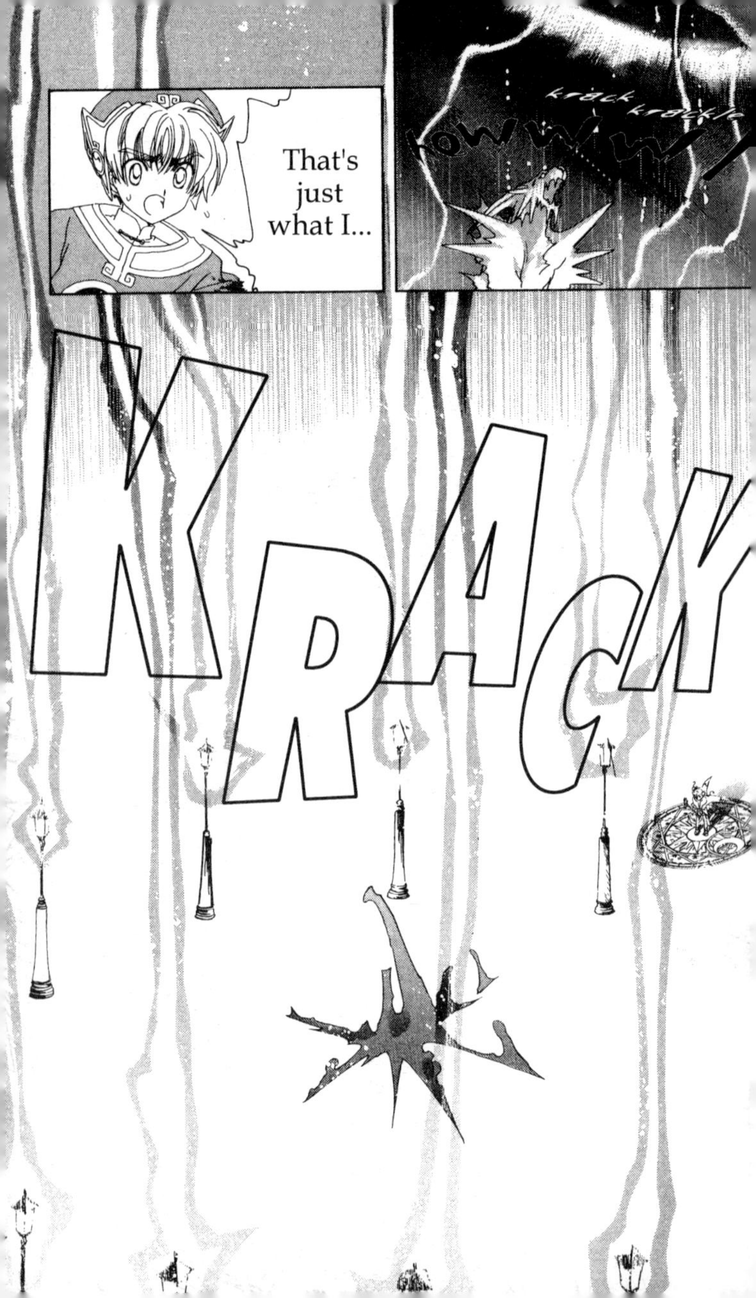
That's just what I...
krack krackle
KRACK

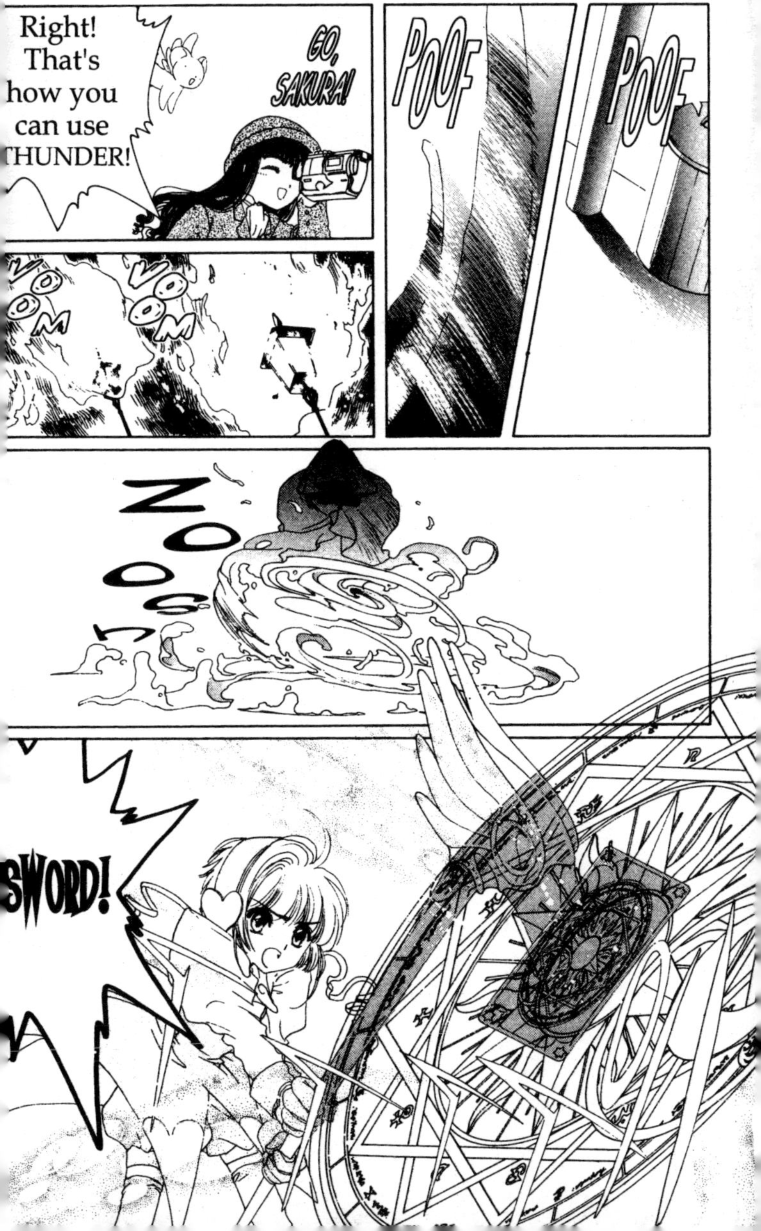

Right! That's how you can use THUNDER!
GO, SAKURA!
POOF
POOF
VOOM VOOM
ZOOOSH
SWORD!

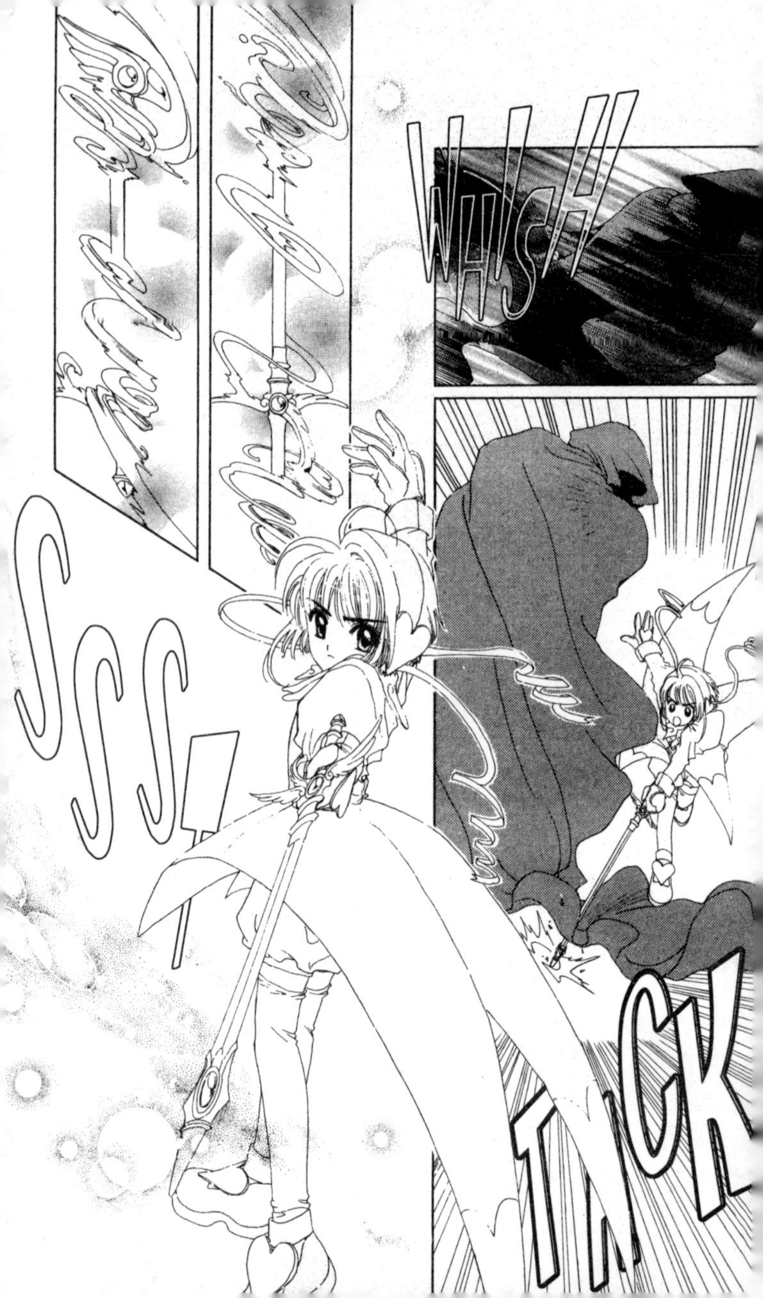
WHISH
SSS!
TACK

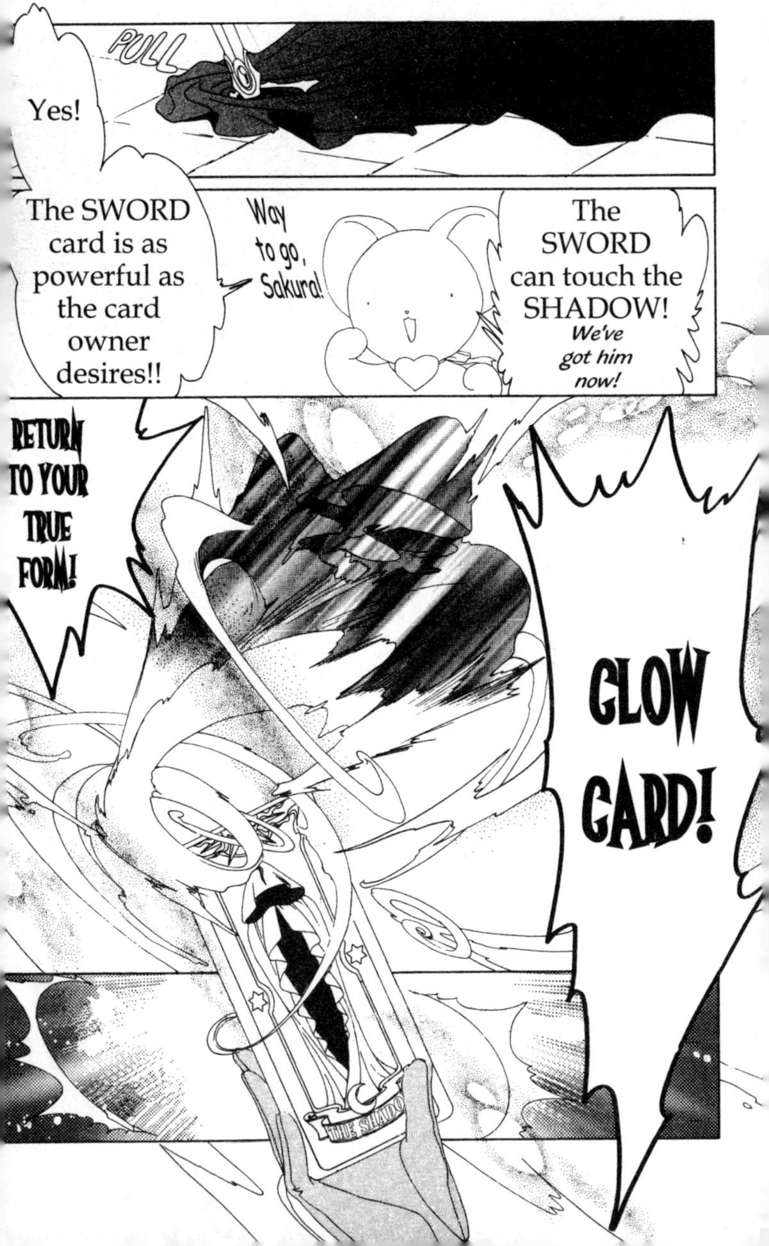
PULL
Yes!
The SWORD card is as powerful as the card owner desires!!
Way to go, Sakura!
The SWORD can touch the SHADOW!
We've got him now!
RETURN TO YOUR TRUE FORM!
GLOW CARD!
THE SHADO

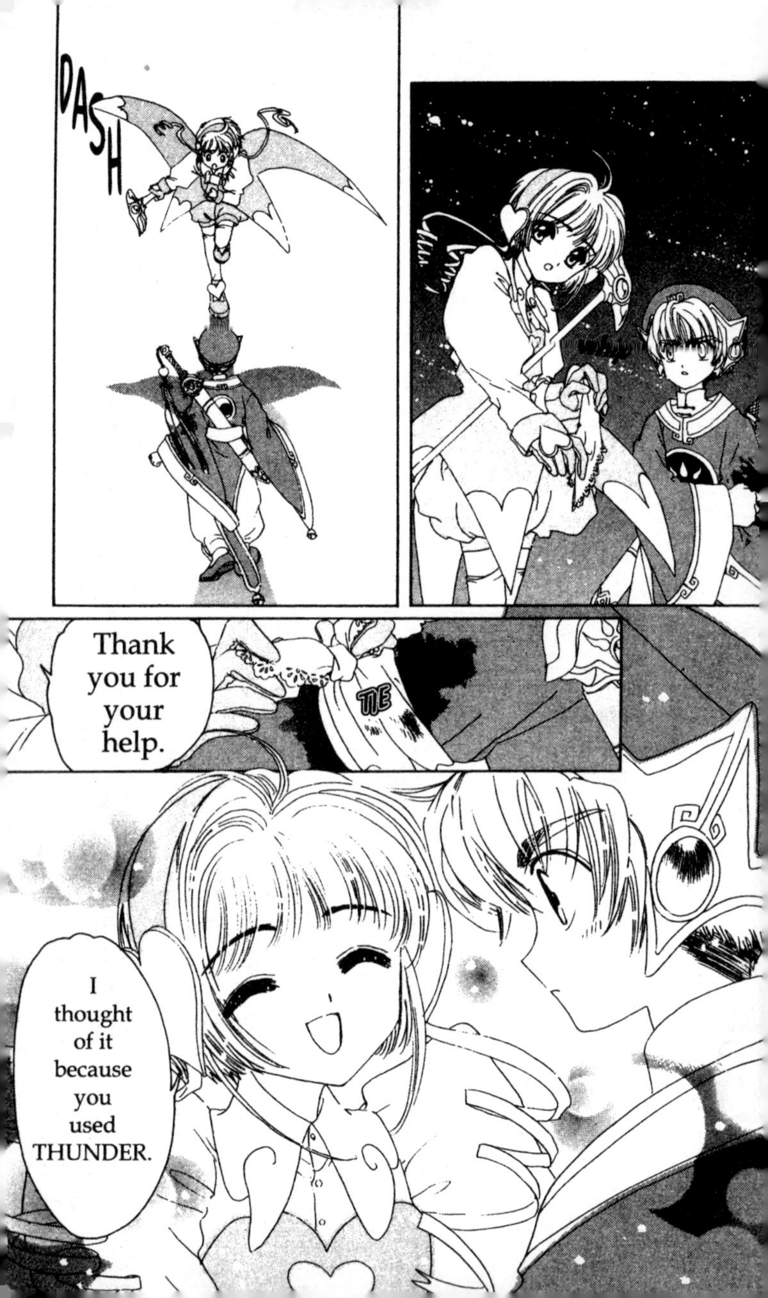
DASH
Thank you for your help.
TIE
I thought of it because you used THUNDER.

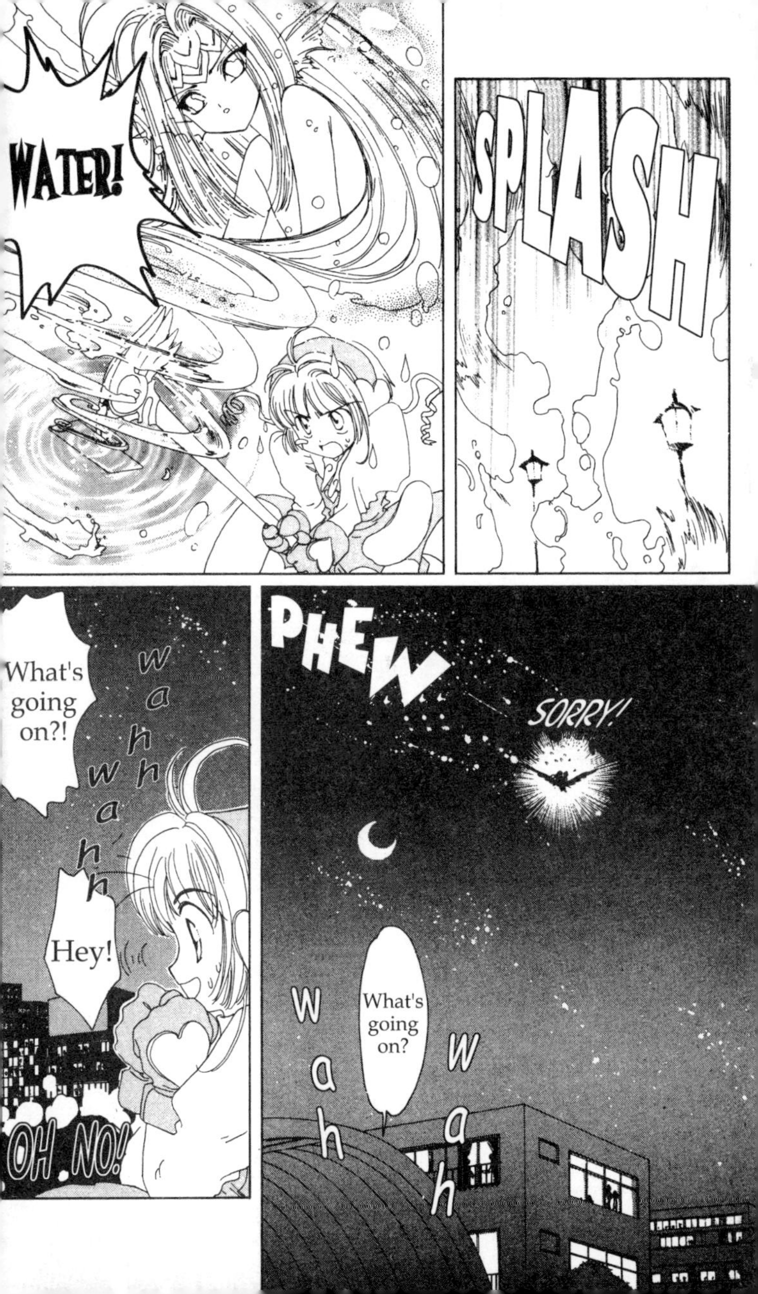

WATER!
SPLASH
What's going on?!
wahh
wahh
Hey!
OH NO!
PHEW
SORRY!
Wah
What's going on?
Wah

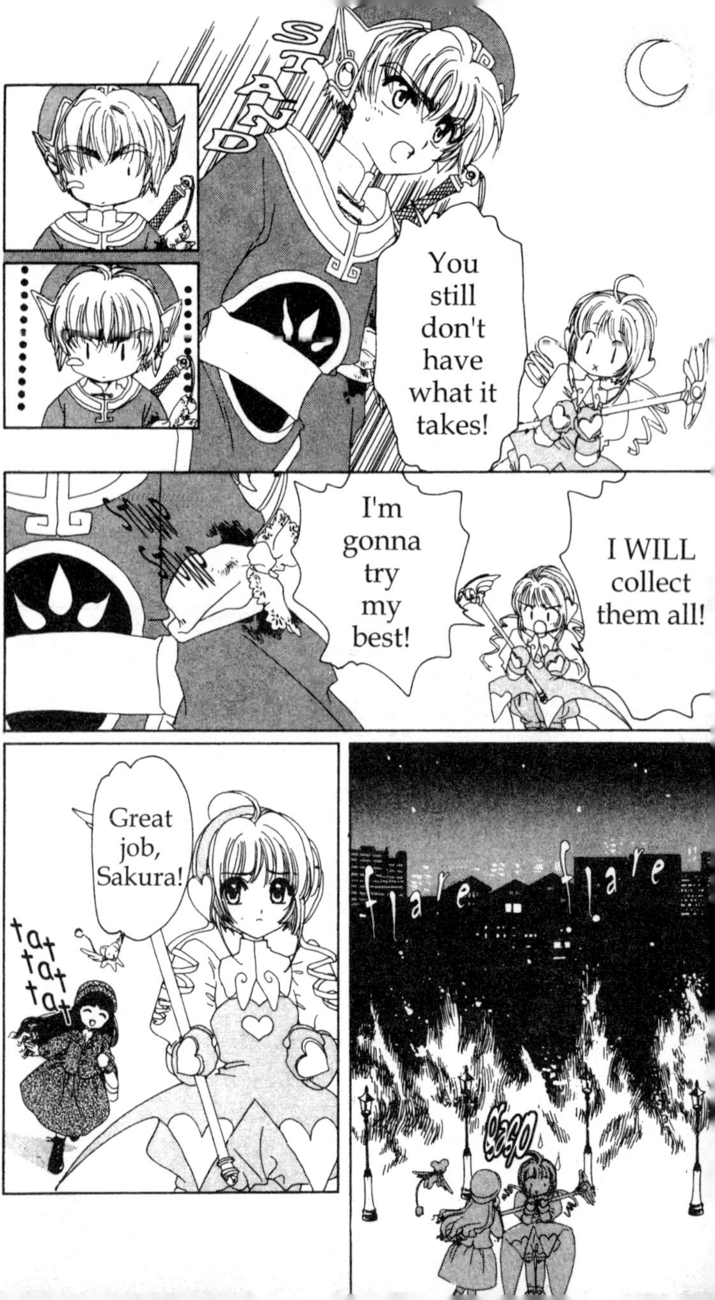
STAND
You still don't have what it takes!
I'm gonna try my best!
I WILL collect them all!
Great job, Sakura!
tat tat tat
flare flare

CHATTER
CHATTER

Here.

I've done this so many times now.

Yeah.

This will be the fifth year.

Really? I always wonder if it's home-made or not.

Thank you!

I don't even get nervous about Valentines anymore.

look

look

If it's home-made, I have to start praying.

SHAKE SHAKE

GR

What did you say?!

Ah ha ha

What is it?

Just wondering if Li's okay...

Li went to the field.

He said he had something to give someone.

Hm?

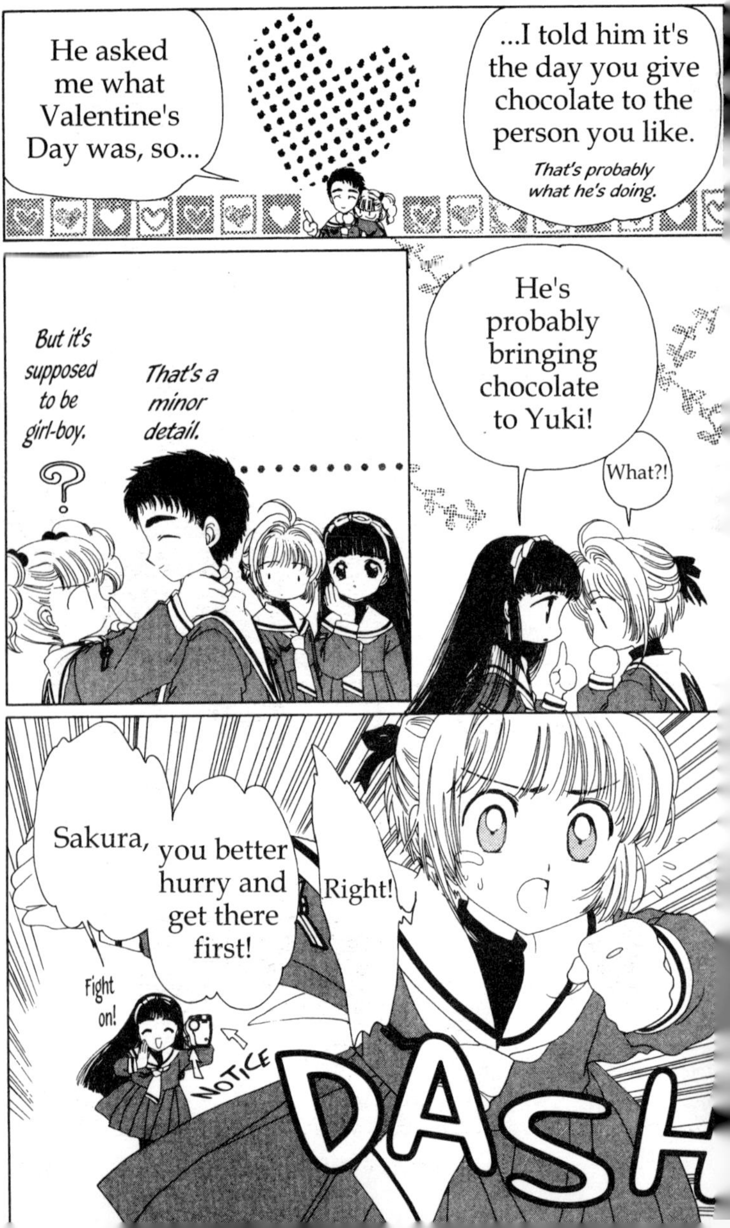
He asked me what Valentine's Day was, so...
...I told him it's the day you give chocolate to the person you like.
That's probably what he's doing.
But it's supposed to be girl-boy.
That's a minor detail.
He's probably bringing chocolate to Yuki!
What?!
Sakura,
you better hurry and get there first!
Right!
Fight on!
NOTICE
DASH

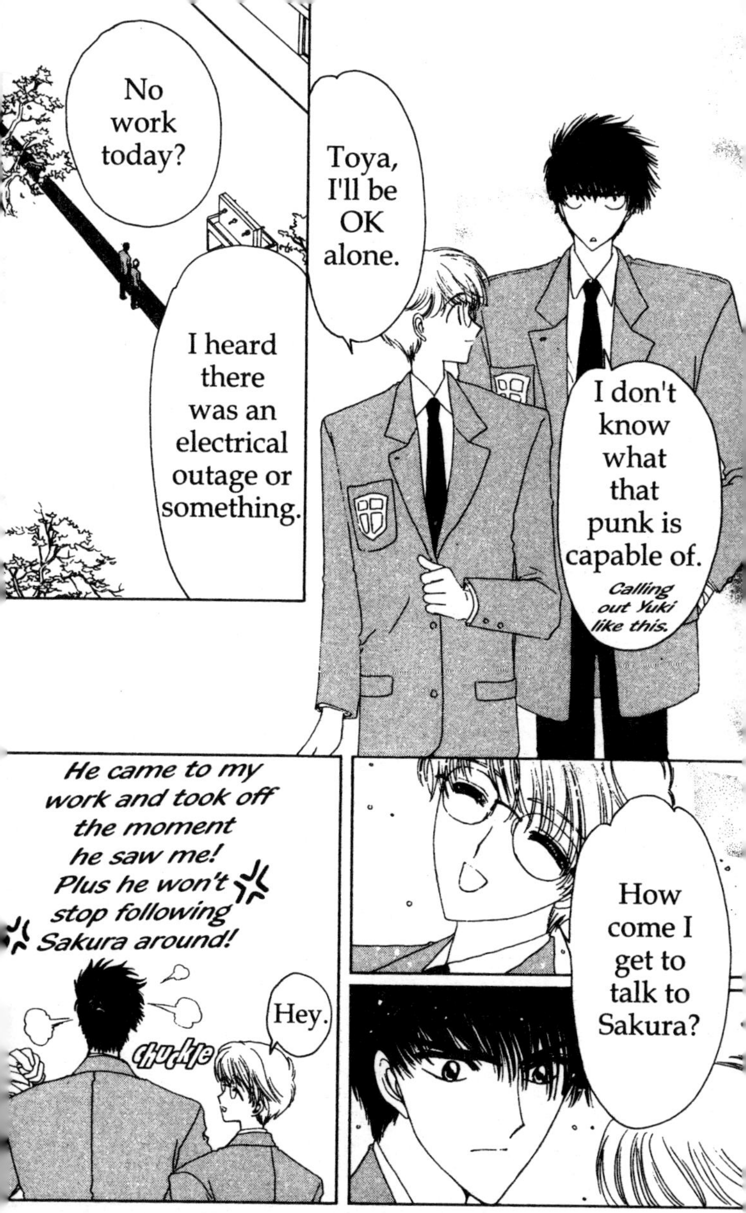
No work today?
I heard there was an electrical outage or something.
Toya, I'll be OK alone.
I don't know what that punk is capable of.
Calling out Yuki like this.
He came to my work and took off the moment he saw me! Plus he won't stop following Sakura around!
chuckle
Hey.
How come I get to talk to Sakura?

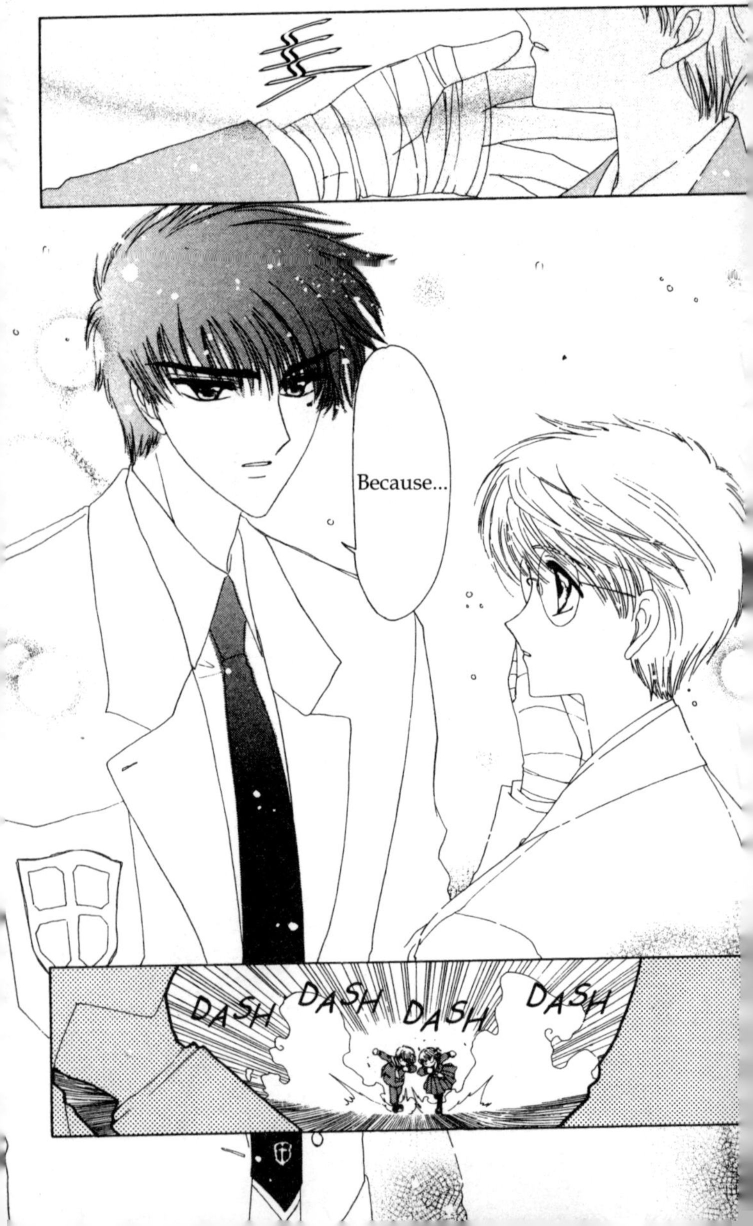
Because...
DASH DASH DASH DASH

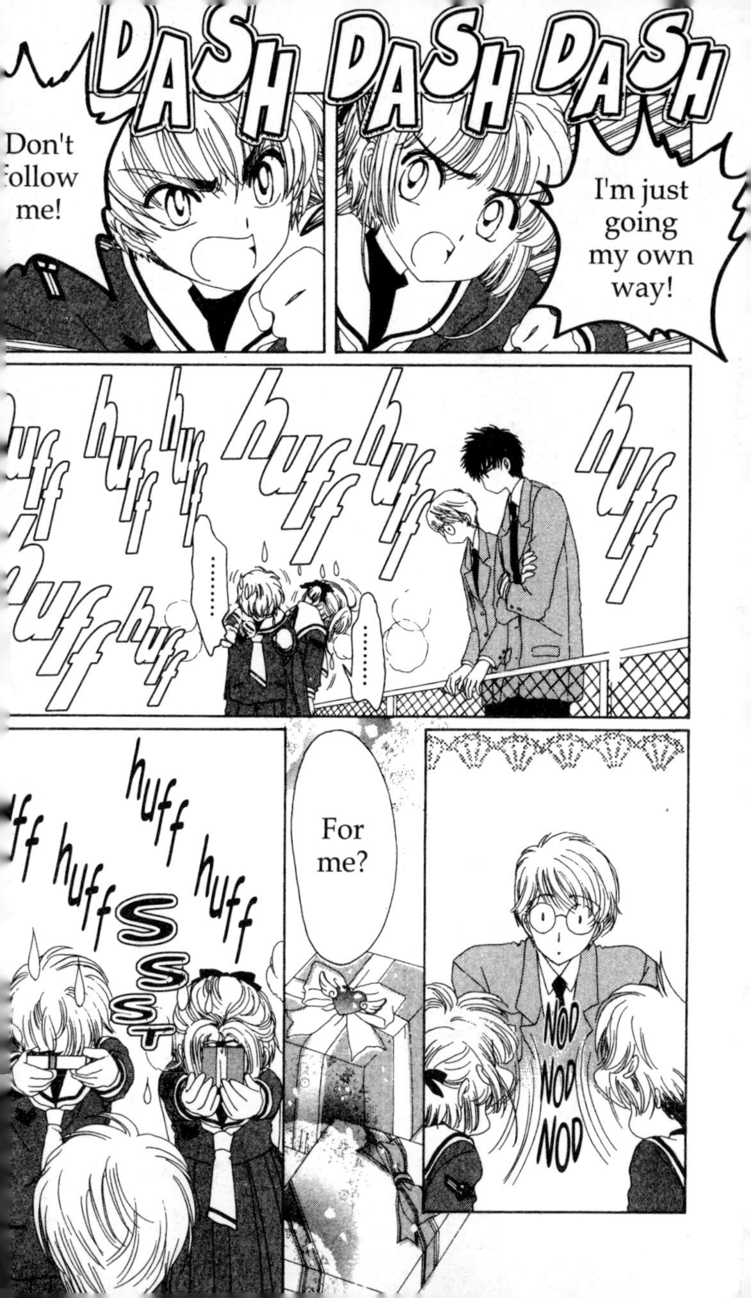
DASH DASH DASH
Don't follow me!
I'm just going my own way!
huff huff huff huff huff huff huff huff huff
……
……
huff huff huff huff
SSST
For me?
NOD NOD NOD

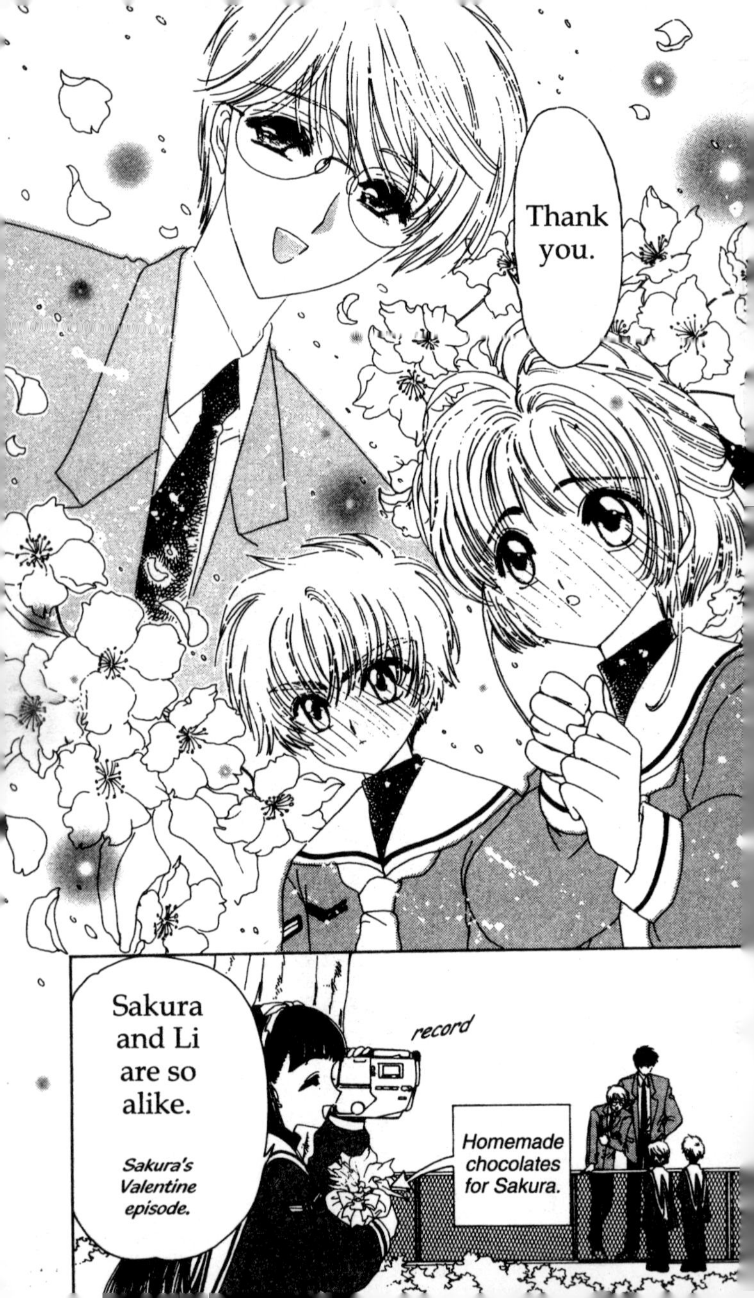
Thank you.
Sakura and Li are so alike.
Sakura's Valentine episode.
record
Homemade chocolates for Sakura.

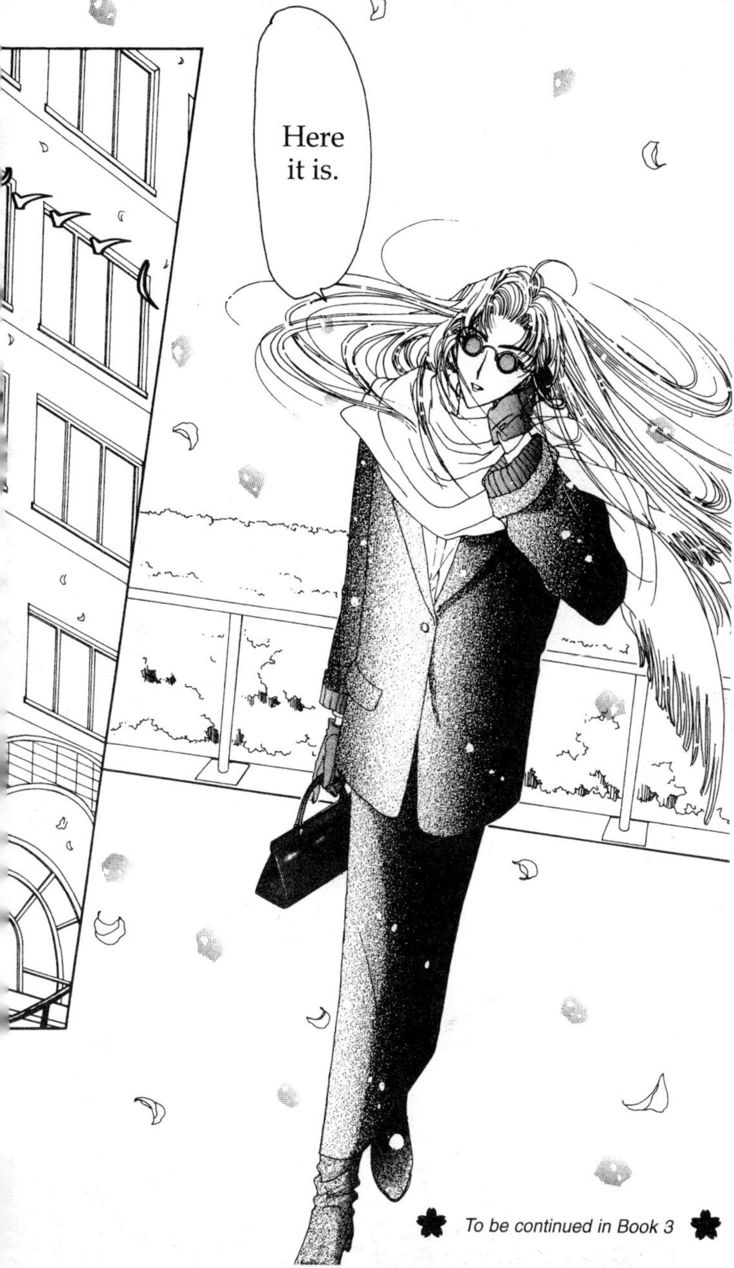
Here it is.

To be continued in Book 3

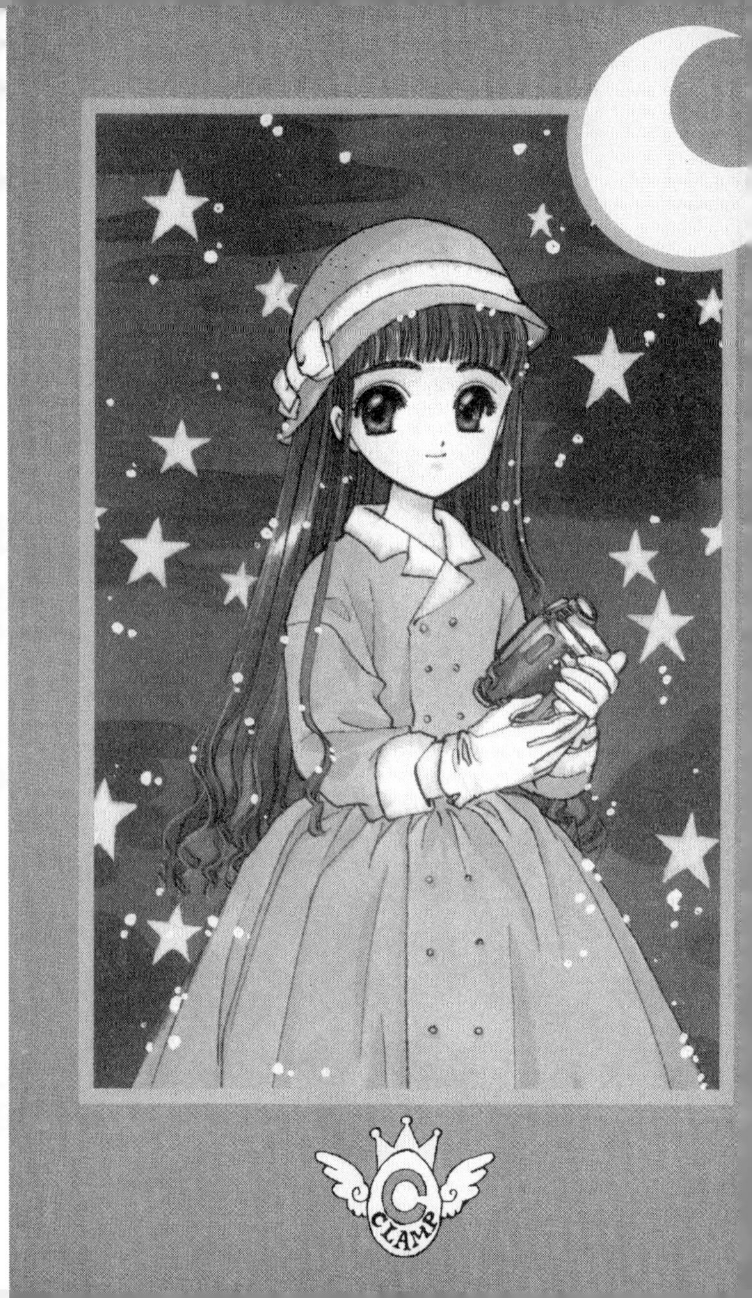

CLAMP